D1190797

ONLY IN
KRAKOW

Duncan J. D. Smith

ONLY IN
KRAKOW

A Guide to Unique Locations,
Hidden Corners and Unusual Objects

Photographs by
Duncan J. D. Smith
except where stated otherwise

**The
Urban
Explorer**

For Roswitha,
without whom the following pages could not have been written,
and my old friend Marek, who helped make them so much better.

"Krakow's urban layout lends it the hallmarks of an ideal city.
A city should not be too big; one has to be able to take in its boundaries.
Its roads should lead to the centre. It is good to have the sense
that one can walk into the heart of the city."
Andrzej Wajda, Polish film and theatre director (1926–2016)

Contents

APPENDICES

Introduction

"Krakow is one of my favorite places on earth.
It is a medieval city full of young people.
A wonderful, striking combination."
Jonathan Carroll, US novelist and writer, b. 1949

Krakow (pronounced *Krak-oof* in Polish) has been called the 'Polish Athens' and the 'Florence of Central Europe'. The early 20th century writer Tadeusz Boy-Żeleński described it as a "city of painters, poets, grand tombs and stained glass…a city of life and art". It is this suggestion of a place where people live and work against a richly storied backdrop that helps explain why Krakow so beguiles many visitors today.

Situated on the banks of the Vistula (Wisła) and straddling several medieval trade routes, Krakow served as the Polish capital until 1596, when King Sigismund III Vasa (Zygmunt III Waza) moved the royal court to Warsaw. Despite this, kings were still crowned in Krakow and it wasn't until 1791 that Warsaw was officially recognised as capital. Krakow instead became capital of the historical region of Lesser Poland (Małopolska) and for many it remains the country's cultural capital, too.

Poland's kings and foreign interlopers have all left their mark. After surviving a Tatar raid in 1241, Krakow received its market charter in 1257. This prompted King Casimir III the Great (Kazimierz III Wielki), last of the founding Piast dynasty that Christianised the country, to initiate a golden age. In 1386, Poland's first female monarch, Jadwiga, married the Lithuanian Grand Duke Ladislaus II Jagiello (Władysław II Jagiełło) producing a union between the two countries. Designed to keep the Austrians out, it didn't prevent a Swedish occupation in the 1650s nor a trio of Partitions that led in 1795 to Krakow becoming part of Habsburg-controlled Galicia. An independent Poland would not exist again until 1918, only to find itself reoccupied in 1939 by Nazi Germany and the Soviet Union. Remarkably the city escaped significant damage during the Second World War and was liberated by the Red Army. In 1952 it fell under Soviet-backed Communist control, which lasted until 1989, when Solidarity leader Lech Wałęsa was made President in the country's first democratic elections.

Only in Krakow is designed for city explorers interested in getting off the beaten track and under the city's skin. This is the Krakow of legendary churches and mysterious monasteries, novel art spaces and industrial remains, colourful customs and candlelit cellars. The hundred or so locations described represent the author's own odysseys through the city – from Kleparz in the north down to Łagiewniki, and from the Wolski Forest (Las Wolski) in the west across to Nowa Huta. Together they reveal the treasures of Krakow old and new.

The story begins on Wawel Hill, where archaeologists have unearthed Stone Age remains. A natural defensive site rising above the Jurassic plain, this is where Poland's earliest kings built their castle in the early 11th century, when Krakow became capital of the first Polish state. Wawel Cathedral (Katedra Wawelska), the country's national sanctuary, was erected alongside it. In the lee of the hill are the Okół and Stradom Quarters, the former boasting Krakow's prettiest street.

One of Krakow's most famous architectural features is its medieval square (Rynek Główny). The largest in Europe, it sits at the heart of the Old Town, one of three distinct settlements that made up medieval Krakow. Together with the surrounding grid-iron of streets, it provides an architectural feast encompassing Romanesque churches and Modernist public buildings. The line of the medieval walls that once surrounded the Old Town is marked today by the Planty park.

South of Wawel is Kazimierz, the second of Krakow's medieval settlements. Once an island in the Vistula, it remained separate until 1800. In 1335 Casimir III the Great encouraged the Jews to settle here and despite their forced removal in 1941, the area retains much Jewish heritage.

Lying on the southern bank of the Vistula is the industrialised district of Podgórze. Founded in 1784 by the Habsburg Emperor Joseph II, this separate town only joined Krakow in 1915. Between 1943 and 1945 it was the location of the Płaszów concentration camp near which stands Oskar Schindler's famous factory.

North of the Old Town is the suburb of Kleparz, the third medieval settlement, annexed in 1792. Here stand some of the many fortresses built by the Austrians during the 19th century, as well as the extensive Rakowicki Cemetery. Farther east is the sprawling Communist-era steelworkers' town of Nowa Huta.

Finally, to the west are the suburbs of Piasek and Nowy Świat. The Communist theme continues with the Hotel Cracovia overlooking the vast Błonia meadow. Farther west, the leafy suburb of Salwator gives way to the sylvan delights of the Wolski Forest (Las Wolski).

Whilst walking is the best way to explore central Krakow, the outer suburbs are easily accessed using the city's network of buses and trams (www.mpk.krakow.pl). Whether climbing mysterious mounds, eating *pierogi* in milk bars, exploring Poland's oldest university, or marvelling at the city's eco-incinerator, *Only in Krakow* will encourage readers to set out on their own urban expedition. Happy Exploring!

Duncan J. D. Smith, Krakow & Vienna

1 History on Wawel Hill

31-001 Kraków (Wawel Hill), the Royal Private Apartments
(Prywatne Apartamenty Królewskie) and State Rooms
(Reprezentacyjne Komnaty Królewskie) at Wawel Royal Castle
(Zamek Królewski na Wawelu)
Tram 6, 8, 10, 13, 18 to Wawel (note: there is a daily limit on tickets
so booking is advised, last entry is an hour before closing and Royal
Private Apartments can only be visited as part of a guided tour)

Krakow's story begins on Wawel Hill (Wawelskie Wzgórze). Here prehistoric man found security on an outcrop of Jurassic limestone overlooking a bend in the Vistula (Wisła). Pagan tribes did likewise during the early Middle Ages followed in the late 10th and 11th centuries by Poland's earliest kings, when Krakow became capital of the first Polish state. They built a castle and cathedral on the hill, and a town on the plain below. Subsequent incarnations of Wawel Royal Castle (Zamek Królewski na Wawelu) have produced the palimpsest seen today.

Most visitors follow in the footsteps of the kings. They traverse the Old Town along the Royal Road (Droga Królewska), bringing them to the Herbowa Gate (Brama Herbowa) (see no. 33). Embedded in the rampart here are inscribed stones commemorating the castle's restoration after the Austrians returned it to Krakow in 1905.

Wawel Royal Castle (Zamek Królewski na Wawelu) on Wawel Hill (Wawelskie Wzgórze)

The towering 16th century bastion on the left supports an equestrian statue of national hero Tadeusz Kościuszko (1746–1814). Beyond is another gate giving access to the castle's outer courtyard. Here the layers of history are apparent: the Renaissance and Baroque cupolas of Wawel Cathedral (Katedra Wawelska) to the left, Gothic defence towers ahead, and in the middle, ruins of buildings demolished in the early 19th century, when the Austrians made the hill a fortress.

What can't be seen is the Stone Age hamlet archaeologists say existed here around 50,000 BC nor the settlement established by Slavic tribes during the 7th and 8th centuries, which legend credits to the dragon-slaying King Krak (see no. 5). And what of the first incarnations of the castle and cathedral? The latter is represented by the 11th century Romanesque St. Leonard's Crypt beneath the present-day cathedral (see no. 4). Of the first castle, vestiges of a late 10th century pre-Romanesque rotunda are preserved as part of the Lost Wawel (Wawel Zaginiony) exhibition (see no. 3). Remains of the 14th century castle built by King Casimir III the Great (Kazimierz III Wielki) (1310–1370) and Ladislaus II Jagiello (Władysław II Jagiełło) (c. 1352–1434) include the Gothic-vaulted Hen's Foot and Danish towers, used today to house the Crown Treasury and Armoury (Skarbiec Koronny i Zbrojownia) (see no. 2). That little else remains beyond defensive works is because the highest, easternmost part of Wawel Hill was always the favoured position for the castle's residential quarters. Thus, when the Gothic residence was damaged by fire in 1499 and replaced by the Renaissance palace seen today, much of it was obliterated.

To explore the palace, visitors pass through a third gate and enter the castle's inner courtyard; in the form of a magnificent Renaissance arcaded quadrangle, one has the impression of suddenly being transported to Florence. This is not surprising since the buildings are largely the work of Florentine architects hired by Jagiellonian King Sigismund I the Old (Zygmunt I Stary) (1467–1548). First on the scene in 1506 was Francesco Fiorentino (?–1516), who began work on the quadrangle's west wing (now used to display an Oriental Art (Sztuka Wschodu) exhibition; see no. 2). He was followed by Bartolomeo Berecci (c. 1480–1537), who completed the north and east sides of the quadrangle in 1536, with a curtain wall and more modest kitchen wing completing the courtyard to the south.

Despite such strong Italian involvement, the quadrangle is not pure Renaissance. Closer inspection reveals it is a fusion of Italian and native elements. Its irregular shape, for example, the vase-shaped imposts, and the function allocated to each storey – ground floor for palace officials, first for royal apartments and second for state rooms – are local

The Renaissance courtyard at Wawel Royal Castle (Zamek Królewski na Wawelu)

features. Similarly, the steep pitched roofs help cope with snowy Polish winters, their eaves extended far out to keep rain off the balconies.

Both first and second floors in the east wing can be visited. Together they provide an impression of royal life during the Golden Age initiated by King Sigismund I the Old, when Renaissance Krakow was a dynamic centre of commerce and the royal household was a centre of cultural life, music and artistic patronage. On the first floor the Royal Private Apartments (Prywatne Apartamenty Królewskie) have been restored to their Renaissance magnificence, with larch wood ceilings, ornate stone doorframes, painted friezes and magnificent Belgian tapestries commissioned by the last Jagiellonian, King Sigismund II Augustus (Zygmunt II August) (1520–1572).

The State Rooms (Reprezentacyjne Komnaty Królewskie) on the second floor were used for court ceremonies and are even more splendid. Whereas the first floor has arcades overlooking the quadrangle, here a double-height balcony with slender Gothic-style columns is deployed. Three rooms warrant special attention, namely the Envoys' Room (Sala Poselska), with its unique coffered ceiling of 1540 adorned with lifelike wooden heads by Sebastian Tauerbach (?–1552), the Tournament Room (Sala Turniejowa) featuring a frieze by Albrech Dürer's brother Hans (1490–1538), and the Senators' Hall (Sala Senatorska), where Sigismund I the Old married the Milanese princess Bona Sforza (1494–1557). She famously introduced tomatoes to Poland!

The latest chapter in Wawel's long history is an esoteric one. According to Hindu philosophers, one of seven sacred stones comprising goddess Shiva's global energy wheel *(chakra)* landed here. Though never seen, it is believed to reside behind the left-hand wall inside the palace quadrangle, where believers linger to soak up the vibe.

Other locations nearby: 2, 3, 4, 5

2 Sceptres and Swords

31-001 Kraków (Wawel Hill), the Crown Treasury and Armoury (Skarbiec Koronny i Zbrojownia) and the Oriental Art (Sztuka Wschodu) exhibition at Wawel Royal Castle (Zamek Królewski na Wawelu)
Tram 6, 8, 10, 13, 18 to Wawel (note: there is a daily limit on tickets so early arrival is advised and last entry is one hour before closing)

The Royal Apartments and State Rooms at Wawel Royal Castle (Zamek Królewski na Wawelu) show how Polish royalty lived and worked during their tenure in Krakow (see no. 1). Elsewhere in the castle complex, however, there are two permanent exhibitions that reveal another side to monarchy, namely their taste in treasure, weaponry and Oriental art.

The first of these, the Crown Treasury and Armoury (Skarbiec Koronny i Zbrojownia), occupies a series of rooms in the north east corner of the castle's Renaissance courtyard. The insignia of royal power, including crowns, sceptres, orbs and swords, have been stored here since the 14th century, where they have provided a visible sign of Polish independence. Largely destroyed by the Prussians in 1795, the present collection was assembled in the 1930s.

The first room (up the stairs) is named for King Casimir III the Great (Kazimierz III Wielki) (1310–1370) and is a unique example of a formal chamber from the castle's 14th century Gothic incarnation. It is part of a three-storey tower with a central vaulted pillar, nicknamed the Hen's Foot Tower. The room today is used to display various royal treasures, including a chalice commissioned by Casimir and the chessboard of Sigismund III Vasa (Zygmunt III Waza) (1566–1632). To the right is the Danish Tower containing what remains of the original Treasury, most notably Poland's original coronation sword *(Szczerbiec)* used to crown most monarchs from 1320 onwards. Sigismund III's Tower was added alongside it around 1600 and contains the insignia of King John III Sobieski (Jan III Sobieski) (1629–1696). To the left, the Room with Ceremonial Weapons contains objects from the king's personal armoury, as well as spoils from various 17th century Polish campaigns.

Thereafter follows a series of rooms that make up the Armoury proper. Here can be found pikes, two-handed swords and decorated halberds used by the court guards, as well as more modern sabres and rapiers. The 17th and 18th century armour includes a magnificent winged Hussar's suit made from articulated scales. Rifles, pistols and crossbows come later in the collection, which concludes in the Gothic and Renaissance cellars with a collection of cannons and mortars, and replicas of banners captured at the Battle of Grunwald (1410).

The second exhibition, Oriental Art (Sztuka Wschodu), can be found in the west wing of the castle. This collection is the result of military and trading contacts with various Near and Middle Eastern countries. Probably the most significant artefacts are those seized during the Battle of Vienna (1683), when the Polish army commanded by King John III Sobieski famously halted the advance of the invading Ottoman Turks. The spoils include trophies, weapons, banners and tents, as well as part of a superb 16th century Persian carpet depicting the Islamic *Garden of Paradise*. Several Turkish banners from the battle are displayed together with the personal sabre of defeated Ottoman

Winged Hussar's Armour in the Crown Treasury and Armoury (Skarbiec Koronny i Zbrojownia) at Wawel Royal Castle (Zamek Królewski na Wawelu)

commander Kara Mustafa (1634/1635–1683). There are also examples of Turkish horse armour, and various Turkish and Caucasian prayer rugs dating from the 18th and 19th centuries.

A separate part of the exhibition is devoted to some magnificent examples of Far Eastern ceramics. There are large Chinese vases on pedestals from the 17th and 18th centuries, including one decorated with the eight Buddhist symbols of prosperity. They are accompanied by various kettles, tea cups and figurines. The collection concludes with a display of Japanese porcelain, mainly of the 18th century *Imari* type, given by Catherine the Great (1729–1796) to a Prussian prince and later inherited by Poland's wealthy Radziwiłł and Potocki families.

Other locations nearby: 1, 3, 4, 5

3 Discovering the Lost Wawel

31-001 Kraków (Wawel Hill), the Lost Wawel (Wawel Zaginiony) exhibition at the Wawel Royal Castle (Zamek Królewski na Wawelu)
Tram 6, 8, 10, 13, 18 to Wawel (note: there is a daily limit on tickets so early arrival is advised and last entry is one hour before closing).

Wawel Royal Castle (Zamek Królewski na Wawelu) stands at the historic heart not only of Krakow but also Poland. The various buildings seen today are impressive but like most ancient places they have their antecedents. The intriguing remains of these earlier structures are preserved in the Lost Wawel (Wawel Zaginiony) exhibition.

The first royal residence on Wawel Hill appeared in the late 10th and early 11th centuries during the reigns of Kings Bolesław I the Brave (Bolesław I Chrobry) (967–1025) and Mieszko II Lambert (c. 990–1034), both members of Poland's founding Piast dynasty. Their pre-Romanesque palace was located on the highest, easternmost part of the hill, where it comprised a hall, a residential wing and the Rotunda of SS. Felix and Adaukt (also known as the Rotunda of the Blessed Virgin Mary). The ruins of this last remarkable structure – one of the best preserved examples of pre-Romanesque architecture in Poland – lie at the heart of the Lost Wawel Exhibition. One of several informative scale models dotted throughout the exhibition shows how the building with its four apses, built directly onto the bedrock, appeared during the Middle Ages.

Later in the 11th century, the main building of Wawel's Romanesque palace was erected. The remains of this two-storey hall with its 24 columns have been discovered under the northern wing of the present palace. The ruins of the church that went with it, the triple-aisled Church of St. Gereon (alternatively Mary of Egypt), were identified beneath the west wing, where it was used until the 13th century.

Later still, during the 14th century, the palace was transformed into a Gothic one, with new buildings and circuit walls erected by Kings Casimir III the Great (Kazimierz III Wielki) (1310–1370) and Ladislaus II Jagiello (Władysław II Jagiełło) (c. 1352–1434). Despite being damaged by fire in 1499, its Hen's Foot, Danish and Jordanka Towers remain containing some fine Gothic vaulting (see no. 2). The present configuration of the palace around a Renaissance courtyard was realised under King Sigismund I the Old (Zygmunt I Stary) (1467–1548)

The ruined Rotunda of SS. Felix and Adaukt is the centrepiece of the Lost Wawel (Wawel Zaginiony) exhibition

(see no. 1). It was during this phase of reconstruction that the Rotunda and the Church of St. Gereon were lost.

A separate room in the exhibition, the Royal Coach House, contains a collection of everyday items reflecting life on Wawel Hill during the Middle Ages, including shoes, belt buckles, tools and various vessels. There is also a tomb slab carved with a *Tree of Life* that came from a second pre-Romanesque rotunda known simply as Church B. The adjacent Small Kitchen contains the remains of the 16th century royal kitchens complete with ovens.

Another important part of the Lost Wawel Exhibition is the multi-roomed Lapidarium, where an array of sculptural fragments from the various incarnations of Wawel's palace is displayed. Also here can be found altar and tomb fragments from Wawel Cathedral (Katedra Wawelska), as well as a collection of 19th century plaster casts taken from sculptures in the cathedral's Sigismund Chapel. Another room contains a superb collection of Renaissance-era ceramic tiles together with models of the stoves from which they came.

Back in the entrance is a scale model of Wawel Hill in the 18th century, which is interesting for the various buildings and gardens that once cluttered the now-open main castle courtyard.

Visitors interested in learning more about the architecture and landscaping of Wawel Hill should take the seasonal Wawel Architecture and Gardens (Budowle i ogrody Wawelu) tour, which departs from just outside the entrance to the Lost Wawel Exhibition between April and September.

Other locations nearby: 1, 2, 4, 5

4 Of Bells and Bones

31-001 Kraków (Wawel Hill), Wawel Cathedral (Katedra Wawelska)
on Wawel Hill (Wawelskie Wzgórze)
Tram 6, 8, 10, 13, 18 to Wawel (note: the Cathedral is free to visit
but a ticket is required for the Sigismund Bell, Royal Tombs and
Cathedral Museum)

A cathedral has stood on Wawel Hill since around 1000 AD. After its first two incarnations were destroyed by fire, the present Gothic structure was begun in 1320 and consecrated in 1364. Poland's spiritual centre, it is here that many of its monarchs have been christened, crowned and buried.

Hanging over the entrance are some old bones. Legend has it they belong to the Wawel Dragon (Smok Wawelski) though in reality they are mammoth, woolly rhino or whale, placed here at a time when worshippers knew no better (see no. 5). Should they be removed it is said the world will end.

Inside the entrance on the right is the Gothic Chapel of the Holy Cross (Kaplica Świętokrzyska) containing the red marble tomb of King Casimir IV Jagiellon (Kazimierz IV Jagiellończyk) (1427–1492) and his Austrian wife Elisabeth von Habsburg (Elżbieta Rakuszanka) (c. 1436–1505) sculpted by Veit Stoss (c. 1450–1533) (see no. 18). The Byzantine-style frescoes were painted by Ruthenian artists brought to Poland after the creation of the Polish–Lithuanian Commonwealth in 1386.

Beneath where the nave and transepts cross stands the canopied Shrine of St. Stanislaus of Szczepanów (Ołtarz św. Stanisława) (c. 1030–1079). Bishop, martyr and patron saint, his revered relics lie in a 17th century silver sarcophagus (see no. 44). Polish kings deposited their spoils of war here, for example King Ladislaus II Jagiello (Władysław II Jagiełło) (c. 1352–1434), who brought the banners of the vanquished Teutonic Knights from the Battle of Grunwald (1410). The chancel beyond contains the 17th century main altar, where Poland's coronations took place.

The southern transept contains the Sigismund Chapel (Kaplica Zygmuntowska), Poland's finest Renaissance structure. Dedicated to the last Jagiellonian kings, notably Sigismund I the Old (Zygmunt I Stary) (1467–1548), it was completed in 1531 to a design by Florentine architect Bartolomeo Berecci (c. 1480–1537) (it can be identified from outside by its golden dome). Nearby in the southern ambulatory is the marble canopied tomb of King Casimir III the Great (Kazimierz III

Wielki) (1310–1370), who built the Gothic incarnation of Wawel Hill, his feet resting on a lion.

The east end of the cathedral holds the Batory Chapel (Kaplica Batorego) where the Blessed Sacrament is adored. The faithful also gather before the Black Crucifix in the north ambulatory, where Christ is said to have instructed the 12-year-old Queen Jadwiga (1374–1399) to marry the Grand Duke of Lithuania – later King Ladislaus II Jagiello (Władysław II Jagiełło) (c. 1352–1434) – facilitating the creation of the Polish–Lithuanian Commonwealth. Leading off the north ambulatory is the medieval Sigismund Tower (Wieża Zygmuntowska), with its Baroque lantern added by architect Kasper Bażanka (c. 1680–1726). The tower's namesake bell (Dzwon Zygmunta) was commissioned in 1520 by Sigismund I the Old and rings on important occasions.

The many towers of Wawel Cathedral (Katedra Wawelska)

This tour finishes back at the main entrance, where a staircase leads down to a series of Royal Tombs (Groby Królewskie). Here kings from the time of Sigismund I the Old onwards are buried. The first and oldest of them, the 11th century St. Leonard's Crypt (Krypta św. Leonarda), is Krakow's finest example of Romanesque architecture. Following the demise of the monarchy, half a dozen national heroes were additionally buried here, including statesman Tadeusz Kościuszko (1746–1814), national poet Adam Mickiewicz (1798–1855) and General Władysław Sikorski (1881–1943). Most recently interred were Polish President Lech Kaczynski (1949–2010) and his wife, who perished in a plane crash in 2010.

Alongside the cathedral is a museum containing a wealth of religious artefacts dating back to the 13th century.

Other locations nearby: 1, 2, 3, 5

5 In the Dragon's Den

31-001 Kraków (Wawel Hill), the Dragon's Den (Smocza Jama) at Wawel Royal Castle (Zamek Królewski na Wawelu)
Tram 6, 8, 10, 13, 18 to Wawel (note: there is a daily limit on tickets so early arrival is advised, last entry is one hour before closing, only open late April until October, not suitable for the infirm and passage is one way)

Like most cities, Krakow has its share of legends. One of the most colourful concerns the Wawel Dragon (Smok Wawelski) that allegedly once lived beneath Wawel Hill. True or not, the legend is important because it alludes to the historical origins of Krakow itself.

The earliest version of the legend is in the *Chronica Polonorum*, a Latin history published around 1200 by historian Wincenty Kadłubek (1150–1223). Probably compiled at the behest of Casimir II the Just (Kazimierz II Sprawiedliwy) (1138–1194), the work includes various legends cited in an attempt to connect contemporary Polish history to antiquity, a practice common among medieval chroniclers.

According to this version "there was in the windings of a certain rock a fierce ferocious dragon". Each week it demanded livestock from the locals and whenever there was a shortfall it took humans instead. Unable to tolerate this, one King Grakch hatched a plan with his two sons to stop the slaughter. Instead of livestock, they sent carcasses stuffed with burning sulphur, inflicting a fiery death on the dragon. Afterwards, the younger son killed his brother, blaming the death on the dragon. This fooled the king into declaring him the victor and giving him the crown. Only later did the deceit come to light and the younger son was banished. In memory of the event, a castle was built over the dragon's lair and named Krakow after the king (see no. 1).

Every good legend has some truth in it. Sure enough beneath the western slope of Wawel Hill there is a winding limestone cave known as Smocza Jama – Dragon's Den. Formed 25 million years ago, it consists of three interconnected chambers around 900 feet in length. The first, Chamber A, is a former well accessed by means of a 132-step staircase inside the Thieves' Tower (Baszta Złodziejska) in the main courtyard at Wawel Royal Castle (Zamek Królewski na Wawelu). Chamber B is the longest and most attractive part of the cave, and was used during the 16th and 17th centuries as the banquet hall of a tavern. Behind an iron grille can be glimpsed muddy pools containing the troglobitic crustacean *Niphargus tatrensis*, a relic of the Tertiary sea that washed over Wawel Hill in Jurassic times.

The third chamber, Chamber C, served as the main room of the tavern. Today it deposits visitors onto the Vistula (Wisła) riverbank by means of a natural opening in the rock. Here stands a fire-breathing statue of the dragon by sculptor Bronisław Chromy (1925–2017) past which a Dragon Parade floats each year.

So the dragon's lair existed – but what about the dragon? Bones purporting to belong to it have hung outside Wawel Cathedral (Katedra Wawelska) for years but are clearly those of a mammoth, woolly rhino or whale (see no. 4). And what of King Grakch? Better known as Krak or Krakus, there is little evidence he ever existed but his part in the legend, like that of the dragon, serves to illustrate Krakow's beginnings in an easy-to-relate and exciting manner. In reality, Wawel Hill has been occupied since the Stone Age, its natural defences always attractive to newcomers. During the 7th and 8th centuries these would have included the Slavic tribe (most likely Vistulans or Avars), led by a Grakch-like figure, who probably fought not a dragon but those eager to seize his hill.

Bronisław Chromy's fire-breathing sculpture of the Wawel Dragon (Smok Wawelski)

Sculptor Bronisław Chromy also designed the Monument to Dżok the Dog (Pomnik Psa Dżoka) farther down the riverbank. It commemorates a loyal pet, which remained at the nearby rondo Grunwaldzkie long after its owner died there of a heart attack.

Other locations nearby: 1, 2, 3, 4

6   Pinball Paradise

31-068 Kraków (Stradom), the Krakow Pinball Museum
(Interaktywne Muzeum Flipperów) at ul. Stradomska 15
Tram 6, 8, 10, 13, 18 to Stradom or Wawel; 22, 52 to Stradom (note:
the museum is in the courtyard at the back of the building)

Concealed in a brick-vaulted cellar at ul. Stradomska 15 (Stradom) is something unexpected. The Krakow Pinball Museum (Interaktywne Muzeum Flipperów) contains more than 60 vintage working pinball machines dating back to the mid-1950s and represents a labour of love on the part of its owners, Marcin Moszczynski and Maciej Olesiak. This is the place to experience an old school games arcade before digital technology changed gaming forever.

The walls of the dimly-lit, brick-vaulted cellar are lined with flashing, chiming pinball machines on which players score points by manipulating a steel ball on a playfield, gathering points along the way. Each machine is free to play once admission has been paid, with re-entry guaranteed throughout the day.

Pinball has ancient origins being derived from outdoor games such as bowls, boules, bocce, and pétanque, which themselves find a common ancestry in the games of ancient Rome. These in turn led to variants that could be played inside, such as billiards, and eventually to table top versions (notably bagatelle in the 1770s) in which moveable wickets were replaced by fixed pins. French soldiers carried bagatelle boards with them when they went to America to help fight the British during the American Revolutionary War, and the game quickly caught on there. It was a British settler, Montague Redgrave, who saw the commercial potential in bagatelle and in 1869 he patented a board with a spring-loaded ball cue. These 'pinball' games became especially popular during the 1930s American depression, when people were eager for affordable entertainment.

The golden age of pinball followed the Second World War, when player-controlled flippers were pioneered by pinball manufacturer David Gottlieb. By the 1960s most machines offered a host of other features, too, including rubberised bumpers, slingshots, targets, and a nudge facility. Sound effects and elaborate light displays were made possible by the introduction of solid-state technology in the 1970s.

The arrival of the video game in the 1980s, however, signalled the end of the pinball boom, and the once-familiar rows of pinball machines were soon ousted by table top video games such as *Space*

Mechanical fun in the Krakow Pinball Museum (Interaktywne Muzeum Flipperów)

Invaders and *Pac-Man*. A selection of these games is available in the museum for good measure, with many more available in the dedicated Krakow Arcade Museum (Interaktywne Muzeum Gier Wideo) at Centralna 41a (Czyzyny). But the simple electro-mechanical pleasures of traditional pinball machines endured and during the 1990s they enjoyed a renaissance on the back of feature film tie-ins such as *Star Trek*, *Indiana Jones*, *Jurassic Park* and *The Addams Family* – the most popular pinball machine of all time – all of which are represented in the museum. Full use was made of the machine's vertical back glass on which eye-catching graphics were used to lure punters away from their video screens. Who can resist pinball machines featuring *The Terminator* (with Arnold Schwarzenegger's voice), *The Creature from the Black Lagoon*, *Medieval Madness* and *Dirty Harry*?

Anyone who remembers queuing enthusiastically in arcades for their turn on a favourite machine should visit the museum, where they can happily spend all day revelling nostalgically in the joys of analogue entertainment.

Gamers of all persuasions will enjoy Cybermachina at ul. Stolarska 11 (Old Town), where everything from card games and board games to Nintendo and Wii are available in a cellar bar. Billiards' devotees should visit The Stage at ul. Łobzowska 3 (Piasek), where they will find seven handsome tables and a well-stocked bar. Football fans wishing to see their favourite teams in action can do so at the Football Heaven Sports Bar at ul. św. Filipa 7 (Kleparz).

7 Finding a Woolly Rhino

31-049 Kraków (Stradom), the Natural History Museum of the Institute of Systematics and Evolution of Animals (Muzeum Przyrodnicze Instytutu Systematyki i Ewolucji Zwierząt) at ul. św. Sebastiana 9
Tram 6, 8, 10, 13, 18 to Wawel

One of Krakow's least-known treasures lurks in a museum in Stradom. The world's only complete preserved specimen of an extinct woolly rhinoceros (*Coelodonta antiquitatis*), it takes pride of place at the Natural History Museum of the Institute of Systematics and Evolution of Animals (Muzeum Przyrodnicze Instytutu Systematyki i Ewolucji Zwierząt) at ul. św. Sebastiana 9.

A branch of the Polish Academy of Sciences (Polskiej Akademii Nauk), the museum came about in 1865, when ornithologist Kazimierz Wodzicki (1816–1889) donated a collection of stuffed birds to the Scientific Society of Krakow (Towarzystwo Naukowe Krakowskie). Soon bolstered with rocks and fossils, the collection opened to the public in 1888 at the Academy's premises at ul. Sławkowska 17 (Old Town), finding its way to its current address in 1993.

The Institute's work combines traditional scientific disciplines with systematics (classification) of living and extinct animals, and genetics. Its holdings number over two million specimens and one of Poland's largest zoological libraries. A representative selection of specimens is displayed in the museum, where visitors are shown both long-dead fossilised creatures and under the same roof living walk-through ecosystems, including a rain forest.

The museum's greatest treasure though is undoubtedly its woolly rhino. It was found in 1929 in an ozokerite pit in the village of Starunia, south-east of Lwów in what is now Ukraine. The ozokerite, a naturally-occurring mineral wax mined for candles, had preserved not only the animal's carcass but also its organs and soft tissues, making it a unique find. Although the adult female's hooves and horns had not survived, and her hair was preserved only in patches, enough remained for a decent reconstruction. Additionally, the remains of plants, insects and small vertebrates found alongside the rhino facilitated a reconstruction of its Late Pleistocene habitat pertaining 30,000 years ago in the Carpathian foothills.

Prior to the discovery of the Starunia specimen, the appearance of the woolly rhino, which died out 12,000 years ago, was known only

This preserved woolly rhino graces a natural history museum in Stradom

from its depiction in prehistoric cave paintings. Roaming Eurasia from the Pyrenees to Siberia, it was the second biggest Ice Age herbivore after the woolly mammoth, growing up to six and a half feet tall, with long dense fur and two huge horns.

It should be mentioned here that it was in Krakow in 1967 that Europe's greatest concentration of mammoth bones was found on ul. Vlastimila Hofmana (Zwierzyniec) near the Kościuszko Mound (see no. 106). Dating back 25,000 years, the bones included a rib in which a manmade flint spearhead was lodged. It is the first direct evidence of how prehistoric man killed these great beasts.

Natural historians will also enjoy the new Centre for Nature Education (Centrum Edukacji Przyrodniczej) at ul. Gronostajowa 5 (Dębniki), an extramural department of the Jagiellonian University (Uniwersytet Jagielloński). Born out of a late 18th century 'Cabinet of Natural Curiosities', it is today a world-class teaching establishment (tours by appointment only www.cep.uj.edu.pl). It also contains the university's Zoology Museum (Muzeum Zoologiczne) and Geology Museum (Muzeum Geologiczne).

One doesn't have to be a geologist to enjoy the Wieliczka Salt Mine (Kopalnia soli Wieliczka) half an hour from Krakow by train (www.wieliczka-saltmine.com). Brine was evaporated here 5,000 years ago and the first shafts were dug in the 13th century by Benedictine monks. Table salt was mined commercially until 1996, since when the labyrinth of tunnels have become a hugely popular UNESCO World Heritage site. Visitors thrill at the salt-cut chapels, statues and chandeliers. When the queues get too long try instead the nearby Bochnia Salt Mine (Kopalnia soli Bochnia), Poland's oldest dating back to 1248.

Other locations nearby: 9

8 The Prettiest Street in Krakow

31-002 Kraków (Okół), a walk along ul. Kanonicza
Tram 1, 6, 8, 13, 18 to Plac Wszystkich Świętych

Officially Krakow's prettiest street is cobblestoned ul. Kanonicza, which runs between ul. Senacka and ul. Padzamcze. A part of Okół, Krakow's oldest medieval trading settlement absorbed into Krakow in 1401, its Renaissance-era palaces, featuring carved portals, *sgraffito* decoration and secretive back gardens, were built for the canons of nearby Wawel Cathedral (Katedra Wawelska). This brief tour (by house number) reveals how much history still resides here:

1. The Palace of Bishop Samuel Maciejowski (Pałac biskupa Samuela Maciejowskiego) was built in the 1530s and features an arcaded gallery by Renaissance stonemason Bartolommeo Berrecci (1480–1537). It today houses the Department of Architectural History and Cultural Heritage Protection of the Tadeusz Kościuszko University of Technology, with a gallery and theatre space in the cellar.

6. The Gothic Knight's House (Dom Rycerski) served formerly as a residence for knights and today houses the Krakow Society of Friends of Fine Arts.

7. The House Under the Three Crowns (Pod Trzema Koronami) was completed in 1523 for Canon Jan Karnkowski. It is rendered in a mixture of Gothic and Renaissance styles, including a portal inscribed *Dominus audiator meus et protector meus* (The Lord hears me and protects me).

9. This stuccoed building was originally two houses, merged after a fire in 1455. During the 18th century it was home to Hugo Kołłątaj (1750–1812), one of the great figures of the Polish Enlightenment, who in 1791 co-wrote the first Polish Constitution, the first such document in Europe.

11. Another former canon's residence with an early 19th century frieze of Napoleonic eagles.

13. Another Gothic-Renaissance canon's house, where a 9th century ducal treasure was unearthed which can be seen in the nearby Archaeological Museum (see no. 11).

15. The Sreniawa Chapter House (Dom Kapitulny Szreniawa) is yet another canon's house, its Renaissance portal adorned with the Krakow Chapter's coat of arms.

16. The House Under the Butterfly (Pod Motylem), a canon's house built in the early 15th century and reworked after the fire of 1455,

is now the Hotel Copernicus. Guests stay in rooms with original frescoes and swim in the vaulted medieval cellar!

17. The Palace of Bishop Erasmus Ciołek (Pałac Biskupa Erazma Ciołka) was considered the grandest resident on ul. Kanonicza. Completed in 1505, it now houses a museum of religious art – a branch of the National Museum in Krakow (Muzeum Narodowe w Krakowie) – including sculptural fragments, icons and Madonnas.

18. The Palace of Florian Mokrski (Pałac Floriana z Mokrska) was built for a Bishop of Krakow during the 14th century, later reconstructed and currently headquarters of the Pope John Paul II Centre (see no. 47).

19-21. These magnificent 16th century Renaissance residences once housed the Deans

Ul. Kanoniza with Wawel Royal Castle and Wawel Cathedral beyond

of Krakow. Italian architect Santi Gucci (1530–1600) added the *sgraffitoed* façade, inscribed portal and arcaded courtyard. Home to Pope John Paul II when he was Poland's youngest bishop, it contains the Archdiocesan Museum of Cardinal Karol Wojtyła (Muzeum Archidiecezjalne Kardynała Karola Wojtyły) (see no. 10).

22. The Hotel Kanonicza offers just three huge rooms, each occupying an entire floor of this 15th century house.

24. The Gorków Palace (Pałac Górków) is two older houses combined, which later served as an Austrian police barracks and a telegraph office. It is today the Office for the Protection of Monuments.

25. The Długosz House (Dom Długosza) was built in the 14th century as a royal bath house then converted for use by canons and named after royal chronicler Jan Długosz (1415–1480). Presently it houses the rectorate of the Pontifical University of John Paul II.

Other locations nearby: 9, 10, 11, 12

9 Little Rome

31-044 Kraków (Okół), the Church of SS. Peter and Paul (Kościół św. Piotra i Pawła) at ul. Grodzka 52A
Tram 1, 6, 8, 13, 18 to Plac Wszystkich Świętych

There are no Renaissance churches in Krakow. This bald fact might seem surprising in a city with so many places of worship but the reason is prosaic. The Gothic era in Krakow was so successful that no further churches were required until the early 17th century. By this time the intervening Renaissance style was waning in favour of Baroque. It was the age of the Jesuits, who had arrived in the city in 1582, and they adopted Baroque as a way of asserting the Catholic Counter-Reformation. The number of Baroque churches built over the ensuing two centuries earned Krakow the moniker of 'Little Rome'.

The city's first and finest Baroque church is the Church of SS. Peter and Paul (Kościół św. Piotra i Pawła) at ul. Grodzka 52A (Okół). Funded by King Sigismund III Vasa (Zygmunt III Wasa) (1566–1632) and completed in 1619, it was Poland's first building designed entirely in the Baroque idiom. The cruciform church was largely realised by Italian Jesuit monk-cum-architect Giovanni Maria Bernardoni (1541–1605). That its pilastered façade resembles the Church of the Gesù, the Jesuit Mother Church in Rome is not surprising since Bernardoni worked on that building, too. Both feature niches containing statues of saints, and over the entrance is the Jesuits' familiar *IHS* emblem. What sets the Krakow church apart though is its eye-catching perimeter wall containing pillars supporting statues of the twelve apostles. Designed originally by Kasper Bażanka (c. 1680–1726) as a wayside shrine for passers-by, the present statues are modern copies.

The interior of the church was designed by royal architect Giovanni Battista Trevano (?–1644). Viewed from the nave, the pillars supporting the dome create the impression of a theatrical stage upon which the liturgy is played out (originally accompanied by a hundred singers!). The stucco work so typical of Baroque interiors was undertaken by Giovanni Battista Falconi (1600–1660) of Milan.

In 2010 the crypt beneath the church was reworked as a national pantheon for Poles distinguished in the arts and sciences. This continued a tradition long carried on at Wawel Cathedral (Katedra Wawelska) and the Skałka Sanctuary (Sanktuarium Skałka) (see nos. 4, 44). The Counter-Reformation polemicist Piotr Skarga (1536–1612) had been interred here in 1612 and in 2013 he was joined by Sławomir Mrożek

Baroque saints grace the Church of SS. Peter and Paul (Kościół św. Piotra i Pawła) in Okół

(1930-2013), Poland's much-loved master of satire and lampoonist of the totalitarian system. His 1964 play *Tango* examining the conflict between conformism and anarchy brought him considerable fame.

Another relatively recent addition is a Foucault pendulum installed in the church in 1949. Consisting of a swinging weight suspended on a 150-foot-long wire, it offers a simple but effective illustration of the Earth's rotation. As the pendulum swings across a clock face marked on the floor, its path appears to rotate, whereas in reality the plane is fixed and it is the Earth that is rotating (demonstrations usually occur on Thursday mornings).

Other Baroque churches in Krakow's Old Town include the beautiful Church of St. Anne (Kościół św. Anny) at ul. św. Anny 11. The collegiate church of the Jagiellonian University, it was built in the late 17th century to a design by Dutch architect Tylman van Gameran (1632–c. 1706), with stucco by Baltazar Fontana (1661–1733) and some marvellous *trompe l'oeil* frescoes. Also well worth visiting are the Piarist Church of the Transfiguration (Kościół Przemienienia Pańskiego) at ul. Pijarska 2, the Church of St. Martin (Kościół św. Marcina) at ul. Grodzka 58, and the Church of St. Bernard (Kościół św. Bernardyna) at ul. Bernardyńska 2.

Other locations nearby: 7, 8, 10, 11, 12

10 Papal Tourism

31-002 Kraków (Okół), a tour of sites associated with Pope John Paul II (Jan Paweł II) including the Archdiocesan Museum of Cardinal Karol Wojtyła (Muzeum Archidiecezjalne Kardynała Karola Wojtyły) at ul. Kanonicza 19–21
Tram 1, 6, 8, 13, 18 to Plac Wszystkich Świętych; 6, 8, 10, 13, 18 to Wawel

In 1978, when Karol Józef Wojtyła (1920–2005) was made Pope John Paul II (Jan Paweł II), he became the first non-Italian pontiff in 455 years. Since his death, the number of places proclaiming a connection to the man has grown, with devotees now following in his footsteps. The result is a local phenomenon known as 'papal tourism'.

Karol was born on May 18th, 1920 in the town of Wadowice, 30 miles south-west of Krakow. The house today is a museum – the Family Home of John Paul II (Dom Rodzinny Ojca Świętego Jana Pawła II) – at the aptly re-named plac Jana Pawła II 5. Unfortunately his mother Emilia and brother Edmund both died whilst he was still a boy.

In 1938, after graduating from high school (famously eating numerous custard *Kremówkas* to celebrate!), Karol enrolled for philology and languages at Krakow's Jagiellonian University (Uniwersytet Jagielloński). He moved with his father into a modest tenement at ul. Tyniecka 10 (Dębniki), where another museum – the Wojtyła Apartment (Mieszkanie Wojtyłów) – has been established. At this time Karol was known more for his poetry and sporting prowess – swimming, skiing and mountaineering – than his religious beliefs.

With the German invasion of Poland in September 1939 Karol's studies were interrupted and he spent his days as a labourer in the Zakrzówek limestone quarry and the Solvay soda plant in Borek Fałęcki (see nos. 46, 47). A continuing interest in the arts though saw him join the Studio 38 theatre company in defiance of Nazi edicts.

It was the death of his father in 1941 – and the example set by Saint Albert Chmielowski (1845–1916) who gave up painting to join the priesthood – that prompted Karol to seek a new life within the Catholic Church. In 1942 he began clandestine seminary studies run by the Archbishop of Krakow, Adam Stefan Sapieha (1867–1951), and attended Mass at the Church of St. Stanisław Kostka (Kościół św. Stanisława Kostki) at ul. Konfederacka 6.

Karol was ordained on November 1st 1946 and delivered his first Mass in the Crypt of St. Leonard beneath Wawel Cathedral (Katedra

Karol Wojtyła occupied this room on ul. Kanonicza before he became Pope

Wawelska) (see no. 4). Later, in 1958 during a kayaking expedition, he heard he had been made Poland's youngest bishop. This necessitated a move to ul. Kanonicza 19 (Okół), where his room, with its desk, record player, skis and cassock is preserved as part of the Archdiocesan Museum of Cardinal Karol Wojtyła (Muzeum Archidiecezjalne Kardynała Karola Wojtyły).

Long a supporter of workers' rights, with a discernible anti-Communist tone to his sermons, in 1959 Karol famously gave the first ever Mass in Nowa Huta, Krakow's Soviet-style steelworks. Construction of the first Catholic church there began a decade later and his role in the subsequent rise of the Solidarity (Solidarność) movement and eventual fall of Communism cannot be overstated (see no. 75).

Karol later occupied the 14th century Bishop's Palace (Pałac Biskupi) at ul. Franciszkańska 3 (Old Town) until his election to Pope on 16th October 1978. Even after becoming Pope and relocating to Rome, he stayed here during visits to the city, with the faithful congregating beneath the Papal Window (now filled with a mosaic). His statue with outstretched arms, one of several in the city, adorns the courtyard, which is open daily.

As Pope John Paul II, Karol's last visit to Krakow was in 2002 culminating in an outdoor sermon that drew 2.5 million people. He died on April 2nd 2005 and was canonized in 2014. The most recent addition to Krakow's papal landscape is the massive John Paul II Centre (Centrum Jana Pawła II) in Łagiewniki (see no. 47).

Other locations nearby: 8, 9, 11, 12

11   Mystery of the Zbruch Idol

31-002 Kraków (Okół), the Archaeological Museum in Krakow
(Muzeum Archeologiczne w Krakowie) at ul. Poselska 3
Tram 1, 6, 8, 13, 18 to Filharmonia or Plac Wszystkich Świętych

The Archaeological Museum in Krakow (Muzeum Archeologiczne w Krakowie) at ul. Poselska 3 (Okół) is one of the city's great unsung attractions. Not only is it housed inside an historic former monastery but it also boasts some fascinating permanent exhibits, including a collection of Egyptian mummies and examples of the first Polish pottery from the 6th millennium BC. The main attraction here, however, is the so-called Zbruch Idol (Bałwan z Zbrucha), the world's only example of a sculpture representing a Slavic god.

From the 9th century onwards, the area occupied by the museum was part of the timber-built settlement of Okół. Only in the 14th century was the area encompassed by Krakow's city wall, parts of which are preserved beneath the museum and in the lovely walled garden. Between the 15th and 18th centuries, the Church of St. Michał and Monastery of the Barefoot Carmelites occupied the site. After the Catholic monks were ejected, the buildings were reused first as a prison and court house, and later a museum.

As far as the early history of Krakow is concerned, the museum's exhibit on the prehistory and Early Middle Ages of Lesser Poland (Małopolska) is most enlightening. The mysterious Zbruch Idol, however, comes from farther afield. Made of grey limestone, this four-sided pillar stands just over eight and a half feet high, with three tiers of reliefs carved on each face. It was unearthed in August 1848 in the dried up bed of the River Zbruch (a tributary of the Dniester) near the village of Liczkowce in what is now Ukraine. The village elder donated it to a Polish Count, Mieczysław Potocki, who in 1850 passed it to the Krakow Scientific Society (Towarzystwo Naukowe Krakowskie), which established the museum the same year.

Ever since its discovery, the Zbruch Idol has prompted discussion as to its purpose and meaning. That it is a pagan religious monument seems clear from it having been deliberately submerged sometime after the Christianisation in 988 of Kievan Rus, the federation of East Slav tribes.

Notions about the idol's meaning are based on its carved reliefs. Three sides of the lowest tier show a kneeling, bearded man supporting the upper tiers on his hands (the fourth side shows an eroded solar symbol). The four sides of the middle tier depict a smaller figure with arms outstretched, one accompanied by a child-like figure. The four sides of the uppermost tier have the largest figures, one carrying a ring, another a horn, and a third on horseback wearing a sword (the fourth is empty-handed). One theory postulates that the four-sided idol represents the pan-Slavic, four-headed god of war, Svetovid (Światowid). Alternatively, the four sides might represent four individual Slavic gods, namely Perun, Mokosh, Lada and Dažbog. Yet again, the three-tiered design of the idol might represent the three levels of the world (underworld/mortal world/heaven), linking it to the Slavic deity, Triglav. Or perhaps the top tier figures represent the four seasons, the horn of plenty signifying Spring and the empty-handed figure, Winter. We'll never know for sure.

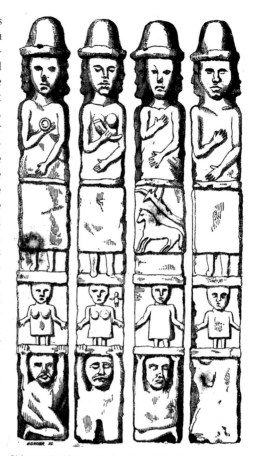

Old engraving showing the four faces of the Zbruch Idol (Bałwan z Zbrucha)

Those unable to visit the museum will find a copy of the Zbruch Idol in plac Bernardyński outside Wawel Royal Castle (Zamek Królewski na Wawelu).

Nearby at ul. Poselka 12 is a wall plaque inscribed thus: "Around 1860, in a house that stood on this site, lived the son of a wandering poet, Józef Konrad Korzeniowski – Joseph Conrad. He brought the Polish soul to English letters." Around the corner at ul. Senacka 3 is a small regional Geological Museum (Muzeum Geologiczne) run by the Polish Academy of Sciences (Polska Academia Nauk).

Other locations nearby: 8, 9, 10, 12

12 Where Medieval Meets Modern

31-004 Kraków (Okół), the Basilica of St. Francis (Bazylika św. Francoszia) at plac Wszystkich Świętych 5
Tram 1, 6, 8, 13, 18 to Plac Wszystkich Świętych or Filharmonia

Krakow at the turn of the 19th and 20th centuries witnessed a period of exciting architectural change. New buildings such as the School of Industry at al. Mickiewicza 5 (Piasek) displayed an innovative penchant for strong vernacular features and folk motifs. Elsewhere old buildings were being renovated in Art Nouveau style, creating a localised synthesis of medieval and modern that still enthralls. The finest example is the Basilica of St. Francis (Bazylika św. Francoszia) at plac Wszystkich Świętych 5 (Okół).

Consecrated in 1269 by Franciscan friars from Padua – hence also being called the Franciscan Church (Kościół Franciszkanów) – the basilica was Krakow's first brick building. It was here that the pagan Grand Duke of Lithuania, Jogaila (c. 1352–1434), was baptised before ascending the Polish throne as King Ladislaus II Jagiello (Władysław II Jagiełło).

It was damage sustained during the Krakow Fire of 1850 that provided an opportunity to transform the building's medieval interior into one of the city's most colourful churches. The project was spearheaded by Krakow's great Art Nouveau practitioner and proponent of the Young Poland (Młoda Polska) movement, Stanisław Wyspiański (1869–1907) (see nos. 18, 31, 90). He deployed modernist stained glass in conjunction with medieval-inspired murals – many by the unsung Tadeusz Popiel (1863–1913) – to create a breath-taking universe of colour within the basilica's strict Gothic confines. Thus beneath a painted blue firmament pricked with golden stars are meadows of sunflowers, roses, violets and geraniums celebrating St. Francis' love of nature, set within a framework of geometric patterns, polychrome rainbows and winged cherubs (see front cover and page 4).

These murals are complimented by Wyspiański's eight stained glass windows in the choir, including one of St. Francis receiving his Stigmata. Most powerful of all is *God the Father – Arise* over the east door showing God as a bearded alchemist in the act of fiery creation (see no. 92). To witness the diminishing rays of a sunset playing through this window is a sight to behold. Elsewhere in the basilica, fellow artist Józef Mehoffer (1869–1946) was responsible for the large Stations of the Cross in the Chapel of the Lord's Passion, with Stefan Matejko (1871–1935) contributing the polychrome murals in the Chapel of Our Lady of Sorrow (see no. 84).

Before leaving the Basilica notice the Chapel of the High Brotherhood of Our Lord's Passion, which contains an exact copy of the Shroud of Turin, and opposite a painting of St. Maximilian Kolbe (1894–1941), a Franciscan monk murdered at Auschwitz. There is also an atmospheric Gothic cloister containing a portrait gallery of Krakow's bishops.

God the Father – Arise by Stanisław Wyspiański in the Basilica of St. Francis (Bazylika šw. Francoszia)

For another taste of Gothic, walk eastwards onto ul. Dominikańska. On the left at ul. Stolarska 12 is the Basilica of the Holy Trinity (Bazylika šw. Trójcy), known also as the Dominican Church (Kościół Dominikanów) after the Bolognese friars that raised it in 1250. Also damaged by the fire of 1850 and only modestly redecorated afterwards, it retains its late-17th century miracle-working shrine of Our Lady of the Rosary and a reputation for plainsong. Additionally the Dominicans administer the much-rebuilt 11th century Church of St. Giles (Kościół šw. Idziego) at ul. Grodzka 67, Krakow's only Catholic church offering Sunday Mass in English. Outside is the Katyń Cross commemorating 21,768 Polish military officers and intelligentsia murdered in 1940 by Soviet secret police (NKVD).

For another example of Wyspiański's talent for restoration, visit the 14th century Church of the Holy Cross (Kościół šw Krzyża) at ul. šw. Krzyża 23 (Old Town), where he restored the late medieval frescoes in the choir. Note the unusual palm tree-like pillar supporting a canopy of rib vaults.

Other locations nearby: 8, 9, 10, 11, 95

13 The Biggest Market Square

31-013 Kraków (Old Town), a walk around Rynek Główny
beginning with the Bonerowski Palace (Pałac Bonerowski)
at number 42
Tram 1, 6, 8, 13, 18 to Plac Wszystkich Świętych; 2, 4, 8, 13, 14,
18, 20, 24, 44 to Teatr Bagatela

Krakow's great architectural superlative is its main square (Rynek Główny). The size of six football pitches, it is Europe's largest medieval marketplace. Although these days it bustles more with tourists than traders, there is much history to be found in the buildings surrounding it.

Laid out in 1257 according to its newly-granted town charter, 'the Rynek' has played a vital role in the city's life. It was here that royal processions passed along the Royal Road (Droga Królewska) to Wawel Royal Castle (Zamek Królewski na Wawelu). It was also here that events of national importance took place, for example in 1794 when freedom fighter Tadeusz Kościuszko (1746–1817) launched his revolt against foreign occupation. On a darker note, during the Second World War the Rynek was briefly renamed Adolf-Hitler-Platz.

Primarily though, the Rynek was a marketplace. Permanent stalls were only permitted with the monarch's consent, with zones allocated to specific trades – ironmongery in front of the Basilica of St. Mary (Bazylika Mariacka), for example, and butchery concealed in Mały Rynek to the rear. Visiting merchants were obliged to sell at a discount to enable local traders to turn a profit.

What follows is an anti-clockwise whistle-stop tour by house number starting on the north side:

42. The Bonerowski Palace (Pałac Bonerowski) is a luxury hotel formed from a 16th century nobles' tenement house. Gothic elements are still discernible despite a sumptuous 19th century makeover that contrasts with the 1920s apartment block next door, which the Nazis rendered less overtly modernist in 1941.

35. The Krzysztofory Palace (Pałac Krzysztofory) is even older and now home to the main branch of the Museum of Krakow (Muzeum Krakowa) (see no. 20).

27. The Palace under the Rams (Pałac Pod Baranami) is also shaped from medieval tenements, one of which was an inn where sheep were traded. Today it contains an upstairs cinema and a famous cellar bar (see nos. 21, 25). Almost in front is the much-photographed sculpture

Eros Bendato (Eros Bound) by Igor Mitoraj (1944–2014) and beyond it Krakow's leaning Town Hall Tower (Wieża Ratuszowa) (see no. 17).

26. The Prince's House (Kamienica Książęca) features a corner statue of St. John of Capistrano (1386–1456), who preached Christianity against the Ottomans and allegedly stayed here.

25. Like most of the buildings on the Rynek's south side, this house was destroyed during the Krakow Fire of 1850 and rebuilt by young Warsaw architect Tomasz Pryliński (1847–1895), who helped shape the Rynek's present appearance. Today it houses an International Cultural Centre (Międzynrodowy Centrum Kultury).

Looking out from the Cloth Hall (Sukiennice) across Rynek Główny

17. The 14th century Hetman House (Kamienica Hetmańska), now the luxurious Szara Gęś restaurant, has an unusually grand Gothic vaulted hall on the ground floor, with ceiling bosses adorned with tournament helmets. Historians suggest it may once have been used by royalty.

13. Pasaż 13 is a townhouse converted into a designer shopping mall, its old walls providing a novel backdrop.

9. The Boner House (Kamienica Bonerowska) features a Renaissance attic overlooking the ancient Church of St. Adalbert (Kościół św. Wojciecha) (see no. 16).

8. The House under the Lizards (Kamienica Pod Jaszczurami) retains its figurative medieval house sign over the entrance.

7. The first Polish international coach post service set out for Venice from here in 1569.

5. The Czynciel House (Kamienica Czyncielów), the Rynek's only Art Nouveau building (1908), rounds out this tour providing a counterpoint to the nearby medieval Basilica of St. Mary, the Renaissance Cloth Hall (Sukiennice) opposite and the neo-Gothic brick façade of the House under the Eagle (Kamienica Pod Orłem) at number 45 (see nos. 15, 18).

Other locations nearby: 14, 15, 16, 17, 18, 19, 20, 21, 22, 23

14 Beneath the Rynek

31-042 Kraków (Old Town), the Rynek Underground (Podziemia Rynku) at Rynek Główny 1
Tram 1, 6, 8, 13, 18 to Plac Wszystkich Świętych; 2, 4, 8, 13, 14, 18, 20, 24, 44 to Teatr Bagatela (note: closed every second Monday of each month, free on Tuesdays, advance booking advised at the information office in the Cloth Hall or www. muzeumkrakowa.pl)

Krakow's main square (Rynek Główny) revels in its reputation as Europe's largest medieval marketplace. Laid out during the mid-13th century, it contains some of the city's most historic structures (see no. 13). Considering its age, it is no surprise that the square has provided rich pickings for archaeologists eager to discern its earlier incarnations. Their findings have been made been made public in the shape of the fascinating subterranean attraction called the Rynek Underground (Podziemia Rynku).

Serious excavation began in the eastern part of the square in 2005, when the discovery of artefacts around the Cloth Hall (Sukiennice) led to speculation about what else might be found. The dig was supposed to last for six months but once the scale and importance of the finds being unearthed was realised, it was extended to five years. The result is a treasure trove of finds that paints a vivid picture of daily life in Krakow over the past thousand years.

The Rynek Underground opened in 2010 to a blaze of publicity. A branch of the Museum of Krakow (Muzeum Krakowa), it has remained enormously popular ever since. Since only 300 visitors can be accommodated at any one time, timed tickets can be bought in advance to avoid long queues. But don't let this put you off. The Rynek Underground may be a tourist hotspot and especially popular with youngsters but it offers something quite unique.

Visitors access the museum by means of a staircase that descends over 13 feet down from an entrance in the Cloth Hall directly opposite the Basilica of St. Mary (Bazylika Mariacka). Immediately they are greeted by a hologram of 14th century Cracovians projected onto a curtain of smoke beyond which medieval Krakow is reborn. What might otherwise have been a difficult-to-interpret archaeological site has been transformed into a walk-through immersive museum, where full use has been made of modern technology – lasers, audio effects and 3-D models of artefacts displayed on touchscreens – to create an

An ancient cobbled street in the Rynek Underground (Podziemia Rynku)

otherworldly atmosphere that helps today's visitors engage directly with the past.

Technology is one thing but ultimately it's all about what's actually been excavated. There are quotidian objects that were once traded here including belt buckles, leather shoes, clothes and jewellery, as well as the coins, scales and weights necessary to do so. There are plentiful structural remains, too, including remnants of medieval market booths (the earliest incarnation of the famous Cloth Hall overhead), as well as the raised cobbled streets with wooden kerbs that serviced them (see no. 15). There are also remains from the time before Krakow received its market charter, including evidence of cottages destroyed in 1241 by raiding Tatars from northern and central Asia (see no. 23). It should be remembered that for at least 150 years before Rynek Główny was laid out, this area was still an urban centre, one of several (including Kazimierz and Kleparz) that existed here in medieval times.

Then there are the remains of an 11th century cemetery. These are of particular interest because they showcase anti-vampire burial methods! According to Polish folklore, potential vampires could be identified by their red hair and extra row of teeth. To prevent them from becoming undead, they were buried in the foetal position, with their hands tied and severed head placed between the feet.

In addition to the useful multilingual labelling of everything on display, there are excellent audio guides in a range of languages. Factor in the short, sub-titled documentaries covering the various epochs of Krakow's history and an automated puppet show for children, and the Rynek Underground has something for everyone.

Other locations nearby: 13, 15, 16, 17, 18, 19, 20, 21, 22, 23

15 The Cloth Hall Story

31-042 Kraków (Old Town), the Cloth Hall (Sukiennice) at Rynek
Główny 3
Tram 1, 6, 8, 13, 18 to Plac Wszystkich Świętych; 2, 4, 8, 13, 14,
18, 20, 24, 44 to Teatr Bagatela

Krakow's famous main square (Rynek Główny) contains a great variety of historic structures. It would be difficult to select a single building as representative although for many the Cloth Hall (Sukiennice) is a serious contender. A superb example of commercial Renaissance architecture, this 750-year-old shopping mall is a must-see on any visitor's itinerary.

The earliest incarnation of the Cloth Hall was erected in the mid-13th century. Archaeological excavations have revealed that it consisted of two rows of market booths separated by a public thoroughfare, with pitched roofs added around 1300. The actual remains can be seen in the Rynek Underground (Podziemia Rynku), a popular visitor attraction beneath the present building (see no. 14).

In the mid-14th century, King Casimir III the Great (Kazimierz III Wielki) (1310–1370) ordered that a larger version of the original structure be built. It's worth noting here that although the name 'Sukiennice' refers specifically to textiles and fabrics, the Cloth Hall at this time saw a great variety of commodities traded by its merchants, including leather, spices, wax, silk, lead, and salt from the famous Wieliczka mines. This new Cloth Hall helped increase Krakow's importance as an East–West trading post, at a time when the city had also become a member of the powerful Hanseatic League.

Later in the mid-16th century, a destructive fire necessitated reconstruction of the Cloth Hall. Consisting this time of a single, two-storey structure, it was rendered in the then-fashionable Renaissance style overseen by Italian sculptor Giovanni Maria Padovano (1493–1574), with rooftop grotesques courtesy of fellow countryman Santi Gucci (c. 1530–1600).

By the 1870s, however, with Poland now partitioned for almost a century, the once imposing Cloth Hall lay abandoned by the occupying Austrians. Krakow's patriotic mayor Mikołaj Zyblikiewicz (1823–1887) took the opportunity to restore his city's prestige by restoring the building (as well as Wawel Castle). Thus between 1875 and 1879, the tawdry lean-tos that had slowly obscured the exterior were swept away and in their place neo-Gothic arcades and projecting wings added by the young Warsaw architect Tomasz Pryliński (1847–1895). Additionally part of the upper floor was given over to the first Polish National Museum, which quickly became a focus for patriotic celebrations.

The exterior of the Cloth Hall has remained the same ever since although the interior has been modernised. It is good to know it still functions as a market albeit one that now sells souvenirs, including Polish lacework and amber jewellery (old fashioned signs in one of the arches recall the fabric merchants they've replaced).

The upper floor is now home to the Gallery of 19th Century Polish Art, a branch of the National Museum in Krakow (Muzeum Narodowe w Krakowie). It is organised

The Cloth Hall (Sukiennice) on Rynek Główny with the towers of the Basilica of St. Mary (Bazylika Mariacka) beyond

like a 19th century salon into four rooms each covering a different theme. Of particular interest are the large-scale historical canvasses of events that occurred in the square outside, notably *Hołd Pruski (Prussian Tribute)* by Jan Matejko (1838–1893) and *Przysięga Kościuszko (Kościusko's Oath)* by Michał Stachowicz (1768–1825). During the summer months it is possible to access the roof of Pryliński's arcades, where Café Szał affords its patrons with a wonderful overview of the square below. Those after an Old Europe vibe should stay downstairs and visit Café Noworolski, with its sumptuous Art Nouveau interior (see no. 87).

Upon leaving the Cloth Hall look for the knife suspended from one of the arcade arches. It symbolises the Magdeburg Rights granted in 1257, which not only gave Krakow its town charter (and so its market square) but also stipulated that thieves would have their ears cut off!

Other locations nearby: 13, 14, 16, 17, 18, 19, 20, 21, 22, 23

16   A Romanesque Rarity

31-042 Kraków (Old Town), the Church of St. Adalbert (Kościół św. Wojciecha) on Rynek Główny
Tram 1, 6, 8, 13, 18 to Plac Wszystkich Świętych

Krakow's famous main square (Rynek Główny) can be explored horizontally and vertically. One can walk across it from side to side, as well as plumb its ancient depths courtesy of the Rynek Underground (Podziemia Rynku) museum (see nos. 13, 14). In one location, the Church of St. Adalbert (Kościół św. Wojciecha), it is possible to do both since it is so old that its floor sits well below the present level of the square.

The old and new parts of the Church of St. Adalbert (Kościół św. Wojciecha)

Located in the southern corner of the square, St. Adalbert's is one of the oldest stone churches in Poland. It was originally built in the 11th century thus preceding the demarcation of the square by almost a century, which explains its seemingly random position.

The church is dedicated to the Bohemian missionary Saint Adalbert of Prague (Wojciech Sławnikowic) (c.956–997), who was martyred in his efforts to convert the Baltic Prussians to Christianity. When the rulers of Bohemia refused to pay the ransom for the body's return, it was acquired instead by Poland's first king, Bolesław I the Brave (Bolesław I Chrobry) (967–1025), who offered its weight in gold and then placed the remains in the Royal Cathedral of Gniezno. Religious relics held considerable power at the time and Bolesław's political power was undoubtedly enhanced as a result.

The architectural history of the church is fascinating. According to the Archaeological Museum of Krakow, a wooden structure occupied the site in the late 10th century (consecrated according to legend by St. Adalbert before he set out on his mission). This was followed by the first stone church in the 11th century, the remains of which can be detected in the lowest parts of the walls. These then became the footings of a second stone church erected at the turn of the 11th and 12th centuries. Both incarnations are precious examples of Polish Romanesque architecture.

Over the following centuries, the level of the surrounding square gradually rose by over six feet as it was repeatedly re-surfaced. Accordingly during the early 17th century, the church walls were heightened to keep pace. These were then stuccoed to hide the join and topped off with a Baroque cupola, which in addition to a vestry and chapel to St. Wincenty Kadłubek (c. 1150–1223) added a century later, resulted in the structure seen today. More recently some of the ancient masonry has been deliberately revealed to aid interpretation (this can be discerned around the original Romanesque portal, as well as around a second entrance built higher up on the west side during the Baroque reworking).

The cramped interior still functions as a church although the old congregation of merchants and nobles is made up today of devout locals and curious visitors. Classical music concerts are performed here and the crypt contains a small underground museum illustrating the long and colourful history of Rynek Główny.

Krakow's ascent to royal capital in the 11th century stimulated construction in the Polish Romanesque style. Other surviving examples include St. Leonard's Crypt beneath Wawel Cathedral (Katedra Wawelska) and the Church of St. Andrew (Kościół św. Andrzeja) at ul. Grodzka 54 (Okół) (see no. 4). Regarded as perhaps the country's best example of Romanesque architecture, the fortress-like walls of St. Andrew's provided a refuge during the Tatar raids of the 13th century, when the building was known as the Lower Castle to distinguish it from Wawel Castle. Like St. Adalbert's, it received a Baroque makeover, including a pair of steeples, stucco decoration by Italian plasterwork maestro Baltazar Fontana (1661–1733) and a Rococo pulpit in the shape of a boat.

Other locations nearby: 13, 14, 15, 17, 18, 19, 20, 21, 22, 23

17 Top of the Town Hall Tower

31-001 Kraków (Old Town), the Town Hall Tower (Wieża Ratuszowa) at Rynek Główny 1
Tram 1, 6, 8, 13, 18 to Plac Wszystkich Świętych; 2, 4, 8, 13, 14, 18, 20, 24, 44 to Teatr Bagatela (note: last entrance 30 minutes before closing and closed every first Tuesday of the month)

A graphic example of how Krakow suffered during the years of foreign occupation can be found in the south-west corner of Rynek Główny. Standing alongside the Cloth Hall (Sukiennice) is a stone and brick tower, all that remains of Krakow's once-imposing medieval Town Hall (Ratusz). A victim of economic and political stagnation, this once-important building was largely demolished in the early 19th century leaving only its tower as a reminder of former times.

The main body of the Town Hall was first constructed in brick in 1313. From that time until the early 19th century, it served as the city's administrative hub and seat of its Great Council and Mayor. As such, it was one of Poland's oldest seats of civic government. To be a suitably representative building, however, it required a dominant visual feature, which it received in 1383 in the form of the tower.

Over the years, the Town Hall was repeatedly enlarged and remodelled (a metal model alongside the tower shows how the building appeared in the 18th century). During the time of the Austrian Partition, however, the building was effectively abandoned. Without adequate maintenance it soon became a hazard to market traffic and in 1820 the Austrians ordered its demolition. Only through vociferous opposition from locals was the tower spared.

A combined belvedere and belfry, the Town Hall Tower (Wieża Ratuszowa) today stands as an important example of so-called Polish Gothic. Rising to a height of 230 feet, it leans almost two feet at the top, the result of a fierce storm in 1703. Its original Gothic dome was lost to lighting in 1680 and replaced shortly afterwards by a Baroque dome. This survived until 1783, when signs of collapse saw it replaced by the smaller dome seen today.

Despite its chequered past and inclination, the Town Hall Tower can still be climbed. Visitors enter via a door in one of the two sides of the tower made of brick (these originally faced inwards onto the Town Hall, as opposed to the two decorated sides facing outwards onto the square). Note the remnants of the original Gothic portal above the door consisting of the city's coat of arms and the emblem of Poland. From here it's a leisurely climb to the top of the tower from where far-reaching vistas can be gained although it's difficult to look downwards onto the square because the tower is tapered. Now a branch of the Museum of Krakow (Muzeum Krakowa), the tower is used to display historic images of the surrounding square, a collection of medieval costumes and information about the tower's clock.

All is not quite as it seems though. The lions guarding the entrance to the tower are not original. They were brought here from a palace in Pławowice during some rather fanciful renovations in the 1960s courtesy of colourful Polish architect and television host Wictor Zin (1925–2007). At the same time he reinvented the bay windows on the tower's second floor and excavated the medieval cellars, which once housed the town jail and torture chamber.

The Town Hall Tower (Wieża Ratuszowa) on Rynek Główny

Krakow's modern City Hall (Urząd Miasta Krakowa) is based in the Wielopolski Palace between plac Wszystkich Świętych and ul. Poselska. Unusual for its crenelated roofline, it was built in the mid-16th century by nobleman and knight, Jan Tarnowski (1488–1561). The building was subsequently home to the aristocratic Wielopolski family. Following the Krakow Fire of 1850, they sold the burned-out building, which was first restored as a café and ball venue, and then in 1864 as Municipal Offices, including the office of the Mayor (Prezydent Krakowa).

Other locations nearby: 13, 14, 15, 16, 18, 19, 20, 21, 22, 23

18 The Veit Stoss Altarpiece

31-042 Kraków (Old Town), the Basilica of St. Mary (Bazylika Mariacka) at plac Mariacki 5
Tram 1, 6, 8, 13, 18 to Plac Wszystkich Świętych; 3, 10, 24, 52
Poczta Główna

The eastern corner of Krakow's main square (Rynek Główny) is dominated by the twin-spired Basilica of St. Mary (Bazylika Mariacka). The city's parish church since the early 13th century, it was built in stages and so presents an informative palimpsest of architectural styles. The interior is no less interesting, its undoubted highlight being the Veit Stoss Altarpiece (Ołtarz Wita Stwosza), the largest Gothic altarpiece in the world.

The basilica began life as a stone Romanesque structure. Destroyed during a Tatar raid in 1241, it was rebuilt in red-brick in the late 14th century, with Early Gothic cross vaults supporting a steeply pitched roof. The Late Gothic towers and adjoining chapels were added in the mid-15th century, the taller tower topped off with an octagonal lantern-spire and gilded Baroque crown. The result is a fine example of the so-called Polish Cathedral style, which served as a model for churches elsewhere, including several in Chicago founded in the late 19th century by Galician immigrants.

According to legend, the reason the towers are different heights is because they were built by two different architects, brothers who fell out when one excelled the other resulting in murder. In reality, whilst the shorter tower belongs to the church, the taller one is a city-owned watch tower from where a bugle known as the *Hejnal* is sounded at the turn of each hour. That its tune stops so abruptly is said to recall the first bugler, who whilst sounding the alarm during the Tatar raid was silenced by an arrow.

Inside, the basilica is known for its colourful late-19th century revamp with astonishing polychrome murals by Jan Matejko (1838–1893) and stained glass by Stanisław Wyspiański (1869–1907) and Józef Mehoffer (1869–1946) (see nos. 30, 84, 92). The greatest treasure, however, is the magnificent Veit Stoss Altarpiece.

Veit Stoss (known in Poland as Wit Stwosz) (c. 1450–1533) is regarded as the greatest late medieval European sculptor. Born in Swabia near Nuremberg, it is thought that a falling out with local authorities there prompted his move to Krakow, where he established a workshop and remained for 20 years. He created the famous altarpiece between

A detail of the Veit Stoss Altarpiece (Ołtarz Wita Stwosza) in the Basilica of St. Mary (Bazylika Mariacka)

1477 and 1489 in return for which he was made an honorary citizen and exempted from paying taxes.

The altarpiece is a triptych comprising a main panel flanked by smaller hinged panels on either side. When fully opened, it measures an impressive 36 feet wide and almost 43 feet high. Size aside, what makes the piece so important is the way Veit Stoss handled the main panel's subject matter. The scene at the bottom shows the death of Mary in the presence of the Twelve Apostles, each 12-foot-high figure realistically carved from a single trunk of soft linden. Their lifelike locks of hair, furrowed brows and straining muscles betray an emotion rare in Gothic art. The scene above depicts the Assumption of Mary into Heaven and at the top, outside the frame, is Mary's coronation witnessed by Poland's patron saints, Stanislaus and Adalbert. The side panels show the six scenes of the Joys of Mary, including the Nativity, which when closed reveal 12 scenes from the life of Jesus and Mary. So visually arresting is the work that Picasso declared it the Eighth Wonder of the World.

The square surrounding the basilica once contained one of half a dozen Old Town cemeteries closed by the Austrians in the late 18th century on health grounds and paved over. Also here is the 14th century Church of St. Barbara (Kościół św. Barbary), with its quaint attached Gothic Gethsemane (Ogrojec) Chapel.

Other locations nearby: 13, 14, 15, 16, 17, 19, 20, 21, 22, 23

19 At Home with the Hipolits

31-042 Kraków (Old Town), the Hipolit House (Kamienica Hipolitów) at plac Mariacki 3
Tram 3, 10, 24, 52 to Poczta Główna

The Hipolit House (Kamienica Hipolitów) at plac Mariacki 3 (Old Town) is one of a handful of historic house museums in Krakow. It is unique in that within a building of medieval origin is displayed a series of recreated bourgeois living spaces from the 17th to the early 20th centuries. As such it acts as a time machine of social history.

The Hipolit House is named after a family of Krakow merchants of the same name, who lived here between the late 16th and the early 17th centuries. Were they to reappear today they would undoubtedly recognise parts of their old home, whilst other parts would be alien to them. The building itself has been remodelled several times in the years prior to 2003, when it became a branch of the Museum of Krakow (Muzeum Krakowa).

A tour of the Hipolit House should really begin in the basement since that's where the oldest remains are to be found. Back in the Middle Ages this was a tenement house and in those days the basement served as the ground floor. This explains why relatively high status features such as a fine stone portal and a stove are preserved here.

The modern ground floor reached directly from the street is also noteworthy for its stone portals. One of them is Gothic and features a 'key' motif; another is Renaissance and is sculpted with the motif of an eye. Note, too, the old fashioned skiing equipment hanging on the wall and the horseshoe hung for good luck. Beyond is a steep staircase leading up to the first floor. That it is protected by the remains of a grille suggests the building was made deliberately secure.

A dozen variously-furnished rooms with different functions follow. One of the most beautiful is the cabinet *(gabinet)*, the walls of which are stuccoed by Italian plasterwork maestro, Baltazar Fontana (1661–1733), whose work graces numerous churches in Krakow (see nos. 9, 12, 16). Together with the rich carpets and academic books, the room reflects the interests and tastes of a wealthy patrician of the time. Another richly-appointed room is the bedroom *(sypialnia)*. Typical of the Rococo period, with its plasterwork, Venetian glass mirror, and faience ornaments, it also includes a marquetry table and chairs for use by visiting guests.

Several less grand but no less important rooms follow. These include the cosily-appointed parlour *(bawialnia)*, which served as a living room and contains furniture in different styles from different periods, as was once the fashion. Decorations include 18th century porcelain figures and portraits of Polish heroes such as Tadeusz Kościuszko (1746–1814) and Józef Poniatowski (1763–1813), reflecting the owners' patriotism. There is also the *salon*, which contains family portraits displayed to impress visitors, the dining room *(jadalnia)*, with its lace curtains and tablecloths made by the female occupants, and the matrimonial

The Hipolit House (Kamienica Hipolitów) on plac Mariacki

bedroom *(sypialnia małżeńska)*. Traditionally off-limits to anyone other than newly-weds, this is also where the lady of the house could retire to do her sewing and needlework.

Two specialised rooms complete the tour. One is the Collector's Room *(Pokój Kolekcjonera)*, which as its name suggests is filled with paintings, sculptures and ornaments. There is also a significant collection of old clocks here making this room appear more like a museum than a living space. The other is the Grandmother's Room *(Pokój Babci)*, which reeks of nostalgia with its sentimental keepsakes, local landscape paintings and wall-hung tapestry.

Afterwards relax at the modern Café Bar Magia on the ground floor of the building, with its concealed courtyard garden.

Other locations nearby: 13, 14, 15, 16, 17, 18, 20, 21, 22, 23

20 The Krzysztofory Cribs

31-011 Kraków (Old Town), the Krzysztofory Palace (Pałac Krzysztofory) at Rynek Główny 35
Tram 2, 4, 8, 13, 14, 18, 20, 24, 44 to Teatr Bagatela; 1, 6, 8, 13, 18 to Plac Wszystkich Świętych

It is fitting that the main branch of the Museum of Krakow (Muzeum Krakowa) is housed in an historic building. The Krzysztofory Palace (Pałac Krzysztofory) at Rynek Główny 35 (Old Town) has an illustrious history making it just as interesting as the artefacts it contains. Like many buildings on Rynek Główny, the palace finds its origins in the merging of several medieval tenement houses. Protected by Saint Krzysztof, hence the building's name, these were owned during the 14th and 15th centuries by various well-to-do merchant families. Only during the mid-17th century were the tenements merged to create a palace and the interiors reworked in Baroque style. This included the installation of the Tuscan arcades in the courtyard and, on the first floor, the imitation marble sculptures *(scagliola)* and ceiling stucco by Italian plasterwork master Baltazar Fontana (1661–1733).

The palace subsequently passed through the hands of Bishop Kajetan Sołtyk (1715–1788) and Jacek Kluszewski (1761–1841), owner of the Stary Teatr, whose presence drew prominent visitors. Later in 1846 it served as a base for Jan Tyssowski (1811–1857), leader of the doomed Krakow Uprising against the Austrians, and in 1914 as a recruiting station for the Polish Legions. During the 1930s, the cellars were used by the avant-garde Grupa Krakowska. Finally in 1965 the palace passed into the hands of the Museum of Krakow.

Since then the building has undergone considerable renovation. Although this work is still ongoing, a permanent exhibit called *Cyberteka (Krakow – Time & Space)* has been opened. Using the latest multimedia technology, it chronicles the urban and spatial development of the city from its earliest days through the granting of the town's charter in 1257 to the absorption of Podgórze in 1915 creating Greater Krakow.

Long associated with the museum is a collection of objects unique to the city. These are the Krakow Cribs *(Szopki krakowskie)* – known locally as Nativity Scenes – and their importance has earned them inclusion on UNESCO's list of Intangible Cultural Heritage of Humanity. The tradition of making cribs in Krakow dates back to the 19th century, when local craftsmen began making them as seasonal decorations to bolster their income during the lean winter months. As

Christmas approached, the cribs would be carried from door to door as part of a mobile nativity play (*Jasełka*). Abandoned during the 1920s and 30s, the tradition was reinvented in 1937 as an annual crib-building contest and except for a break during the Second World War, it's been going strong ever since.

From 1946 onwards, the contest has been orchestrated by the Museum of Krakow. On the morning of the first Thursday of December over 150 participants of all ages bring their cribs to Rynek Główny and display them around the statue of national poet Adam Mickiewicz (1798–1855). Each is given a registration number and the crowd gathers to marvel at their intricate craftsmanship. What makes the Krakow Cribs unique is that they incorporate miniaturised elements of the city's historic architecture – Gothic spires, Renaissance façades, Baroque domes – as well as its legendary characters, all rendered from everyday materials such as cardboard and coloured foil.

Preparing to display a Krakow Crib (*Szopka Krakowska*) in Rynek Głowny

At midday the cribs are taken to the Krzysztofory Palace for judging. Prizes are awarded in four size categories for the best designed crib made by a child, teenager and adult. The winning cribs are then displayed in the museum until February although during the building's current renovation they are displayed in the Celestat at ul. Lubicz 16 (Wesoła). Those deemed particularly attractive are acquired by the museum and added to its permanent collection (see no. 104).

Other locations nearby: 13, 14, 15, 16, 17, 18, 19, 21, 22, 23

21 Big Screen Krakow

31-010 Kraków (Old Town), a selection of historic cinemas
including Kino Pod Baranami at Rynek Główny 27
Tram 2, 4, 8, 13, 14, 18, 20, 24, 44 to Teatr Bagatela or 1, 6, 8, 13,
18 to Plac Wszystkich Świętych

Krakow may not be the Hollywood of the East – that accolade usually
goes to Prague – but it does have a long cinematic tradition. Several
internationally successful films have used the city as a backdrop, notably Krzysztof Kieślowski's *Double Life of Veronique (Podwójne życie
Weroniki)* (1991) and Steven Spielberg's *Schindler's List* (1993). Additionally Krakow's Academy of Fine Arts (Akademia Sztuk Pięknych
w Krakowie) nurtured the Father of Polish Cinema, Andrzej Wajda
(1926–2016), whose powerful films including *Człowiek z żelaza* (Man
of Iron) (1981) about the rise of the Solidarity (Solidarność) movement
and *Katyń* (2008) have helped put Polish cinema on the map.

These days Krakow is home to a buoyant arthouse and independent cinema scene, with screenings in a range of venues both historic
and modern. Unfortunately at the time of writing, Krakow's oldest
working cinema Kino ARS has just closed. Established in a converted
town house at ul. św. Tomasza 11 (Old Town) in 1916, it was originally
called Kino Sztuka ('sztuka' means art) and re-named in 1980. Although the building is now slated to become part of a new hotel, there
is talk that Kino ARS may be reborn elsewhere.

Now Krakow's only remaining Old Town cinema is Kino Pod
Baranami at Rynek Główny 27. This, too, is located inside a domestic
building but in this case a former palace with medieval origins (see no.
13). The cinema, however, is relatively young having only opened in
1969. A popular arthouse cinema hosting international films, festivals
and themed seasons, it offers three screens set across two floors and
an open-air summer screen in the courtyard. Reached by a sweeping
staircase, the grand Sala Czerwona (Red Salon) features Pullman seating and a carved wooden ceiling. Punters waiting for a film are encouraged to loiter in the foyer where comfortable armchairs are set against
a backdrop of film posters and vintage projectors.

Krakow's oldest purpose-built cinema building is Kino Wanda at
ul. św. Gertrudy 5 (Stradom). Although it has been used as a supermarket since 2003, the exterior remains intact, including a 1950s-style
neon sign. Opened in 1912, when the city was still under Austrian
rule, the *Art Nouveau* stained glass windows suggest the influence of

the Vienna Secession movement. The old entrance foyer to the left of the main façade is extant, as is the glamorously curved upstairs circle overlooking what is now the shop floor. Worth mentioning here is Teatr Bagatela at ul. Karmelicka 6 (Piasek), which opened in 1919. After being damaged by fire in 1928, it was remodelled as the Scala Kinoteatr and used during the Second World War to screen German language-only films. Returning thereafter to its use as a theatre, this is where in the 1940s a young

In the Sala Czerwona (Red Salon) at Kino Pod Baranami

Roman Polański (b. 1933) made his stage debut before finding fame as a film director.

Other interesting cinemas built during the 1950s and 60s can be found in Krakow's suburbs. They include Kino Kijów Centrum at al. Krasinskiego 34 (Salwator), Kino Agrafka at ul. Krowoderska 8 (Kleparz), and the aptly-named Kino Mikro squeezed beneath an apartment block at ul. Juliusza Lea 5 (Nowa Wieś). Originally used by Communist militia, in 1984 the Mikro became one of the first cinemas to show independent films as Communism lost its grip. Of Krakow's new independent cinemas, the intimate Kinokawiarnia Kika at ul. Krasickiego 18 (Podgórze) is an admirable example.

Krakow hosts several film festivals, including the Off Camera festival of independent cinema in April, the Krakow Film Festival (Krakowski Festiwal Filmowy) in May, and the Silent Movie Festival (Festiwal Filmu Niemego) in December.

Other locations nearby: 13, 14, 15, 16, 17, 18, 19, 20, 22, 23

22 Dough Rings and Floating Wreathes

31-001 Kraków (Old Town), obwarzanki street carts around the Town Hall Tower (Wieża Ratuszowa) at Rynek Główny 1
Tram 1, 6, 8, 13, 18 to Plac Wszystkich Świętych; Tram 2, 4, 8, 13, 14, 18, 20, 24, 44 to Teatr Bagatela

Ancient customs are an important part of modern Krakow and two of them can be described here. One is a humble dough ring that is probably the progenitor of the world-conquering bagel; the other is a floating wreath that has morphed since pagan times into a major annual festival.

Stroll around central Krakow, especially around the Town Hall Tower (Wieża Ratuszowa) in Rynek Główny, and you will come across *obwarzanki*. These oval braided dough rings, sprinkled with salt, poppy or sesame seeds, are sold by older vendors from blue-painted street carts. A staple street food, the name derives from the Polish verb *obwarzać* meaning 'to parboil' since that is what happens to the dough before baking. This gives the finished product a moist, sweetish centre encased in a crunchy, golden-brown crust. Around 200,000 *obwarzanki* are baked daily in Krakow and locals will tell you they are best eaten before midday.

It is this parboiling that connects *obwarzanki* with the non-braided, circular bagel first documented in Krakow's Jewish community in 1610. *Obwarzanki*, however, are much older being first mentioned in 1394 in the court records of King Ladislaus II Jagiello (Władysław II Jagiełło) (c. 1352–1434), when some are delivered to his wife, Jadwiga (1374–1399). In 1496, King John I Albert (Jan I Olbracht) (1459–1501) granted Krakow's bakers' guild a monopoly on baking *obwarzanki* during Lent, which remained in place until the reign of King John III Sobieski (Jan III Sobieski) (1629–1696). The decree only regulated sales within the city walls though, and so during the early 17th century the Jews of Kazimierz began baking their own, which they called *bajgiel* from the Yiddish *bagel*.

The rules of baking *obwarzanki* were relaxed during the 19th century so that today anyone can bake them and at any time. Since 2010 they have even been officially recognised as a protected regional food, as is revealed at the Obwarzanek Museum (Żywe Muzeum Obwarzanka) at ul. Paderewskiego 4 (Kleparz), where visitors can try making their own.

Down on the Vistula (Wisła), where the river bends beneath Wawel Hill, an even more ancient custom is observed. In its current form, *Wianki* is a mass cultural event managed by Krakow City Hall on Midsummer Eve (23rd June) consisting of open-air concerts, firework displays and beer tents. In ancient times, however, it was a Slavic pagan rite known as *Noc Kupały* (Kupala Night).

Derived from the Slavic word for bathing, Kupala Night marked the summer solstice – the shortest night of the year – when floral wreathes *(wianki)* were cast onto the river to promote fertility and purification. After the adoption of Christianity in Poland, Kupala Night was coerced into the Christian calendar as *Noc Świętojańska* (St. John's Night). John the Baptist's act of baptising people through full im-

Detail of a street cart selling fresh *obwarzanki*

mersion found a useful parallel in Kupala Night, which thus became a native Christian tradition infused with Slavic folklore.

Elements of the original rite remained. Wreathes were still floated (often lit with candles) and girls would interpret their relationship fortunes from the way in which they drifted away. Later during Poland's annexation by Austria, St. John's Night became a patriotic ritual, when Wanda, the princess of Prince Krak, legendary founder of Krakow, was commemorated. Today's *Wianki* only came about after the Second World War reaching its current more boisterous manifestation following the welcome repeal of Martial Law in 1983.

Krakow boasts several traditional bakeries *(piekarnia)* including Piekarnia Pochopień at ul. Krupnicza 12 (Piasek), with its mouth-watering chocolate wafers, and Piekarnia Mojego Taty at ul. Beera Meiselsa 6 (Kazimierz), which specialises in rye sourdough loaves.

Other locations nearby: 13, 14, 15, 16, 17, 18, 19, 20, 21, 23

23 The Hobby Horse Parade

31-001 Kraków (Old Town), the Lajkonik parade on Rynek
Główny
Tram 1, 6, 8, 13, 18 to Plac Wszystkich Świętych; 2, 4, 8, 13, 14,
18, 20, 24, 44 to Teatr Bagatela

One of Krakow's most colourful customs occurs on the first Thursday after Corpus Christi, which falls in either May or June. It consists of a local man in pseudo-Oriental dress parading through the city on a wooden horse, with a boisterous retinue and band in attendance. Known as *Lajkonik* ('hobby horse'), the custom commemorates Krakow's citizens saving their city from Tatar raiders.

The historical origins of the *Lajkonik* parade are difficult to pin down. Certainly Krakow was prey to raids by Tatars from northern and central Asia during the 13th century and three of them are well documented. It is thought that the parade commemorates the last of them in 1287, as this was the only raid during which the Tatars were successfully repelled.

According to tradition, the raiders were routed whilst asleep by a group of Vistula raftsmen *(włóczkowie)* from the Krakow suburb of Zwierzyniec. They commandeered the Tatars' belongings and one of the raftsmen dressed up in the fancy garb of the Tatar general. Emboldened by their actions, the raftsmen then mounted a comic attack on Krakow as a means of ridiculing the would-be attackers, attracting applause from locals as they went. In appreciation of the raftsmen's actions, the procession became an official annual event.

The inclusion of the wooden horse in the *Lajkonik* parade is only recorded in the 18th century though the reasons are unclear. It might be a relic of pagan ceremonies, when Svetovid (Światowid), the Slavic god of war, was celebrated as he circumnavigated the world on horseback (see no. 11). Alternatively, the Polish artist and writer Stanisław Wyspiański (1869–1907) in his play *Achilles* suggested that the rider had prehistoric origins, relating him to Indo-European water worshippers. Others have sought a more recent origin citing arcane medieval guild ceremonies, with their penchant for oriental costumes, as well as the 17th century fascination with cultures of the Far East. It's worth noting here that customs similar to *Lajkonik* have been recorded elsewhere, notably in Asia and South America, where they are associated with agricultural societies and their need to propitiate the gods for rain and crop fertility.

The *Lajkonik* parade begins around 1pm at the Norbertine Monastery (Klasztor norbertanek) on the banks of the Rudawa, a tributary of the Vistula (Wisła), where the raftsmen were once based (see no. 99). Today's horseman wears embroidered red robes designed in 1904 by Wyspiański, a pointed hat adorned with a crescent and a bushy black beard. After paying tribute to the Mother Superior, the parade continues along ul. Kosciuszko, ul. Zwierzyniecka, ul. Franciszkanska and ul. Grodzka. Eventually it reaches the main square (Rynek Główny) (Old Town), where *Lajkonik* dances the fast-paced *Krakowiak* folk dance,

The annual *Lajkonik* parade on Rynek Główny

bestowing good luck by tapping onlookers and shopkeepers with his golden baton. The parade culminates around 7pm in front of the Town Hall Tower (Wieża Ratuszowa), where the mayor toasts *Lajkonik* and the city's continuing good fortune (see no. 17). So beloved is Lajkonik today that his image even adorns Krakow's public transport upholstery and his name is used for a chain of bakers.

Another colourful annual tradition not only in Krakow but across Poland is *Dzien Trzech Króli* (Three Kings Day). This Catholic holiday on January 6th sees families attending Mass and children walking the streets dressed as the three wise men, Kaspar, Melchior and Balthazar. They carry with them a piece of blessed chalk, which they use to scribe the letters K + M + B over front doors in return for a few coins. This guarantees health and happiness to the home owners in the year to come.

Other locations nearby: 13, 14, 15, 16, 17, 18, 19, 20, 21, 22

24 The First University in Poland

31-007 Kraków (Old Town), a walk through the Jagiellonian University (Uniwersytet Jagielloński) beginning at ul. Gołębia 16
Tram 2, 4, 8, 13, 14, 18, 20, 24, 44 to Teatr Bagatela

Krakow is home to Poland's oldest university founded in 1364 by King Casimir III the Great (Kazimierz III Wielki) (1310–1370). Known originally as the Academy of Krakow (Akademia Krakowska), it became the fully-fledged Jagiellonian University (Uniwersytet Jagielloński) in 1400, when the Pope granted the right to run a theology department. Strolling its peaceful quadrangles today is like stepping back in time. This walk begins outside the 15th century Collegium Opolski at ul. Gołębia 16 (Old Town), which today houses the Polish Philology Department. Almost opposite is the rear entrance to the Collegium Kołłątaja (originally the Collegium Physicum). Here in 1883 two university professors, Karol Olszewski (1846–1915) and Zygmunt Wróblewski (1845–1888), first liquefied oxygen, nitrogen and carbon dioxide in a stable state leading to new advances in science and industry. The building today houses the University's Centre for Language Teaching and the University Archives.

Continue to ul. Gołębia 11 and the 15th century Collegium Minus. This originally housed Krakow's first art faculty established in 1882, where Poland's renowned painter Jan Matejko (1838–1893) studied before becoming director of the Academy of Fine Art (Akademia Sztuk Pięknych w Krakowie) on plac Jana Matejki (Kleparz). The University's Institute of Archaeology is based here today.

Around the corner at ul. Jagiellońska 15 is the red-brick Collegium Maius (Great College), the oldest surviving university building in Poland. Its history dates back to 1400, when King Ladislaus II Jagiello (Władysław II Jagiełło) (c. 1352–1434) acquired a noble's tenement house for conversion into a university (although adjacent buildings were subsequently purchased to create the more complex structure seen today, fragments of the tenement's limestone outer wall still line the street). Inside there is a superb albeit much reworked late-Gothic arcaded courtyard (open daily dawn to dusk), with a clock that chimes the old student song *Gaudeamus Igitur* at 1pm.

Originally the Collegium Maius provided accommodation for science professors, with a library upstairs and a lecture hall downstairs. It subsequently housed the departments of Theology and Liberal Arts, as well as a medical school. Today it is used for ceremonies and conferences, and contains the fascinating Jagiellonian University Museum (Muzeum Uniwersytetu Jagiellońskiego), which can be visited as part of a weekday guided tour. Among the scientific instruments displayed is a 16th century globe showing the newly-discovered America and astronomical equipment used by former student Nicolaus Copernicus

The courtyard of the Collegium Maius (Great College) on ul. Jagiellońska

(Mikołaj Kopernik) (1473–1543) (see no. 103). His heliocentric theory formulated in 1510 was a major scientific milestone. Between April and October, a painted passage leads from the courtyard to the contemplative Professors' Garden (Ogród Profesorski).

Now turn left onto ul. Św. Anny (passing a sculpture-filled courtyard along the way) to reach the Collegium Nowodworskie at number 12. The city's first grammar school established in 1588, it is now houses the University's Medical College. Directly opposite is the University's Church of St. Anne (Kościół św. Anny), considered Krakow's loveliest Baroque building (see no. 9).

This walk concludes by turning left along the Planty to reach the 19th century Collegium Novum (New College), where a stately oak marks freedom from Austria. The neo-Gothic building contains a gallery of famous professors, several of whom were arrested here in 1939 and deported during the Nazis' *Sonderaktion Krakau*, an operation designed to eliminate Polish intelligentsia (see no. 79). Jan Matejko's *Astronomer Copernicus (Astronom Kopernik)* (1873) hangs inside.

The university today sprawls across different parts of the city, including the Collegium Iuridicum at ul. Grodzka 53 (Old Town), with its head by sculptor Igor Mitoraj (1944-2014) and the Pedagogical Institute (Instytut Pedagogiki) at ul. Stefana Batorego 12 (Piasek), with its concealed back garden.

Other locations nearby: 25, 26, 27, 28

25 Cellar Pubs and Clubs

31-009 Kraków (Old Town), a tour of cellar clubs and pubs including Piec'Art Acoustic Jazz Club at ul. Szevska 12
Tram 2, 4, 8, 13, 14, 18, 20, 24, 44 to Teatr Bagatela

The centuries-old architecture of Krakow's Old Town lends itself perfectly to cellar pubs and clubs. With their sturdy brick vaults, good acoustics and constant temperature, these atmospheric hideaways are a magnet for drinkers, music lovers and those drawn to things subterranean. Many are a product of the post-Communist free market, when local entrepreneurs bought up unused basements and reinvented them for a new generation.

That said, Krakow's oldest cellar bar dates back to 1956. The Piwnica Pod Baranami (Cellar under the Rams) is housed in the 14th century cellar of a former palace at Rynek Główny 27 8see no. 13). It was here in 1956 that Warsaw-born Piotr Skrzynecki (1930–1997) founded his famous literary and political cabaret, a den of humorous yet subversive activity throughout the oppressive Communist era and still going strong today. Despite a smattering of curious visitors, the Polish-language performance every Saturday at 9pm still draws mostly local artists, academics and bohemians, who fit right in among the eclectic furnishings. A bronze statue of the colourful Skrzynecki sits outside what was his favourite café, Vis à Vis, two doors along at number 29.

Lacking political pretence but no less atmospheric is the Piec'Art Acoustic Jazz Club at ul. Szevska 12. Opened in the 1990s and considered one of the city's best jazz venues, the stage here plays host not only to Polish performers but also to many from farther afield. The cellar arches adorned with moody black-and-white photos of musicians and the cosy corner bar add an intimacy rarely found in conventional concert halls. More underground jazz can be enjoyed at the U Muniaka club at ul. Floriańska 3 and Camelot at ul. św. Tomasza 17, where another cabaret, Loch Camelot, performs at weekends. Also on ul. św. Tomasza at number 4 is Społem, a different sort of cellar bar. Being named after a chain of Communist-era shops, it revels in its themed decoration, which consists of Soviet propaganda posters and a DJ spinning records from a Soviet-era truck.

Krakow's other cellar bars cater for a variety of audiences. At the smarter end of things is the Polski Pub at Rynek Główny 44, boasting plush booths, the city's largest sports television and beer from the his-

A concert in full swing in the Piec'Art Acoustic Jazz Club on ul. Szevska

toric Tyskie Brewery in Silesia. More boisterous are the Pod Papugami Irish pub at ul. św. Jana 18, the student-filled Klub Kulturalny at ul. Szewska 25, and Klub Re at ul. św. Krzyża 4, which hosts indie bands and has a leafy beer garden at street level. There is even a branch of McDonalds at ul. Szewska 2, where diners have the option of eating their burgers in a 13th century cellar!

This tour finishes with an oddity. Stary Port (The Old Port) at ul. Straszewskiego 27 (entrance from ul. Jabłonowskich) is Krakow's only nautical-themed bar, where sea shanties are sung on Fridays and some Saturdays in honour of Poland's distant coastline.

The default drink in a Krakow cellar is vodka. The Poles have been distilling it since the Middle Ages, when potatoes were used instead of grain. Pure vodka should be drunk ice-cold. Otherwise flavoured vodkas are popular, including sweet cherry Wiśniówka, honey-infused Krupnik, herby amber-coloured Żołądkowa Gorzka, and floral Żubrówka containing a blade of grass from the Białowieża Forest (with apple juice it is called tatanka). Pickled herring (śledzia) is said to go well with vodka, which explains the curiously-named Ambasada Śledzia bar at ul. Stolarska 8 (Old Town), opposite the American Embassy. Other popular bar snacks (zakąski przekąski) include kiełbasa (sausage), galaretka (jellied pig trotters) and the ubiquitous pierogi.

Other locations nearby: 24, 26, 27, 28

26   A Shock in the Old Town

31-011 Kraków (Old Town), the Contemporary Art Gallery
Bunker (Galeria Sztuki Współczesnej Bunkier) at plac
Szczepański 3A
Tram 2, 4, 8, 13, 14, 18, 20, 24, 44 to Teatr Bagatela

It is often remarked that Krakow's Old Town is an open air museum of architecture. Certainly one can't escape the area's matchless Gothic, Renaissance and Baroque buildings in every shape and size. So it comes as something of a shock to walk into plac Szczepański and find the Contemporary Art Gallery Bunker (Galeria Sztuki Współczesnej Bunkier). One of the few modern buildings in the area, it is rendered in late-20th century Brutalist style.

Brutalism flourished between the 1950s and 70s having sprung from the early 20th century Modernist movement. The name is derived from the French word for 'raw' after Brutalist pioneer Le Corbusier (1887–1965) described his preferred material as being *béton brut* (raw concrete).

Krakow had brushed previously (and uneventfully) with Modernism in suburban buildings such as the National Museum (Muzeum Narodowe w Krakowie) and Jagiellonian Library (Biblioteka Jagiellońska) on al. Adama Mickiewicza (Czarna Wieś), as well as the Press Palace on ul. Wielopole (Stradom). But Brutalism was an extreme form of Modernism and the Contemporary Art Gallery Bunker was situated in the city's hallowed Old Town. Needless to say, when it was unveiled in 1965 there was quite an uproar.

The term 'bunker' was initially applied to the building in a pejorative way. Those opposed to what originally was called Pawilon Wystawowy (Exhibition Pavilion) felt its jagged concrete façade, with the impression of wooden shuttering left deliberately visible, resembled a wartime air raid shelter. The building seemed all the more brutal when viewed together with its neighbour, the graceful Art Nouveau-styled Palace of Art (Pałac Sztuki) (see no. 27). After a few years, however, the 'bunker' name stuck and in time the building was accepted as something new and exciting. Certainly there was nothing else like it in Krakow at the time and even today it raises the eyebrow of passers-by. The chunky façade topped off with a lightweight clerestory still works, as does the novel incorporation of an old tenement house.

The art displayed inside the Contemporary Art Gallery Bunker in line with the original ethos of the building, namely ground-breaking modern and contemporary art by Polish and international artists. Temporary exhibitions are staged across three floors and exhibition catalogues are sold in the small mezzanine bookshop. After viewing the art on display, be sure to enjoy a coffee or something stronger in the gallery's café-cum-bar. Whilst not Brutalist in design, this part of the building is also architecturally innovative, being in the form of a bold, iron-framed conservatory.

The Contemporary Art Gallery Bunker was not the first building to cause a stir in plac Szczepański. On the corner of the square with ul. Reformacka stands a modest skyscraper erected in 1936. Its strident Modernist design and the fact that a medieval tenement house was swept away to make room for it upset many preservationists. As a result, the main investor was coerced into paying a large fine that was put towards the construction of the National Museum (Muzeum Narodowe w Krakowie) at al. 3 Maja 1 (Czarna Wieś).

The Brutalist façade of the Contemporary Art Gallery Bunker (Galeria Sztuki Współczesnej Bunkier)

Those who appreciate the Contemporary Art Gallery Bunker's mix of architecture, art and café will find locales with similar facilities elsewhere in Krakow. One of them is the Mostowa Artcafe at ul. Mostowa 8 (Kazimierz). Concealed behind the sturdy but peeling façade is a sleek gallery space arranged beneath stripped-back brick vaults. The identically-appointed café spills out onto the pavement during the summer months. Devotees of contemporary art should also be aware of Krakow's contemporary arts festivals, including Sacrum Profanum in September and Unsound in October (the latter is part of a broader musical celebration).

Other locations nearby: 24, 25, 27, 28

27   A Total Work of Art

31-011 Kraków (Old Town), the Palace of Art (Pałac Sztuki) at plac Szczepański 4
Tram 2, 4, 8, 13, 14, 18, 20, 24, 44 to Teatr Bagatela (note: last entry 30 minutes before closing)

Krakow's Palace of Art (Pałac Sztuki) is one of those places where the building is every bit as engaging as the objects it contains. The city's first Art Nouveau building, it is a fine example of what German-speakers call a *Gesamtkunstwerk* (total work of art), in which different artistic styles and techniques are synthesised to create a satisfying and coherent whole. To this day it is considered one of the city's most prestigious exhibition spaces, with regularly changing displays of contemporary art.

Located at plac Szczepański 4 (Old Town), the Palace of Art is the seat of Krakow's Friends of the Fine Arts Society founded in 1854, the oldest such organisation in Central Europe. The building was completed in 1901 to a design by Franciszek Mączyński (1874–1947), one of the most prolific architects of fin-de-siècle Krakow.

Born in Wadowice in southern Poland, Mączyński got off to an early start professionally. In 1900 he won an international architectural competition with a design for a wooden villa in the ethnic Zakopane style. This enabled him to study at Krakow's Academy of Fine Arts (Akademia Sztuk Pięknych w Krakowie) on plac Jana Matejki (Kleparz), as well as in Vienna and Paris. The commissions that followed included churches, civic structures and cultural institutions.

His first and perhaps finest public building was the Palace of Art. Predominantly rendered in Polish-infused Art Nouveau, the striking façade also displays elements of neo-Classicism and a foretaste of Modernism, the whole creating the impression of a contemporary Greek temple to the arts. The gold bas-reliefs wrapping around the exterior depicting the highs and lows of the creative process were executed by artist Jacek Malczewski (1854–1929), the Father of Polish Symbolism. They show a successful artist crowned with laurel in the presence of the Muses and Pegasus, as well as a failed artist's passage through Pain and Despair. The reliefs are accompanied by busts of some of Poland's most celebrated artists including Jan Matejko (1838–1893) and Stanisław Wyspiański (1869–1907) (see nos. 30, 90). A large head of Apollo crowns the main entrance.

Mączyński never exclusively deployed Art Nouveau in his work.

Take, for example, his former Chamber of Commerce and Industry – also known as the House under the Globe (Dom Pod Globusem) – on the corner of ul. Basztowa and ul. Długa (Kleparz). Completed in the same year as the Palace of Art, it fuses neo-Gothic features with Modernist influences yet lacks excess ornament beyond its namesake globe-topped spire. Likewise the Basilica of the Sacred Heart of Jesus (Bazylika Najświętszego Serca Pana Jezusa) at ul. Kopernika 26 (Wesoła), completed in 1912, references neo-Romanesque and neo-Gothic motifs, with modern elements including sculptures by Xawery Dunikowski (1875–1964). One of the largest churches in Krakow, it features a 223-foot-tall tower and a huge mosaic frieze above the high altar.

Entrance to the Palace of Art (Pałac Sztuki) on plac Szczepański

Mączyński undertook several commissions with fellow Polish architect Tadeusz Stryjeński (1849–1943), who also studied in Paris, as well as in Zurich under German architect Gottfried Semper (1803–1879). In 1906, they redeveloped the Stary Teatr (Old Theatre) in one corner of plac Szczepański. Originally a neo-Renaissance building of 1843, they reworked it in the form of a Venetian palace, with a floral stucco frieze and a striking steel portico over the entrance. The pair also designed the Press Palace (Pałac Prasy) (1921) at ul. Wielopole 1 (Stradom), with its remarkable central atrium and open-plan stairwells. For his part, Stryjeński is remembered as the architect of the District Savings Bank at ul. Pijarska 1 (Old Town) and his own villa, Pod Stańczykiem, at ul. Stefana Batorego 12 (Piasek).

Other locations nearby: 24, 25, 26, 28

8 Mummies at the Monastery

31-012 Kraków (Old Town), the Church of St. Casimir the Prince (Kościół św. Kazimierza Królewicza) and Monastery of Reformed Franciscans (Klasztor Franciszkanów Reformatorów) at ul. Reformacka 4
Tram 2, 4, 8, 13, 14, 18, 20, 24, 44 to Teatr Bagatela (note: the crypt is only opened on All Souls' Day (November 2nd) and by appointment)

The Old Town street name 'ulica Reformacka' takes its name from the Order of Reformed Franciscans, who built their monastery here in the mid-17th century. Like their brethren the Capuchins they sought a return to the ascetic way of life practiced by the order's founder, St. Francis of Assisi (see no. 85). Accordingly these so-called *Reformati* ate cooked food only twice a week and scourged themselves frequently.

Riding the wave of the Counter-Reformation, they arrived from Italy in 1622, settling outside Krakow's walls in an area called Garbary. Thanks to a generous donation they were able to complete their first church here in 1640 in which was displayed a miraculous painting of the Madonna. The building didn't last long though and was soon destroyed during the Swedish occupation (the so-called 'Deluge').

Rather than rebuilding, in 1658 the friars relocated inside the city walls to a small manor on what would become ul. Reformacka. It was given to them by the castellan of Krakow, Stanisław Warszycki (1600–1681), who did much to develop the town at this time. Here they built the present monastery and in 1666 the auxiliary Bishop of Krakow, Mikołaj Oborski (1611–1689), laid the foundation stone for a new church dedicated to St. Casimir the Prince (Kościół św. Kazimierza Królewicza). Remarkably it was just one of 193 churches consecrated by the bishop, who also ordained nearly 3,000 priests!

Financed by local nobleman Franciszek Szembek (1625–1693), the new church was consecrated in 1672. The church interior would originally have been fairly plain in keeping with the still-modest exterior. However, much subsequent decoration has taken place, notably the addition of a series of opulent Baroque side altars installed in the 1740s and a painted ceiling undertaken in 1904 by local artist Aleksander Mroczkowski (1850–1927). Artworks surviving from the original iteration of the interior include a portrait of Saint Casimir (1458–1484) by Gdańsk painter Daniel Schultz (1615–1683) and a painting of Christ entombed that is said to be miraculous. In 1707 during the last great

Stacked coffins in the crypt of the Church of St. Casimir the Prince (Kościół św. Kazimierza Królewicza)

outbreak of plague in Krakow, Christ is said to have emerged from the painting to pray with the friars. After he while he cried "enough" and the plague was lifted.

Of special albeit ghoulish interest is the church crypt though it is only opened once a year on All Souls' Day (November 2nd). Here between 1680 and 1870 a thousand bodies were laid to rest, including church benefactors (notably the noble Wielopolscy, Szembekowie and Morsztynowie families), as well as some 250 friars. Whilst some lie in coffins and sarcophagi, the friars all lie beneath the chancel on bare ground, their legs covered with sand and their heads supported on wooden blocks. The microclimate in the crypt has desiccated around 50 of the bodies so that they remain in an eerily good state of preservation.

Two of these 'mummies' warrant special attention. One is the body of Countess Domicella Skalska, who was employed by the monastery as a housemaid for 20 years. Her noble origin was only revealed shortly before her death in 1864. The other is the body of an unnamed Napoleonic soldier, formally dressed in full uniform. Oral tradition holds that he died at the monastery in 1812 after the rigours of the long march back from Moscow.

Across from the church is an unusual set of outdoor Stations of the Cross. Each station consists of its own miniature chapel, with wooden doors concealing paintings completed in 1816 by Michał Stachowicz (1768–1825). Next door is a humble bread kitchen for the poor.

Other locations nearby: 24, 25, 26, 27

29 A Museum of Pharmacy

31-019 Kraków (Old Town), the Museum of Pharmacy (Muzeum Farmacji) at ul. Floriańska 25
Tram 2, 4, 14, 18, 20, 24, 44 to Stary Kleparz or Teatr Słowackiego

Medical museums may not to everyone's taste but it would be a shame to miss Krakow's Museum of Pharmacy (Muzeum Farmacji). Located inside a lovely Renaissance-era tenement house at ul. Floriańska 25 (Old Town), this specialist collection holds several surprises. The museum's origins go back to 1946, when the director of Krakow's District Chamber of Pharmacists, Dr. Stanisław Proń (1892–1971), asked his fellow pharmacists to send him items of historical interest. These were safeguarded in the chamber's headquarters at ul. Basztowa 3 (Piasek) and in 1956put on public display. In 1978 after becoming a part of the Faculty of Pharmacy at Krakow's College of Medicine (Collegium Medicum), the city authorities provided the 15th century Renaissance house on ul. Floriańska. That the museum became a university collection in the 1990s explains the wall plaque outside carrying the crest of the Jagiellonian University (Uniwersytet Jagielloński), namely crossed maces topped with a crown.

The entrance to the museum is suitably adorned with a statue of *Hygeia*, the Greek goddess of health and hygiene. Beyond are countless artefacts pertaining to the history of pharmacy and pharmaceutical technology spread across the building's five storeys. These include everything from vintage pharmacy equipment – mortars, scales, herb slicers and pill-making machines – to full-size pharmacy interiors salvaged from various buildings. The latter come in a variety of styles – Baroque, Empire and Biedermeier – with pride of place going to the reconstructed Golden Elephant Pharmacy (Pod Złotym Słoniem), its shelves laden with majolica jars. The Latin names on the jars include *Blatt. Orient. Pulv.* (powdered cockroaches), *Cantharides* (Spanish flies) and even *Cran. Humn. PPT.* (ground human skull).

Of particular interest is the reconstructed alchemist's laboratory in the cellar, with its copper kettles and glass retorts, and the wonderfully-fragrant apothecary's attic at the top of the house, with its wooden racks for drying herbs. Dotted around are various other items of interest, including trade signs, ground-breaking medieval herbal treatises and even an electrical device for sterilizing prescriptions to prevent the spread of germs.

Old fashioned medicine bottles in the Museum of Pharmacy (Muzeum Farmacji)

Visitors to the museum will also learn about several important Polish pharmacists. One is Jan Józef Ignacy Łukasiewicz (1822–1882), who studied at the Jagiellonian University. His remarkable achievements include the invention of the modern kerosene lamp (1853), the construction of the world's first oil well (1854) and the building of the first oil refinery (1856). Another is Marian Zahradnik (1848–1901), who in 1893 patented special pharmaceutical weights to measure ingredients less than one gram, which are still used today. A third is brave Tadeusz Pankiewicz (1908–1993), who operated a pharmacy in the Krakow Ghetto during the Second World War (see no. 53). And we shouldn't forget Sister Konstancja Studzińska (1787–1853), a Krakow pharmacist who in 1824 became the first woman to receive a university diploma, which now hangs in the museum.

Directly behind the museum at ul. Szpitalna 24 is the Russian Orthodox Church of the Assumption of the Blessed Virgin (Cerkiew Zaśnięcia Najświętszej Maryi Panny). Housed in a former Jewish synagogue, it is a reminder that not all churches in Krakow are necessarily Catholic.

The Jagiellonian University's other medical museums include the Museum of the Faculty of Medicine (Muzeum Wydziału Lekarskiego) at ul. Radziwiłłowska 4, with its antique stethoscopes, the Museum of Anatomy (Muzeum Anatomii) at ul. Mikołaja Kopernika 12 filled with jars of preserved organs, and the Museum of Anatomopathology (Muzeum Anatomopatologiczne) at ul. Grzegórzecka 16, which contains Poland's oldest anatomical specimen, namely a foetus presented as a curiosity of nature in 1691 to King John III Sobieski (Jan III Sobieski) (1629–1696). All can be visited by appointment (www.en.uj.edu.pl).

Other locations nearby: 30, 31, 32, 33, 34

30 Tribute to the National Painter

31-019 Kraków (Old Town), the Jan Matejko House (Dom Jana Matejki) at ul. Floriańska 41
Tram 2, 4, 14, 18, 20, 24, 44 to Stary Kleparz or Teatr Słowackiego

Krakow-born Jan Alojzy Matejko (1838–1893) is probably Poland's best known artist. His large-scale historical works adorning several of the country's major galleries have become standard depictions of various key events in Polish history. No surprise then that his former home has been preserved in tribute to the man known as Poland's 'national painter'.

Matejko was born the ninth of eleven children on 24th June 1838. His father was Czech, his mother half-Polish, half-German. The house in which they lived at ul. Floriańska 41 (Old Town) was a typical well-to-do townhouse (*kamienica*) built in the 16th century and subsequently remodelled. It was from here in 1846 that the young Matejko witnessed the Krakow Uprising against Austrian forces leading in 1848 to a siege that extinguished the Free City of Krakow.

Matejko studied at Krakow's Academy of Fine Arts (Akademia Sztuk Pięknych w Krakowie) in Kleparz under Władysław Łuszczkiewicz (1828–1900), whose influence prompted his choice of historical painting as a specialisation. His graduation project in 1858 was a suitably ambitious work entitled *Zygmunt I nadaje szlachectwo profesorom Uniwersytetu Jagiellońskiego* (Sigismund I the Old ennobles the professors of the Jagiellonian University).Thereafter he received scholarships to study in Munich and Vienna but returned early to open his own studio in the family home.

His first taste of success came in 1862, when he sold several works and completed another entitled *Stańczyk*. The latter marked an important stylistic watershed between merely illustrating historical events and instead imbuing them with a patriotic message at a time when Poland was partitioned and powerless. Now in the Warsaw National Museum, the work depicts a court jester musing on Poland's loss of Smolensk to the Grand Duchy of Muscovy, while the royal family dance obliviously in a neighbouring room, a sombre and moonlit Wawel Castle visible through the window.

Ill health prevented Matejko from participating in the January Uprising (1863) against Imperial Russia but he offered financial support. He married the same year and began attracting international attention with his detailed historical canvasses. Typical was *Unia Lubelska* (Union of Lublin) depicting the creation of the Polish–Lithuanian Commonwealth (1569).

From 1872 onwards, Matejko served as rector at the Academy of Fine Arts, influencing budding artists such as Józef Mehoffer (1869–1946) and Stanisław Wyspiański (1869–1907). He also continued painting, including *Polonia, Rok 1863* (Poland, 1863) in the Princes Czartoryski Museum (Muzeum Książąt Czartoryskich) showing a female 'Poland' shackled by Russian officers and *Hołd Pruski* (Prussian

This memorial to artist Jan Matejko can be found in the Planty near the Barbakan

Tribute) in the Cloth Hall (Sukiennice), which earned him honorary citizenship (see nos. 15, 32).

Matejko's renown ensured that when he died in 1893 he was buried beneath an imposing monument in Krakow's Rakowicki Cemetery (Cmentarz Rakowicki) (see no. 76). In 1979 to mark the centenary of the Academy's founding, it was renamed in Matejko's honour (Akademia Sztuk Pięknych im. Jana Matejki) and a memorial erected in the nearby Planty depicting the artist sitting inside a picture frame.

Matejko's former home was opened to the public in 1898 as the Jan Matejko House (Dom Jana Matejki). Here visitors will find the minutiae of the artist's life, including his spectacles, brushes and palette, and even his wife's engagement ring. More effects are displayed in the Jan Matejko Manor (Dworek Jana Matejki) at ul. Wańkowicza 25 in the village of Krzesławice (Nowa Huta), where he came to escape the city bustle.

To see an unchanged Gothic-Renaissance *kamienica* on ul. Floriańska visit the Desa auction house at number 13, its first floor salons retaining their wall murals and decorated roof beams.

Other locations nearby: 29, 31, 32, 33, 34

31 The Birthplace of Young Poland

31-019 Kraków (Old Town), Café Jama Michalika at ul. Floriańska 45
Tram 2, 4, 14, 18, 20, 24, 44 to Stary Kleparz or Teatr Słowackiego

Between 1895 and 1918, the modernist movement known as Art Nouveau swept Europe. Pioneered in Paris, where its application was essentially aesthetic, its variants farther east carried a discreet political purpose. Called the Secession in Austria and Jugendstil in Germany, the Polish version was known as Młoda Polska (Young Poland).

Młoda Polska came about as a result of strong aesthetic opposition to the foreign partition of Poland. Science-based ideas of Positivism, which had emerged following the suppression of the January Uprising (1863) against Russian occupation, were rejected. Instead members of Młoda Polska sought to revive Polish national spirits by championing the humanities, which in artistic terms meant bohemian decadence, symbolism, Impressionism and the increasingly fashionable Art Nouveau. Within a few years, the movement permeated not only Poland's visual arts and architecture but also its literature, theatre and music.

If anywhere can lay claim to being the birthplace of Młoda Polska it is Krakow's Café Jama Michalika at ul. Floriańska 45 (Old Town). Opened as a confectionary shop in 1895 by entrepreneur Jan Michalik from Lwów (today Ukraine's Lviv), it was within easy walking distance of the Academy of Fine Arts (Akademia Sztuk Pięknych) on plac Jana Matejki (Kleparz). Thus it provided the perfect place for artists and other creatives to congregate and soon became one of several unofficial headquarters for the movement.

It was one of these Academy-trained artists, the painter and stage designer Karol Frycz (1877–1963), who created the café's *fin-de-siècle* interior when the shop became a café proper. Having studied in Vienna, Paris and at the decorative arts' company of William Morris in London, he utilised a variety of design elements including organic Art Nouveau-style woodwork, modernist stained glass and furniture inspired by Charles Rennie Mackintosh. Additionally there is original artwork by Młoda Polska artists, some of it painted directly on the walls. An example is *St. Florian's Gate* by Henryk Szczygliński (1881–1944), its wobbly perspective the result of it having been painted while inebriated! The balloon in the painting is a reference to the café's Parisian-style literary cabaret, the Little Green Balloon (Zielony Balonik), where attendees poked fun at the establishment through satirical sketches, comic songs and absurdist puppet shows.

Several Młoda Polska members frequenting the café went on to leave a considerable artistic footprint in Krakow. Chief among them were stained glass supremo Stanisław Wyspiański (1869–1907) and muralist Józef Mehoffer (1869–1946), who between them reworked several of the city's Gothic church interiors (see nos. 18, 84, 90, 92). Others included the modernist painters Jan Stanisławski (1860–1907) and Leon Wyczółkowski (1852–1936), who did much to reaffirm the uniqueness of Polish art during the Polish Partitions,

The storied Café Jama Michalika on ul. Floriańska

and collector Feliks Jasieński (1861–1929), whose penchant for Japanese art can be appreciated at the Manggha Museum in Dębniki (see no. 45).

The Café Jama Michalika today hosts mainly tourists, who come for the history as well as the extensive menu of traditional food, accompanied between June and December by twice-weekly performances of folk dancing.

In the Krakow suburb of Bronowice Małe there is a villa at ul. Tetmajera 28 built by Młoda Polska painter Włodzimierz Tetmajer (1861–1923). He married Anna Mikołajczykówna, a peasant's daughter, and together they entertained various Młoda Polska disciples, who believed that folk traditions had a part to play in Poland's revival. Among them was playwright and poet Lucjan Rydel (1870–1918), whose marriage to Anna's sister Jadwiga provided inspiration for Wyspiański's famous play Wesele (The Wedding). In 1908, Rydel bought the house, which is named Rydlówka in his honour.

Other locations nearby: 29, 30, 32, 33, 34

32 The Lady with an Ermine

31-015 Kraków (Old Town), the Princes Czartoryski Museum
(Muzeum Książąt Czartoryskich) at ul. Pijarska 6
Tram 2, 4, 14, 18, 20, 24, 44 to Stary Kleparz or Teatr
Słowackiego

An attractive cluster of neo-Gothic buildings stands at ul. Pijarska 6 in the northern reaches of Krakow's Old Town. Linked by a Venetian-style 'Bridge of Sighs', it comprises the Princes Czartoryski Museum (Muzeum Książąt Czartoryskich) and the city's former Municipal Arsenal (Arsenał Miejski). With the museum recently reopening after renovations, it is a good time to tell its colourful story.

It begins in the 1770s, when Polish noblewoman Princess Izabela Czartoryska (1746–1835) turned her husband's palace in the city of Puławy in eastern Poland into a centre for the Polish Enlightenment. When the Kościuszko Uprising (1794) failed to prevent partition of the Polish–Lithuanian Commonwealth and Puławy fell into Russian hands, the patriotic princess expressed her opposition by creating a museum to nurture national sentiment. It included Turkish trophies seized by King John III Sobieski (Jan III Sobieski) (1629–1696) at the Battle of Vienna (1683) and a garden temple in which she installed royal relics and the Grunwald Swords from the famous 15th century battle.

Inevitably the museum closed during the abortive November Uprising (1830), an anti-Tsarist insurrection against Russian partition. With Poland returned to the Russian fold, Izabela's son, Adam Czartoryski (1770–1861), spirited the collection to safety in Paris. There it remained until 1876, when his son, Władysław Czartoryski (1828–1894), brought the collection to Austrian-administered Krakow, where Poles enjoyed greater autonomy than under the Russians.

When Poland re-emerged as a sovereign state in 1918, the Czartoryski Museum continued as a privately-owned museum up until the Second World War, when the country lost 70% of its cultural heritage. Over 800 artworks disappeared from the museum, including Raphael's *Portrait of a Young Man*. Fortunately American soldiers recovered many pieces, including the jewel in the Czartoryski collection's crown, Leonardo da Vinci's *Lady with an Ermine*. One of only a handful of the artist's surviving oil paintings, it was painted around 1490 and is thought to depict Cecilia Gallerani (c. 1473–1536), the reputed mistress of the Duke of Milan, who commissioned the work (the ermine alludes to the duke, who was known as the White Ermine). The work was originally acquired by Adam Czartoryski in 1800 during a holiday in Italy.

Unfortunately, when the works arrived back in Poland, their rightful owner, Prince Augustyn Czartoryski (1907–1946), was not there to receive them having sought refuge in Spain. Instead the collection became a branch of the National Museum in Krakow (Muzeum Narodowe w Krakowie) managed by Poland's Moscow-backed Communist regime. Only in 1991 after the fall of the Iron Curtain did the newly-formed Czartoryski Foundation reclaim the collection, albeit with the National Museum continuing to finance its upkeep.

A lack of funds, however, prevented the Foundation from making the museum independent again and instead

Da Vinci's *Lady with an Ermine* hangs in the Princes Czartoryski Museum (Muzeum Książąt Czartoryskich)

in 2016 it was sold to the Polish state. The museum on ul. Pijarska and the Municipal Arsenal opposite, which had also contained part of the collection, were mothballed and Leonardo's *Lady with an Ermine* was acquired by the Polish state and removed to its own room in the National Museum's Main Building (Gmach Główny) at al. 3 Maja 1 (Czarna Wieś) (see no. 90). Now, however, with the museum renovated and reopened, its charming mix of Old Masters, Polish curiosities and ancient relics can be appreciated once again by visitors, with Leonardo's great painting taking centre stage.

Afterwards those interested can also visit the Princes Czartoryski Library (Biblioteka Książąt Czartoryskich) around the corner at ul. św. Marka 17, which contains books, prints and manuscripts dating back to the 1770s.

Other locations nearby: 29, 30, 31, 33, 34

33 The Old Town Wall

30-547 Kraków (Old Town), the Florian Gate (Brama
Floriańska) and Defence Walls (Mury Obronne) on ul. Pijarska
and the Planty
Tram 2, 4, 14, 18, 20, 24, 44 to Stary Kleparz or Teatr
Słowackiego (note: the Defence Walls are only open April to
October)

It's hard to imagine today that Krakow's Old Town was once surrounded by a defensive wall. Erected during the medieval period, it was almost entirely dismantled in the early 19th century and replaced by the Planty. This chain of 30 interconnected parks dotted with specimen trees, memorials and water features has been enjoyed by locals and visitors ever since its inauguration in 1830.

The medieval wall was built during the 13th and 14th centuries. Almost two miles in length, it was pierced by eight gates and fortified with 47 towers and a moat fed by a tributary of the Vistula (Wisła). By the start of the 19th century, however, the growing city needed space to expand. Additionally, the wall had fallen into disrepair following the Third Partition of Poland (1795), when Krakow found itself administered by the Austrians, who set about building new fortifications out in the suburbs (see no. 80). With this in mind, the Habsburg Emperor Franz Joseph I (1830–1916) ordered the dismantling of the wall.

This was not the end of Krakow's medieval wall though. In 1817, Professor Feliks Radwański (1756–1826) of the Jagiellonian University (Uniwersytet Jagielloński) convinced the city fathers to save the most important part of the wall, namely the Florian Gate (Brama Floriańska), its flanking walls and towers, and the formidable outlying fortification known as the Barbican (Barbakan). Together they now form a seasonal branch of the Museum of Krakow (Muzeum Krakowa) called the Defence Walls (Mury Obronne) affording today's visitors a good impression of how Krakow's fortifications once looked.

The Florian Gate was built in the early 14th century as a safeguard against Ottoman invasion. Its grandeur and importance is explained by the fact that it gave onto the so-called Royal Road (Droga Królewska) – ul. Floriańska, Rynek Główny, ul. Grodzka and ul. Kanonicza – which was used as a processional way by kings on their way to being crowned at Wawel Royal Castle (Zamek Królewski na Wawelu). That Saint Florian is one of Krakow's protective patron saints explains why this important gate was named in his honour. The gate's three flanking towers, as with all the wall's towers, were originally maintained by individual craftsmen's guilds, hence their names: Haberdashers' Tower (Baszta Pasamoników), Joiners' Tower (Baszta Stolarska) and Carpenters' Tower (Baszta Ciesielska).

The Florian Gate was originally connected by a drawbridge to the Barbican, which was added in the late 15th century. Note the arrow slits and the overhanging upper storey, useful for pouring boiling liquids onto enemies below.

Running north from the Barbican into the former medieval suburb of Kleparz is Plac Matejko. This elongated square is named after the great Polish painter, Jan Matejko (1838–1893), who taught here at the Academy of Fine Arts (Akademia Sztuk Pięknych w Krakowie)

The Florian Gate (Brama Floriańska) carries a relief of its namesake saint

(see no. 30). Also on the square is the Grunwald Monument (1910), erected to mark the quincentenary of the Polish–Lithuanian victory against the Teutonic Knights. Farther out is the Church of St. Florian (Kościół św. Floriana), where in 1184 according to legend the oxen bringing the saint's relics to Krakow halted and refused to go further. The end of the First World War and Poland's return to independence is marked on the square each November 11th.

Little else remains of the wall except for occasional fragments incorporated into the backs of Old Town buildings, footings identified by inscribed stones, and a lofty blocked-up gateway on Westerplatte. Instead the Old Town today is protected by a green wall formed by the sturdy chestnut trees of the Planty.

Other locations nearby: 29, 30, 31, 32, 34, 78

34 A Magnificent Stage

31-023 Kraków (Old Town), the Juliusz Słowacki Theatre
(Teatr im Juliusza Słowackiego) at plac Świętego. Ducha 1
Tram 2, 3, 4, 10, 14, 20, 24, 44, 52 to Teatr Słowackiego
(note: guided theatre tours are only available in July)

For over a century now, Krakow's Juliusz Słowacki Theatre (Teatr im Juliusza Słowackiego) has been a focus for the city's cultural life. More than just an entertainment venue, this is where the Young Poland (Młoda Polska) movement manifested itself in theatrical terms, and where nationally-prominent artists have made their names.

Known originally as the Municipal Theatre (Teatr Miejski), it opened on 21st October 1893. Its address on plac Świętego Ducha recalls the Monastery of the Holy Spirit, which was demolished to make way for it. This caused much consternation among Krakow's conservationists prompting artist Jan Matejko (1838–1893) to vow never to exhibit his paintings in the city again.

The theatre was designed by local architect Jan Zawiejski (1854–1922) in the exuberant if backwards-looking Historicist style prevalent across the Austro–Hungarian Empire (this explains the abundance of neo-Baroque motifs). It was the costliest construction in 19th century Krakow as well as the city's first building illuminated by electricity. Fittingly in 1896 it hosted the first presentation of the Lumière brothers' *Cinématographe* attracting some 10,000 excited viewers.

The theatre is just as flamboyant inside as is revealed on guided tours given in July (Thursday to Sunday). At its opening the auditorium offered 940 seats layered and segregated from floor to ceiling according to social class (the current capacity is 540). On the first floor opposite the stage was an imperial box, although the Austrian Emperor Franz Joseph I (1830–1916) never used it. Instead it served honorary guests, including celebrated Polish Marshal Józef Piłsudski (1867–1935) and visiting French Marshal Ferdinand Foch (1851–1929). During the Second World War, it was occupied by Nazi officials enjoying *Nur für Deutsche* (Only for Germans) performances.

The auditorium is separated from the stage by a magnificent curtain painted by the Polish artist Henryk Siemiradzki (1843–1902). Known for his monumental depictions of the Classical world, it measures almost 40 feet across and evokes drama, comedy, music and dance.

The theatre is not only magnificent but also significant. The synthesis of drama, music and light pioneered here was considered avant-

No expense spared at the Juliusz Słowacki Theatre (Teatr im Juliusza Słowackiego)

garde at the time. It was also here in the early 1900s that the theatrical strand of the Young Poland (Młoda Polska) movement was born. An aesthetic reaction to the foreign occupation of Poland, the movement sought to revive the Polish national spirits by championing new works by Polish playwright Stanisław Wyspiański (1869–1907), whose play *Wesele* (The Wedding) premiered here in 1901. It also revived the Polish Romantic tradition, including works by poet and playwright Juliusz Słowacki (1809–1849), for whom the theatre was renamed in 1909.

Today the theatre is known for staging works by everyone from Sophocles and Arthur Miller to Pope John Paul II, whose political play *Brat naszego boga* (Our God's Brother) about St. Albert Chmielowski (1845–1916) was premiered in 1980. It has also opened other performance spaces aimed at a younger audience, namely the intimate Miniatura Stage in 1976 in the theatre's old power plant, and in 2012 the Małopolska Garden of the Arts (Małopolski Ogród Sztuki) at ul. Rajska 12 (Piasek) (see no. 83). There is also the House of Theatrical Crafts (Dom Rzemiosł Teatralnych) at ul. Radziwiłłowska 13 (Wesoła), which acts as a theatrical store and rehearsal room.

Krakow's other theatres include the venerable Stary Teatr (Old Theatre) (1781) at ul. Jagiellońska 1 (Old Town) and the Łaźnia Nowa at Osiedle Szkolne 25 (Nowa Huta) opened only in 2005. From 2020, the previously nomadic KTO theatre company will have its own stage in the former Kino Wrzos at ul. Jana Zamoyskiego 50 (Podgórze).

Other locations nearby: 29, 30, 31, 32, 33

35 The Kazimierz Synagogues

31-053 Kraków (Kazimierz), a Jewish history walk beginning
with the Remuh Synagogue (Synagoga Remuh) at
ul. Szeroka 40
Tram 3, 17, 19, 24 to Miodowa or Św. Wawrzyńca

Before the Second World War there were around 60,000 Jews living in Krakow. That was a quarter of the population, a figure that rises to a third if those with Jewish roots are included. The Holocaust, post-war pogroms and Communist persecutions expunged the community, as it did across Poland. From a total of 3.3 million Jews just 20,000 survived the horrors (see nos. 53, 57).

Poland's Jews have ancient origins. Their ancestors first appeared north of the Alps with the Romans. Of those who settled in Germany, particularly along the Rhine, many were expelled eastwards. They settled in what became Poland and Lithuania, bringing with them their own medieval German language known as Yiddish.

It was a Piast High Duke, Bolesław V the Chaste (Bolesław Wstydliwy) (1226–1279), who first granted them privileges. These were extended in 1334 by King Casimir III the Great (Kazimierz III Wielki) (1310–1370) allowing them trading concessions and outlawing forced Christianisation. Henceforth Jews began settling in Poland in greater numbers.

In Krakow, they congregated on an island in the Vistula (Wisła). Established in 1335 as an independent town, Kazimierz was named in the king's honour. Here for just over 600 years Jewish life flourished peacefully alongside Krakow's Christian population. With the granting of equal rights in 1867, many of the city's most successful businesses were soon helmed by Jews.

Today, Kazimierz's remaining Jewish heritage is protected by a hundred or so guardians. Cynics might say the district has become a museum devoid of actual Jews but visit during the Jewish Culture Festival in June/July and the streets are undeniably alive. At other times, old Jewish Kazimierz can be experienced through its synagogues, three of which stand on ul. Szeroka.

The Remuh Synagogue (Synagoga Remuh) at number 40 opened in 1553 and sits alongside an older Jewish cemetery (see no. 36). Not only is it the smallest synagogue but also the only active one, with Shabbat services each Friday. Across the road at number 14 is the house where cosmetics' queen Helena Rubinstein (1872–1965) was born. Next door at number 16 is the Renaissance-style Popper Synagogue (Synagoga Popper) built in 1620 and now home to a branch of the Austeria Bookshop (another is at ul. Józefa 38). The Old Synagogue (Synagoga Stara) at number 24, Poland's oldest synagogue, was completed a century earlier to a design by Florentine architect Mateo Gucci and is now a branch of the Museum of Krakow (Muzeum Krakowa). It retains the octagonal stepped *bimah* from where the Torah was read and segregated prayer rooms that now contain a museum of Jewish ceremonial items (a detour from here to the Galicia Jewish Museum (Żydowskie Muzeum Galicja) at ul. Dajwór 18 reveals Jewish life in southern Poland and western Ukraine between 1772 and 1918).

Entrance to the Remuh Synagogue (Synagoga Remuh) in Kazimierz

The walk continues on ul. Józefa with a former prayer house at number 42, the 16th century High Synagogue (Synagoga Wysoka) at 38, and the Cheder café and cultural centre at 36 serving mint tea and hummus. Turn right to reach the Jewish-Baroque Izaac Synagogue (Synagoga Izaaka) at ul. Kupa 18 (the founder's home at ul. Ciemna 15, now the Eden Hotel, boasts Poland's only working *mikveh* ritual bath).

Farther along on ul. Miodowa is the richly-painted Kupa Synagogue (Synagoga Kupa) at number 27 and the Temple Synagogue (Synagoga Tempel) at 24, alongside a well-supported Jewish Community Centre (Centrum Społeczności Żydowskiej). The walk concludes around the corner on ul. Beera Meiselsa with the Judaica Foundation (Fundacja Judaica) at number 17 and Hevre at 18, a Jewish-themed bar in another former prayer house

Other locations nearby: 36, 37, 38, 39, 40

36 The Jewish Stones Speak

33-332 Kraków (Kazimierz), a tour of Jewish cemeteries including the New Jewish Cemetery (Nowy cmentarz żydowski) at ul. Miodowa 55
Tram 3, 17, 19, 24 to Miodowa (note: visitors to the cemeteries should cover their heads, women with a scarf and men with a skullcap or kippah)

Krakow's old synagogues tell only half the story of the city's Jews. To people them, one must explore the cemeteries where their former worshippers are buried. It's a poignant but necessary experience in order to understand the vicissitudes of a community that brought so much to Krakow yet suffered so greatly in the process.

The city's oldest Jewish cemetery sits alongside the Remuh Synagogue (Synagoga Remuh) at ul. Szeroka 40 in Kazimierz. Opened in 1535, it predates the synagogue, which was only established in 1553 at the behest of eminent Ashkenazic Rabbi Moses Isserles (1530–1572) (see no. 35). Until the cemetery's closure in 1800, many influential rabbis and heads of the Krakow Talmudic Academy were laid to rest here. Isserles, whose Hebrew acronym gives the synagogue its name, is among them. One of Poland's greatest Jewish scholars, he was not only a respected Talmudist and legal adviser *(posek)* but also a student of history, astronomy and philosophy. His grave has long been a place of pilgrimage and its survival during the Second World War, when the Nazis desecrated the cemetery, has been taken by the faithful as a sign of his importance. Since then, the cemetery has undergone restoration, its remaining headstones (many inscribed with hands, jugs and crowns symbolising various professions) re-erected in rows, and fragments reused to create a 'wailing wall' along ul. Szeroka.

When the Remuh Cemetery reached capacity in 1800, a New Jewish Cemetery (Nowy cmentarz żydowski) was opened not far away at ul. Miodowa 55. Five times the size of the old cemetery and covering some 11 acres, there are over 10,000 tombs here in which a cross-section of Jewish society is represented. There are rabbis, including Ozjasz Thon (1870–1936) of the Tempel Synagogue, Jewish mystics *(Tzadiks)*, members of the rabbinical court *(Beth din)*, as well as writers, scientists, artists and doctors.

As with the Remuh Cemetery, the New Jewish Cemetery was desecrated by the Nazi regime. Headstones were uprooted and used as construction material, sculptural stonework was sold off to local masons, and graves were opened with bones left in disarray. The cemetery caretaker, who lived on the premises, was taken to the nearby Płaszów Concentration Camp and shot.

Only in the late 1950s did restoration of the cemetery begin. The brick-built funerary hall of 1903 was renovated and a pyramid-shaped Holocaust Memorial erected alongside it using fragments of smashed headstones, topped off with a block of black marble. Many of the still-standing headstones recall entire families murdered during the Holocaust. Occasionally a candle is left burning at one of them, or a handful of pebbles left on top, but the fact that most now lack mourners means they're often unkempt and more poignant for that.

From the early 1930s onwards, as the New Jewish

Broken Jewish headstones form a Holocaust Memorial in the New Jewish Cemetery (Nowy cmentarz żydowski)

Cemetery also began filling up, burials were directed to a pair of Jewish cemeteries in Podgórze. The Old Podgórze Jewish Cemetery on ul. Abrahama had opened in 1887, when Podgórze was still an independent city. The smaller New Podgórze Jewish Cemetery, with its monumental domed funerary hall, was opened in 1932 just north of it, by which time Podgórze was a part of Krakow. Both were bulldozed by the Nazis to make way for the construction of the Płaszów Concentration Camp, their headstones removed by forced Jewish labourers and reused to pave the camp roads (see no. 57). The Old Cemetery's funerary hall is today just a pile of rubble beyond which lie the shattered foundations of the New Cemetery containing the solitary leaning headstone of one Chaim Jakub Abrahamei (d. 1932).

Other locations nearby: 35, 37, 38, 61

37 Crazy about Klezmer

31-053 Kraków (Kazimierz), the Klezmer Hois at ul. Szeroka 6
Tram 3, 17, 19, 24 to Miodowa

No genre of music so clearly defines a district as *klezmer* does Kazimierz. Driven by its clarinet, violin, upright bass and cimbalom, this energetic brand of Central and East European folk music has ancient Jewish origins. Extinguished by the Nazi regime, it experienced a revival during the 1970s and a *klezmer* concert is now an important part of many a visitor's Kazimierz itinerary.

The earliest murmurings of *klezmer* are shadowy. Born out of the haunting melodies of medieval Jewish cantors, it was probably pioneered by travelling Ashkenazi musicians, who performed at weddings and other celebrations. Over the years they absorbed a variety of musical influences as they went, including Ottoman Turkish modes, Balkan gypsy stylings and boisterous Russian dances. The emergence of the esoteric Hassidic movement in 18th century Poland and Galicia (present-day Ukraine) added impassioned melodies *(nigunim)* based on improvised and repetitive vocal sounds to the mix.

Klezmer evolved significantly in the early 20th century, when Jewish immigrants took it to the United States. There elements of Yiddish theatre and American Jazz, both of which were flourishing at the time, were incorporated into the sound. Back in Europe, however, the wholesale destruction of Jewish communities by the Nazis meant that *klezmer* disappeared in its homeland.

The word *klezmer* is a combination of two Hebrew words – *kli* (tool or utensil) and *zemer* (to make music) – and means 'vessels of song'. Originally used to describe the instruments, only later was it colloquially applied to the musicians, who became known as *klezmorim*. And only much later in the late 1970s and 80s, when young musicians in Europe and America began experimenting with its largely forgotten sounds, was the word finally used to denote the genre.

Poland's *klezmer* revival occurred during the 1990s. Centred squarely on Krakow, it was spearheaded by now legendary local bands such as Kroke (Yiddish for 'Krakow') and the Bester Quartet (formerly the Cracow Klezmer Band). Whilst paying respectful homage to the *klezmer* of yore, such bands brought a new energy and interest to the genre, reinventing it for a new and more secular generation.

Today there are many bands performing a mix of vocal and instrumental *klezmer* in the cafés, museums and synagogues of Kazimierz.

Archive photo showing a *klezmer* band of yesteryear

Some replicate perfectly the plaintive strains of traditional central and East European *klezmer*, whilst others enjoy fusing it with contemporary genres such as Afro-pop, rock and hip hop. Few band members are Jewish though, with many hailing instead from the city's Academy of Music (Akademia Muzyczna w Krakowie). They view *klezmer* as a branch of World Music but one with a local twist.

Klezmer concerts have become an intrinsic part of Krakow's Jewish heritage tourism. They occur daily in restaurants such as Dawno Temu Na Kazimierzu at ul. Szeroka 1 and Ariel nearby at number 18 (see no. 38). Some of the best though are to be had in the Klezmer Hois at number 6, where concerts take place at 8pm. As well as serving kosher Jewish Galician dishes straight out of the 19th century, the building itself is of interest since it once functioned as a Jewish ritual bath house (*mikveh*) and contains many fascinating pictures and artefacts.

> Another opportunity to listen to *klezmer* is during Krakow's annual Jewish Culture Festival (www.jewishfestival.pl). Staged in Kazimierz in late June or early July, its aim is to educate people not only about the Jewish culture that flourished here before the Holocaust but also about modern Jewish culture thriving today. Music takes centre stage with plenty of food, theatre, art and other events too

Other locations nearby: 35, 36, 38, 39, 40

38 Once Upon a Time

31-056 Kraków (Kazimierz), Dawno Temu Na Kazimierzu at
ul. Szeroka 1
Tram 3, 17, 19, 24 to Miodowa

Originally a town in its own right, Kazimierz is a great draw for visitors to Krakow. Most come to discover the area's Jewish heritage, which despite the Nazi regime's attempts at expunging it, lives on through its synagogues, cemeteries and museums (see nos. 35, 36). A unique venue is Dawno Temu Na Kazimierzu (Once Upon a Time in Kazimierz) at ul. Szeroka 1, where a row of traditional shop fronts conceals a unique visitor attraction.

These shop fronts, however, are not all they seem. Their signboards have been salvaged from around the district, restored and relocated here to form a clever pastiche of how the streets of Kazimierz would have looked during the early 20th century. Enter the shops and the well-meaning deception continues. Although each contains fixtures and fittings pertinent to the trade sign outside, the partition walls between the shops have been removed. The resulting single space contains a cosy café-restaurant and a unique one at that. It is the owner's intention that Polish and Jewish food and drink be enjoyed here by Jews and non-Jews alike. This acts as a reminder that before the Nazis forced the Jews out of Kazimierz, Christians and Jews lived and worked alongside each other here harmoniously regardless of differences in their faith and culture.

Despite the obvious need for tables and chairs, it's remarkable how each shop space has still been convincingly fitted out according to its intended function. Take Stanisław Nowak's grocery store *(Sklep Spo ywczy)*, with its inviting shop window filled with bottled produce. Inside hangs a portrait of the proud shopkeeper, whilst alongside the counter a gilded plaque advertises the fact that smoked meats and sausages are always available. Next door is Benjamin Holcer, joiner and carpenter *(Stolarz)*. Here patrons can sit at a work bench surrounded by tools of the woodworking trade and items of half-restored furniture. The shop window contains a wooden rocking horse and on the wall is a portrait of real-life Krakow carpenter, Mordechaj Gebirtig. Next comes Szymon Kac, tailor *(Kraviec)*, whose *Salon mód* (fashion salon) is adorned with examples of his nimble handiwork, as well as an ancient sewing machine. Then just around the corner is Chajim Kohan's general store *(Skład Tomarów Różnych)*, with its long-forgotten brands

The tailor's shop at Dawno Temu Na Kazimierzu on ul. Szeroka

such as *Koter* and *Fabot*, and an antique stove embossed proudly with the Star of David. Other shop fronts include seller of fancy goods Aron Weinberg *(Towary Galanteryjne)* and merchant Abraham Rattner *(Kupiec)*.

One of Krakow's smaller restaurants, Dawno Temu Na Kazimierzu contains barely a dozen tables, so booking is recommended. Many dishes are Ashkenazi Jewish in origin, including *gefilte fish* made from minced carp, *cholent* beef and bean stew, and *cymes (tzimmes)* carrot and fruit stew. Dining here is a memorable experience since one is surrounded by so many playful yet poignant reminders of the area's past, and the mood is made more palpable by the traditional Jewish music *(klezmer)* played live most evenings (see no. 37). All in all, it's a novel yet admirable attempt at raising the visitors' awareness of what's been lost here.

For a modern incarnation of a traditional Kazimierz street walk along ul. Józefa between ul. Estery and ul. Bożego Ciała. This colourfully shabby thoroughfare is lined with idiosyncratic boutiques, independent galleries, antique shops and café-bars. Look out for Szpeje at number 9, which offers original Communist-era collectibles, and Galerie d'Art Naif at number 11, which specialises in local 'outsider' art.

Other locations nearby: 35, 36, 37, 39, 40

39 In a Square in Kazimierz

31-056 Kraków (Kazimierz), the Rotunda (Okrąglak)
on plac Nowy
Tram 6, 8, 10, 13, 18, 52 to Stradom

Rynek Główny, Krakow's splendid main square, is rightly the city's most famous public space. After all, it's Europe's largest medieval marketplace and a veritable textbook of architectural styles (see no. 13). However, the city also has other squares, which though far less grand are no less interesting. One is plac Nowy in Kazimierz. With its plain functional architecture and predominantly local life, it is the opposite of tourist-filled Rynek Główny – and that's what makes it special.

Plac Nowy, or 'New Square', was integrated into the Kazimierz Jewish quarter in the late 17th century although it didn't assume its current shape until the early 19th century. Its main feature, the central circular pavilion nicknamed Okrąglak (meaning 'saucepan') because of its shape was not added until 1900. For generations the square was known locally as plac Żydowski (Jewish Square) since not only did it serve as the main Jewish marketplace in Kazimierz but the pavilion served as the Jews' ritual poultry slaughterhouse. It remained in business right up until the Nazi occupation of Krakow.

Although the slaughterers have long since departed there's still a buzz in and around the pavilion. Those in the know queue patiently in front of small sales' hatches, eager to buy what is arguably the best *zapiekanki* in town. Created in the 1970s, this legendary Polish fast food is essentially an open-faced French bread pizza topped with melted cheese, mushrooms and other savoury ingredients. Much like Vienna's famous sausage stands, its consumption is a democratic pastime, attracting all types of customers from partygoers to police officers.

Various makeshift market stalls surround the pavilion and there's usually something being sold here on most days. It's less about the produce on offer though – an arbitrary selection of vegetables, sweets, vintage ephemera and novelties – and more about the communal experience. This is especially clear during the square's weekly themed sales, including a caged bird market early on Friday mornings, a flea market on Saturdays, and a clothing market on Sundays.

Once the stallholders close shop for the day, plac Nowy takes on a different guise as the centre of Kazimierz nightlife. Idiosyncratic bars such as Alchemia and Singer at ul. Estery 5 and 20 respectively revel in a particular Kazimierz aesthetic of guttering candles, well-worn furniture and faded photos. Together with Mleczarnia at ul. Beera Meiselsa 20 and Eszeweria at ul. Józefa 9, they make for a memorable pub crawl, where in the wee small hours table tops often double as dancefloors and wild *klezmer* music is *de rigueur*.

It should be mentioned that unfortunately there plans are afoot to revamp plac Nowy. Already rubber-stamped, the new design would see the historic square's market stalls swept away, a permanent stage installed to one side, and parking prohibited. Whilst such plans might well work elsewhere (notably in squares that have entirely lost their

Comings and goings at the Rotunda (Okrąglak) on plac Nowy

appeal), plac Nowy buzzes with life just as it is. Currently there are not the funds to commence the work and it is hoped by many that this will remain the case indefinitely. Should the plans ever be realised fingers are crossed that developers will look to the likes of the recently-opened Plac Nowy 1 restaurant, a new-build that has been sensitively adapted to its surroundings, for inspiration.

Another idiosyncratic bar in Kazimierz is Propaganda several streets from plac Nowy at ul. Miodowa 20. It is distinguished by its collection of Communist-era artefacts hanging on the wall, everything from old street signs and propaganda posters to vintage radios and portraits of Lenin. It may be rough and ready but it's another facet of Kazimierz life.

Other locations nearby: 35, 37, 38, 39, 40

40 Pierogi Please!

31-056 Kraków (Kazimierz), a selection of traditional restaurants including Restauracja Starka at ul. Józefa 14
Tram 6, 8, 10, 13, 18, 52 to Stradom

Traditional Polish food sometimes gets a bad rap for being stodgy and redolent of the Soviet era. Whilst on occasion this may be true, when well prepared it's just as tasty as any other national cuisine. Additionally it reflects the many nationalities that have called the country home from Lithuanians, Ukrainians and Russians to Jews and Germans.

Polish starters can be meals in themselves. They include *kiełbasa* (sausage), grilled *oscypek* sheep's cheese from the Tatra Mountains, and *smalec* (salty pork lard) served on chunky bread. Soups include the distinctive żurek made using fermented rye flour and *barszcz* made from beetroot.

Barszcz czerwony, pierogi and *smalec* served up at Restauracja Starka in Kazimierz

Half a dozen main courses should be mentioned here. *Pierogi* (from an old Slavic word meaning 'feast') are boiled filled dumplings resembling large ravioli. Originally peasant food, they today transcend social boundaries due to the fact they can be filled with almost anything. The holy trinity are *pierogi ruskie* (cottage cheese, potato and onion), *pierogi z kapusta i grzybami* (cabbage and mushrooms) and *pierogi z miesem* (seasoned meat). *Gołąbki* (literally 'little pigeons' because of their shape) are boiled cabbage leaves stuffed with meat, onion and rice, baked and served with a creamy tomato or mushroom sauce. *Bigos* is a hearty winter stew made from cabbage, prunes, sausage, onions and herbs. *Golonka* is cured pork knuckle that is boiled or roasted and traditionally served with horseradish. *Kotlet Schabowy* resembles the Viennese schnitzel being a breaded and fried pork chop served with mashed potato and sauerkraut. Finally, *placki ziemniaczane* are fried potato cakes topped with goulash and sour cream.

Krakow offers many types of restaurant from smart historic townhouses and traditional dining rooms to converted cellars and cult cafés. Those at the top end include Wierzynek, Szara Gęś and Hawełka at Rynek Główny 16, 17 and 34 (Old Town) respectively, where patrons dine in considerable grandeur, and Jarema at plac Matejki 5, which offers Polish–Lithuanian dishes in similar surroundings (both Old Town). Pod Baranem at ul. św. Gertrudy 21 (Stradom) has a reputation for game and fish.

Other restaurants revel in their traditional Polish cuisine. One of the best is Restauracja Starka at ul. Józefa 14 (Kazimierz), where generous affordable portions are served against a cosy backdrop of red walls and Heinrich Zille sketches, and washed down with homemade vodka. Other recommendations include Kuchnia u Doroty at ul. Augustiańska 4 (Kazimierz) and U Babci Maliny at ul. Szpitalna 38 (Old Town), which is known for the fact that during the Second World, when it functioned as the Café Cyganeria, members of the Jewish Combat Organisation (Żydowska Organizacja Bojowa) planted a bomb here that killed 11 SS and Gestapo members. For good *smalec* in a recreated mountain hut visit Chata at ul. Krowoderska 21 (Kleparz).

Krakow has cornered the market in cellar venues and several cater for diners. At the top end is Chimera at ul. św. Anny 3 (Old Town) and Pod Aniołami at ul. Grodzka 35 (Okól), where patrons eat like kings. More modest is Sąsiedzi at ul. Miodowa 25 (Kazimierz), whilst those on a tight budget should head for Bar Smak, a legendary café at ul. Karmelicka 10 (Piasek) offering piles of *pierogi* for a pittance. For an entirely different dining experience climb aboard one of the converted barges moored along the Vistula (Wisła), including *Barka* and *Mauretania* at Bulwar Kurlandzki.

Poles love their sweets, which are best purchased in good local confectioners *(cukiernia)* including the long-established Cukiernia Jagiellońska at ul. Jagiellońska 5 (Old Town) and Cukiernia Karmelowa at ul. Karmelicka 23 (Piasek). Specialities include *pączek* (rose jam filled doughnuts), *sernik* (cheesecake) and *szarlotka* (apple short bread).

Other locations nearby: 39, 41, 42, 43

41 All Manner of Machines

31-060 Kraków (Kazimierz), the Museum of Municipal Engineering (Muzeum Inżynierii Miejskiej) at ul. św. Wawrzyńca 15
Tram 6, 8, 10, 13 to Plac Wolnica

Anyone interested in things mechanical should head south to Krakow's Museum of Municipal Engineering (Muzeum Inżynierii Miejskiej). Suitably housed since 1998 in the city's oldest tram depot, it contains all manner of machines, as well as plenty of hands-on activities for children.

The museum is located at ul. św. Wawrzyńca 15 (Kazimierz), which during the early 1900s lay at the heart of one of Krakow's most industrialised areas. Not only was the tram depot located here but also the city's electrical power plant and gas works.

At the heart of the museum is its collection of historic trams, housed inside the oldest part of the depot built in 1882. This was the year that horse-drawn trams were introduced into Krakow. Visitors are encouraged to clamber on board the various vehicles displayed, which can also be ridden around the city during the summer months on the museum's dedicated Line 0 (www.muzealna.org).

The rest of the depot consists of further sheds added up until the 1930s and used to house more trams, workshops, offices and eventually buses. At the time of writing several of these are being renovated to provide space for new and improved displays. Once reopened, the various exhibits will reveal Krakow's rich industrial legacy. The oldest artefacts include pieces of wooden water pipe used during the 17th and 18th centuries, as well as early forges, machine tools and printing presses. A highlight is a production line from the A. Rothe candle company. More recent times are represented by a battery-powered radio from 1929 manufactured by the Polish branch of the Marconi Wireless Telegraph Co., and a *Wisła* television set produced in the 1950s under Soviet license. There are household objects, too, including a Polish *Gamma II* vacuum cleaner dating from 1960.

Visitors wishing to roam further can follow the museum's Krakow Technology Trail (Krakowski Szlak Techniki), which highlights another 16 industrial sites of interest. South of the museum these include the Krakow Gasworks at ul. Gazowa 16, which first lit Krakow's streets in 1860, the 19th century stone abutments of the Podgórski Bridge (replaced in 1933 by the iron-trussed Piłsudski Bridge), the former Podgórze power plant on ul. Nadwiślańska (now the Cricoteka), and the famous factory of Oskar Schindler (see nos. 52, 59). North of the museum, the trail takes in the still-active Krakow Power Plant (1905) on ul. Dajwór, the rail viaduct over the infilled Old Vistula (Stara Wisła) on ul. Józefa Dietla, a neo-Gothic fire station (1879) on Westerplatte that is still used but has a horse-drawn fire tender in its foyer, the Ludwig Zieleniewski Machine & Instrument Factory (1856) (Krakow's oldest industrial complex though unfortunately not yet open open to the public) at ul. św. Krzyża 16, another power plant (1893) on plac Świętego Ducha once used to supply the Juliusz Słowacki Theatre (Teatr im Juliusza Słowackiego), the converted Götz-Okocimski Brewery (1840) at ul. Lubicz 17, and Krakow's Old Main Railway Station (Stary Dworzec Główny) in plac Jana Nowaka Jeziorańskiego (see nos. 34, 63, 65, 67).

A vintage tram rattles out of the Museum of Municipal Engineering (Muzeum Inżynierii Miejskiej)

Youngsters can roam farther afield to the seasonal Stanisław Lem Science Garden (Ogród Doświadczeń im. Stanisława Lema) at al. Pokoju 68 (Czyżyny), with its Newton Disc, whirlpool and gyroscope.

Across the road from the museum another part of the old tram depot is used today by the Stara Zajezdnia (Old Depot) brewery and beer hall, which boasts Krakow's longest bar. Likewise the former bus depot around the corner at ul. Gazowa 4 now houses the Studio Qulinarne restaurant.

Other locations nearby: 39, 42, 43

42 Some Glorious Gothic

31-064 Kraków (Kazimierz), the Church of St. Catherine
(Kościół św. Katarzyny) at ul. Augustiańska 7
Tram 6, 8, 10, 13, 18, 52 to Stradom (note: the church is only
open between May and October)

Krakow's Old Town is rightly described as an open air museum of architecture. Buildings in a variety of styles line its streets, including some glorious Gothic churches. Purists, however, may have a problem since some of them, including the famous Basilica of St. Mary (Bazylika Mariacka) at plac Mariacki 5, have had their interiors reworked (see no. 18). To discover Gothic in its unadulterated form one should instead visit Kazimierz, where two churches retain their original atmosphere and with fewer visitors to detract from it.

The churches stand in the old Christian quarter of Kazimierz, which abuts the well-known Jewish town at the symbolic juncture of ul. Beera Meisela and ul. Bożego Ciała (the former is named after Krakow's Chief Rabbi from 1832 to 1856; the latter means 'Corpus Christi Street'). Both churches were founded by King Casimir III the Great (Kazimierz III Wielki) (1310–1370), who established the eponymous town of Kazimierz on what at the time was an island in the Vistula (Wisła).

The first, the Church of St. Catherine (Kościół św. Katarzyny) at ul. Augustiańska 7 (entrance from ul. Skałeczna), is considered by many the city's finest Gothic church. It was built between 1345 and 1378 for the neighbouring Augustinian monastery of which it forms a part. The building's slender pillar buttresses, soaring arches and tall pointed windows make for a sublimely clean interior that typifies the Gothic idiom. That said the uncluttered appearance is in part because most of the original furnishings were lost during the 19th century, when the Austrians slated the building for demolition after it had twice been damaged by earthquakes. Fortunately it survived and what does remain inside is important since it includes a Baroque high altar of 1634, with its mystical painting *The Marriage of St. Catherine*, and some masterful stonework in the south porch.

The monastery, which is contemporary with the church, is worth visiting for the medieval murals adorning its cloister. Note particularly that of the Virgin in the Sanctuary of Our Lady of Consolation (Sanktuarium Matki Bozej Pocieszenia), with canonical crowns a blessed by Pope John Paul II in the Vatican added in 2000. On leaving the church visit the unusual freestanding belfry built in the 15th century from brick and timber, which now contains a shop selling devotional items (many on a theme of roses) related to the Augustinian nun Saint Rita of Cascia (Ryta z Cascii).

The second great Gothic church of Kazimierz stands a few streets away to the east. The Basilica of Corpus Christi (Bazylika Bożego Ciała) at ul. Bożego Ciała 26 was founded in 1340. Late Gothic in style, the building's exterior appears somewhat fussy in comparison with the determined simplicity of St. Catherine's. Inside the two churches again differ, with Corpus Christi's triple nave exhibiting a panoply of carved wood and gilded ornamentation. Two features really stand out, namely the pulpit in the form of a golden boat replete with oars and mast, and a towering golden altarpiece. The Florentine architect Bartolomeo Berecci (c. 1480–1537), who transformed Wawel Castle from a Gothic fortress into a Renais-

Soaring Gothic vaults inside the Church of St. Catherine (Kościół św. Katarzyny)

sance palace, was buried here after his mysterious murder in Krakow's Rynek Główny.

Afterwards walk around the south side of the building to see the Gethsemane Chapel (Ogrojec), which acts as a repository for Gothic funerary sculptures removed from the former graveyard that once surrounded the church. This has now been replaced by a walled garden with parterres that provides a pleasant place to relax during the summer months.

Other locations nearby: 43, 44

43 Folk Dress and Easter Eggs

31-060 Kraków (Kazimierz), the Ethnographic Museum (Muzeum Etnograficzne) at plac Wolnica 1
Tram 6, 8, 10, 13 to Plac Wolnica

In a city with so many galleries and museums, it's easy to overlook Krakow's Ethnographic Museum (Museum Ethnograficzne). This would be a pity since it contains a collection of objects that provides a fascinating insight into Polish folk culture and rural traditions.

The museum was established in 1911 by teacher, anthropologist and folklore enthusiast Seweryn Udziela (1857–1937). For him such a museum should "help us understand what kinds of peoples inhabit God's earth, how they live, how they dress, what they concern themselves with, what their habits and traditions look like". With this in mind, the collection grew in earnest as artefacts were accumulated from as far away as Vilnius, Zakopane and Kołomyja. Ever larger premises were occupied around Krakow until in 1947 the museum moved to its current location in the former town hall of Kazimierz at plac Wolnica 1.

Over the years curators have come and gone and the collections have been reorganised with them. Each has sought to reinterpret the collection in the light of contemporary political events. A good example was the *History of the Countryside* exhibition staged in 1951, which in line with the ruling Soviet-backed Polish People's Republic (Polska Rzeczpospolita Ludowa) overtly condemned the centuries-old oppression of Polish peasants whilst simultaneously extolling their strengths. Another exhibition in the 1960s celebrated the art of Poland's national minorities, including Russian rosaries, Jewish paper-cutting and Slovakian glass painting, whilst another in the early 1980s during the years of Martial Law offered visitors hope in the form of folk images of the famous Black Madonna of Częstochowa.

Today's visitors to the museum are in for a treat especially as much of the labelling is in English. Under the slogan "My museum, a museum about me", the permanent collection is currently organised in four thematic sections. The first, *Od Środka* (Inside), is perhaps the most intriguing since it reveals how ethnographers perceive and preserve the rural past – for example reconstructed cottage and workshop interiors – so that it makes sense for a modern audience.

The second section, *Rytm Życia* (Rhythm of Life), focuses on the importance of Spring rites in the Polish countryside. A straw doll per-

Krakow village folk dress in the Ethnographic Museum (Muzeum Etnograficzne)

sonifying winter is symbolically burned, then a decorated tree is paraded through the village marking the arrival of the new season. In hand with such seasonal rituals go traditional crafts, including the spinning wheel, grain quern and shoulder plough, which help measure out life itself.

The third section, *Rzeczy Ludzkie* (Human Objects), invites the visitor to focus on one unique object, whether it is an illiterate farmer's prayer book, a painted Easter egg from an Orthodox monastery or a bark basket used to collect wild strawberries. Also here is Krakow's oldest Christmas crib (1890s) and some beautifully made folk costumes.

The final section, *Nieobjęta Ziemia* (Unattainable Earth), comprises works of folk art accompanied by the words of Nobel prize-winning poet and author Czesław Miłosz (1911–2004). Here can be found various woodcuts, icons, religious carvings and even painted wooden beehives in the form of life-sized figures of saints and a honey-seeking bear.

The museum also has two outposts. One, the Dom Esterki (Esther's House) around the corner at ul. Krakowska 46, opened in 1986 and houses the museum library and temporary exhibits. The other is a newly-acquired former estate building at ul. Babiński 29 (Dębniki), which is in the process of being converted for use as a novel exhibition space.

Every August Krakow hosts a lively Folk Art Fair (Targi Sztuki Ludowej) in Rynek Głowny featuring countryside crafts, traditional dance and village cooking.

Other locations nearby: 41, 42, 44

44 Where Stanislaus was Slain

**31-065 Kraków (Kazimierz), the Skałka Sanctuary
(Sanktuarium Skałka) at ul. Skałeczna 15
Tram 6, 8, 10, 13 to Plac Wolnica then walk along ul. Skałeczna**

On the riverbank south of Wawel Hill is among Krakow's most sacred spots. The Skałka Sanctuary (Sanktuarium Skałka) in Kazimierz marks the place where in 1079 one of the country's patron saints, Stanislaus of Szczepanów (Stanisław Szczepanowski) (1030–1079), was martyred. The various churches that have since occupied the site have long been popular with pilgrims.

During the medieval period, Kazimierz was an island in the Vistula (Wisła) (see no. 63). Three distinct settlements existed here of which the most important was a pre-Christian Slavic shrine at the western, upstream end of the island. Its setting on a low crag overlooking a pool subsequently gave rise to the name Skałka, which means 'little rock'.

During the 11th century, the site was Christianised and a Romanesque Church of St. Michael the Archangel erected. It was in this building that the martyrdom of Saint Stanislaus took place. Born the son of a nobleman in the village of Szczepanów in southern Poland, Stanislaus rose to become Bishop of Krakow under King Bolesław II the Generous (Bolesław II Szczodry) (c. 1042–c. 1082). Unfortunately his numerous achievements, including bringing papal legates to Poland, eventually created conflict with the king. This came to a head when Stanislaus rebuked the monarch for his promiscuity, excommunicating him from the Church (some historians have suggested he may even have been planning to overthrow the king altogether). In response, Bolesław accused the bishop of treason and, when he failed to appear at court, had him assassinated at Skałka whilst he was celebrating Mass. In some accounts it was Bolesław himself who wielded the sword.

According to legend, Stanislaus was then dismembered and thrown into the pool in front of the church. Here, watched over by four guardian eagles, the bishop's mutilated body was miraculously reassembled. Subsequent outrage over the bishop's murder led to Bolesław losing his crown and Stanislaus eventually being canonised.

The cult of Saint Stanislaus appeared immediately after his death and grew stronger when Poland's feudal fragmentation began in 1138, which many viewed as punishment for the murder. Although the relics of Stanislaus were removed to Wawel Cathedral (Katedra Wawelska) in the 13th century, pilgrims still came to Skałka, and in the following century King Casimir III the Great (Kazimierz III Wielki) (1310–1370) raised a new Gothic church. In 1472 the sanctuary was taken over by the Pauline Fathers, who built a monastery alongside it. Later between 1733 and 1751 the church received the extensive Baroque makeover that greets pilgrims today as they walk down from the cathedral each March 8th to mark the anniversary of Stanislaus' death.

Known officially as the Basilica of SS. Michael the Archangel and Bishop Stanislaus the Martyr (Bazylika św. Michała Archanioła i św. Stanisława Biskupa i Męczennika), the church holds many memories of Stanislaus. Outside can still be seen the sulphurous pool into which his remains were thrown, now adorned with a statue of the saint. The modern courtyard alongside it contains an altar adorned with large statues not only of Stanislaus but also

Shrine to Saint Stanislaus in the Skałka Sanctuary (Sanktuarium Skałka)

Saint Adalbert (another of Poland's patron saints), Pope John Paul II and other saintly personages. Inside the church is an altar-cum-shrine marking the place where Stanislaus fell. It incorporates the wooden stump, on which he was purportedly dismembered, with three dark spots under glass on the wall nearby said to be his blood.

Beneath the church is a crypt containing many distinguished Poles, including royal chronicler Jan Długosz (1415–1480), poet-painter Stanisław Wyspiański (1869–1907), and Nobel Laureate for literature Czesław Miłosz (1911–2004).

Other locations nearby: 42, 43

45 A Passion for Japan

30-302 Kraków (Dębniki), the Manggha Museum of Japanese Art and Technology (Muzeum Sztuki i Techniki Japońskiej Manggha) at ul. Konopnickiej 26
Tram 17, 18, 22, 52 to Rondo Grunwaldzki

Krakow might seem an unlikely place for a museum dedicated to things Japanese. Yet here can be found the Manggha Museum of Japanese Art and Technology (Muzeum Sztuki i Techniki Japo skiej Manggha). Born out of one man's obsession with the Land of the Rising Sun, it is a world-class institution that provides a counterpoint to the city's prevailing penchant for Western art.

The museum's origins go back to 1901, when Polish writer and art collector Feliks Jasieński (1861–1929) arrived from Warsaw and began assembling a collection of graphics, ceramics and fabrics, with a particular fondness for anything Japanese. His well-to-do ancestors had been envoys in the Great Sejm (1788–1792), the parliamentary body made up of aristocratic nobles that dominated political life during the Polish–Lithuanian Commonwealth. This meant he was wealthy, too, enabling him to travel extensively and to move freely within the country's literary and artistic establishment.

The museum came into being in 1920, when Jasieński donated his collection of more than 6,000 Japanese artefacts to the National Museum in Krakow (Muzeum Narodowe w Krakowie). It would eventually be named after a collection of Jasieński's essays entitled *Manggha* (1901) (meaning 'sketches'), which was also Jasieński's nickname.

One condition of Jasieński's bequest was that the collection be made accessible to the public. Accordingly it was placed in one of the museum's branch properties, namely the Szołayski House (Kamienica Szołayskich) at plac Szczepański 9 (Old Town). Inadequate conditions, however, meant that the public were admitted infrequently. Indeed only briefly in 1944 was the collection properly displayed in an exhibition staged in the Cloth Hall (Sukiennice) by the occupying Germans.

One of those fascinated by the exhibition was a young man called Andrzej Wajda (1926–2016), who forty years later became a world-renowned film and theatre director, with awards from Cannes and Venice. In 1987 he was awarded the prestigious Kyoto Prize for his achievements and he donated the not inconsiderable winnings to Krakow's National Museum. This facilitated the construction of a new museum to display Jasieński's Japanese art and to promote Japanese culture in general (the Szołayski House is now used by the National Museum as a temporary art space). With additional support from both the City of Krakow and the Government of Japan, the new Manggha Museum of Japanese Art and Technology opened in 1994. Sitting unobtrusively on the banks of the Vistula (Wisła), directly across from Wawel Hill, it was designed by Japanese architect Arata Isozaki (b. 1931), with assistance from Polish postmodernist Krzysztof Ingarden (b. 1957). Perhaps the most striking feature of the sleek structure is its roof resembling an ocean wave, a motif made famous by Japanese artist Hokusai two centuries earlier.

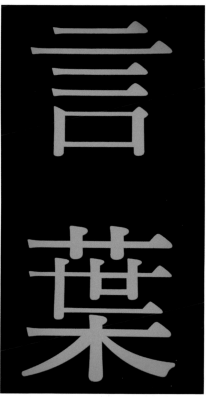

Neon light in the Manggha Museum of Japanese Art and Technology (Muzeum Sztuki i Techniki Japońskiej Manggha)

This fusion of old and new was a deliberate gesture by the architects since the building contains two distinct yet related exhibition spaces. One shows objects taken from Jasieński's collection of historic Japanese art; the other celebrates Polish works inspired by Japanese art (displayed in the separate Europe–Far East Gallery). Illustrating the ongoing synthesis between East and West is an important function of the Manggha Museum.

The building also contains meeting places, where living Japanese culture is promoted, including tea ceremonies, music, language and calligraphy.

Anyone with an interest in postmodern architecture should stray deeper into Dębniki to see the Higher Seminary of the Resurrectionists (Wyższe Seminarium Duchowne Zmartwychwstańców) at ul. Księdza Stefana Pawlickiego 1 (admission by entry buzzer). Krakow's first postmodern building, it was built in 1993 to a design by Dariusz Kozłowski (b. 1942) and features a deliberately cracked façade and various other quirky elements designed to assist students in their journey to God.

46 The Blue Lagoon

30-373 Kraków (Dębniki), the Zakrzówek Lagoon (Zalew
Zakrzówek) on ul. Twardowskiego
Tram 18 from Filharmonia or 22, 52 from Starowiślna
to Kapelanka then walk west along ul. Twardowskiego

Where do Krakow's adventure-seekers go during the summer months?
A favourite destination has long been the Zakrzówek Lagoon (Zalew
Zakrzówek) in Dębniki. This flooded former quarry is beloved by
swimmers and divers, and the surrounding wild landscape draws
walkers and climbers. Mix in mysterious caves, some important natural history, a tenacious legend and even a memorial to Elvis, and the
place makes for an exciting day out.

The Zakrzówek Lagoon was created by accident in 1990, when
quarry workers inadvertently pierced the water table. Before that, the
quarry had supplied limestone for a variety of purposes, including the
Solvay soda plant in Borek Fałęcki, which opened in 1906, and the
construction of the early 20th century flood defences along the banks
of the Vistula (Wisła).

The lagoon is a figure-of-eight in shape, with clear, turquoise water
framed by near-vertical cliffs. Although swimming and cliff-diving is
officially prohibited, scuba diving was until recently permitted through
an approved dive centre. Divers loved the fact that the lagoon reaches
105 feet at its deepest and is littered with manmade objects, from cars
and sunken boats to a light aircraft and the former changing rooms of
the quarry workers. There is also a granite plaque in the depths commemorating the fact that Karol Wojtyła (1920–2005), later Pope John
Paul II, worked at the quarry from September 1940 until October 1941
(see no. 10).

With the dive centre's licence having expired in 2019, there are
plans to turn the lagoon into a municipal recreational facility, with all
the invasive infrastructure that would inevitably bring. Environmental-
ists are among those keen that the area retains its wild aspect citing its
importance as the habitat of rare butterflies and the Smooth snake (Co-
ronella austriaca). These creatures inhabit the extensive wooded area
surrounding the lagoon, which is dotted with limestone bluffs. Geo-
logically speaking these are made of Jurassic limestone created tectoni-
cally about 150 million years ago at the foot of the then-forming Carpathians. Today the area forms part of the eastern edge of the Bielany-
Tyniec Landscape Park (Bielańsko-Tyniecki Park Krajobrazowy).

The Zakrzówek Lagoon (Zalew Zakrzówek) in Dębniki

One bluff north of the lagoon is known as Twardowski Rocks (Skałki Twardowskiego). It is popular with rock climbers, whose steel pitons can be seen hammered into the crevices. The name reflects the local claim that a cave here once contained the workshop of Krakow's legendary 16th century alchemist and occultist Pan Twardowski, who sold his soul to the devil in exchange for special powers. The story was probably inspired by the real-life English alchemists John Dee (1527–1608) and Edward Kelley (1555–1597), both of whom lived in Krakow for a time. Other caves are man-made bunkers dating from the 19th century, when Austrian troops were fortifying Krakow against possible Russian attack (see no. 80). Most of have now been sealed for safety reasons.

A wholly unexpected sight not far from the northern reaches of the lagoon is a memorial to rock'n'roll singer Elvis Presley (1935–1977). Erected in 2006 by the Krakow Elvis Presley Fan Club and consisting of a craggy boulder containing Elvis' face half-submerged in silicon, it can be found on al. Elvisa Presleya, a forested track that leads northwards away from the lagoon to eventually join ul. Jana Pietrusińskiego.

Another flooded quarry popular with pleasure-seekers is the Kryspinów Lagoon, a former sand pit just outside the western city limits. It can be reached by taking Bus 209 or 269 from the Salwator tram terminus to Budzyń Zalew na Piaskach or Budzyń Plaża Główna respectively. Yet another is Bagry Lagoon (Zalew Bagry) reached by taking tram 20 to Rzebika.

47 Have No Fear!

30-610 Kraków (Łagiewniki), the John Paul II Centre (Centrum Jana Pawła II) at ul. Totus Tuus 34
Tram 8 from Stradom to Borek Fałęcki; 19, 22 from Starowiślna to Borek Fałęcki

People hold different opinions as to who was history's greatest Pole. Was it King Casimir III the Great (Kazimierz III Wielki) (1310–1370), who along with his niece Jadwiga (1374–1399) did so much to develop the country? Or was it brave bishop and martyr Saint Stanislaus (1030–1079)? Or freedom fighter Tadeusz Kościuszko (1746–1817)? What is certain is that every Pole's favourite pope is John Paul II (1920–2005). Effigies, museums and institutions of the man born Karol Wojtyła are everywhere in Krakow, the city where he spent his formative years. Indeed in recent years an entire 'papal tourism' industry has built up around sites associated with him. The latest addition to the itinerary is the John Paul II Centre (Centrum Jana Pawła II) at ul. Totus Tuus 34 in the southern district of Łagiewniki.

Built on the former site of the Solvay soda plant, where Wojtyła toiled as a young man, the project was initiated in 2008 by Krakow's former Archbishop a close advisor to John Paul II, Cardinal Stanisław Dziwisz (b. 1939). In essence a self-contained community, the complex primarily accommodates pilgrims and enlightens visitors about John Paul II's many and varied achievements. Among the growing number of facilities (some free, others with an admission charge) are a hotel and conference centre, a meditation park and observation tower (open April to October), a rehabilitation centre, a pilgrims' café and a priests' house.

There are three main visitor attractions in the complex. Most important is the Sanctuary of Blessed John Paul II (Sanktuarium šw. Jana Pawła II), its great bronze doors carrying reliefs depicting the man's life including his work at the soda plant. The cavernous octagonal shrine here has enormous mosaics on each wall, with a marble altar containing a phial of the late pope's blood. Also here is the much-revered blood-soaked cassock he was wearing in 1981 following an assassination attempt in the Vatican. Personal effects belonging to the pope are displayed in the second attraction, namely the John Paul II Museum (Muzeum Jana Pawła II). A branch of the city's Archdiocesan Museum of Cardinal Karol Wojtyła (Muzeum Archidiecezjalne Kardynała Karola Wojtyły), it includes samples of the many gifts he received during his world travels (see no. 10). The third attraction is the John Paul II Institute (Instytut Jana Pawła II), where visitors get the chance to see a copy of the famous and controversial Shroud of Turin.

The full name of the complex is actually the John Paul II Centre 'Have No Fear!' ('Nie lękajcie się!'). The quotation is taken from a speech given by the pope in October 1978 during the inauguration of his pontificate: "Have no fear! Open wide the doors for Jesus Christ and His saving power. Open the borders between countries, economic systems, regimes, and civilization directions. Have no fear!"

It's worth noting that John Paul II echoed these words a year later during a speech in Warsaw. According to Lech Wałęsa (b. 1943), the founder of the Solidarity (Solidarność) movement and the first post-Communist

The Sanctuary of Blessed John Paul II (Sanktuarium św. Jana Pawła II) in Łagiewniki

President of Poland, the pontiff said to the crowd "Do not be afraid… Let your Spirit descend and change the image of the land…this land." Such spiritual inspiration provided the catalyst for a peaceful revolution in Poland, indeed it is now acknowledged by all sides that Pope John Paul II was instrumental in bringing down Communism in Europe. Soviet leader Mikhail Gorbachev (b. 1931) went on to say that "the collapse of the Iron Curtain would have been impossible without John Paul II." With the benefit of hindsight, it was perhaps Karol Wojtyła's greatest achievement.

Other locations nearby: 48

48 The Miracle of Saint Faustyna

30-420 Kraków (Łagiewniki), the Sanctuary of Divine Mercy (Sanktuarium Bożego Miłosierdzia) at ul. św. Siostry Faustyny 3
Tram 8, 22 from Stradom to Sanktuarium Bożego Miłosierdzia; 19 from Starowiślna to Sanktuarium Bożego Miłosierdzia (note: no visits during Mass)

Pope John Paul II (1920–2005) commissioned many new churches in Krakow during his long tenure as head of the Roman Catholic Church. Probably the most impressive is the Sanctuary of Divine Mercy (Sanktuarium Bożego Miłosierdzia) in Łagiewniki. Built to honour Saint Faustyna Kowalska, it is visited annually by over two million pilgrims. Saint Faustyna was born Helena Kowalska (1905–1938) in the village of Głogowiec near Łódź. From an early age she felt drawn to the conventual life but being from a poor family was instead forced by her parents to work as a housekeeper. This she did dutifully until her nineteenth year, when everything changed: while at a dance with her sister she experienced a vision of the suffering Christ. Realising immediately how empty her life was, she moved to Warsaw and shortly afterwards joined the Congregation of the Sisters of Our Lady of Mercy (Zgromadzenie Sióstr Matki Bożej Miłosierdzia). There she took the religious name of Sister Maria Faustyna of the Blessed Sacrament, 'Faustyna' being a diminutive of Fausta (meaning 'fortunate').

Faustyna spent the next 11 years travelling from convent to convent with the Sisters, usually working as a cook and gardener. During this time she reported frequent visions and conversations with God, revealed stigmata, experienced bilocation and claimed to read people's souls. Unfortunately she also suffered tuberculosis, which led to her eventually being admitted to the Infectious Diseases Hospital in Krakow's Prądnik district. Her recovery there was deemed a miracle although Faustyna believed her illness to have been punishment for her sins. Following a relapse she died aged just 33 in the Convent of the Sisters of Our Lady of Mercy (Klasztor Sióstr Matki Bożej Miłosierdzia) in Łagiewniki.

Pope John Paul II was a longstanding admirer of Faustyna. During the Second World War, whilst still a cleric, he prayed regularly at the convent where she died. Later in 1999 as Pope he ordered construction of the Sanctuary of Divine Mercy at the site to handle the increased number of pilgrims expected in the wake of Faustyna's canonisation a year later. Based on the remarkable contents of her 700-page diary, she is the only saint ever given the status of 'Secretary of Divine Mercy'.

The Sanctuary of Divine Mercy consists of a huge ellipsoidal basilica completed in 2002 to a design by local architect Witold Cęckiewicz (b. 1924) (see no. 91). Resembling a boat with room for 5,000 worshippers, it is accompanied by a freestanding 250 foot-high observation tower that resembles a mast, as well as a modern pilgrims' hotel. Above the basilica's altar hangs *Divine Mercy*, an image of Christ with red and white shafts of light streaming from his heart. It was painted in 1944 by Polish artist Adolf Hyła (1897–1965) and based on earlier works depicting Faustyna's visions.

Pilgrims at the Sanctuary of Divine Mercy (Sanktuarium Bożego Miłosierdzia)

Still standing nearby is the Sisters' red-brick convent. Faustyna's remains reside in a tomb in the church at which not only Pope John Paul II but also Popes Benedict XVI and Francis have prayed. It was here in 1981 that pilgrim Maureen Digan of Massachusetts claims to have been relieved of persistent pain caused by Lymphedema. Doctors were confounded and her miraculous healing paved the way for Faustyna's beatification.

During the 1980s and 90s, architect Witold Cęckiewicz (b. 1924) designed several other suburban churches in Krakow, all in his preferred Modernist concrete idiom. They include the Church of St. Brother Albert (Kościół św. Brata Alberta) in Czyżyny, the Church of the Pentecost (Kościół Zesłania Ducha Świętego) in Ruczaj, and the Church of the Divine Mercy (Kościół Miłosierdzia Bożego) in Krzesławice.

Other locations nearby: 47

49 A Red-Brick Masterpiece

30-523 Kraków (Podgórze), the Church of St. Joseph (Kościół św. Józefa) at ul. Zamojskiego 2
Tram 6, 8, 10, 13 to Korona

It's easy to think that central Krakow has a monopoly on the city's historic churches since the concentration there of such buildings is so impressive. There are churches farther afield, however, that should not be missed, including the Church of St. Joseph (Kościół św. Józefa) in Podgórze. Dubbed the Cathedral of Podgórze and ranked one of the city's most beautiful places of worship, it is definitely worth crossing the Vistula (Wisła) for.

Before visiting the church though, it's worth exploring the cobblestoned triangular square in front of it. Rynek Podgórski was laid out in the late-18th century by the Austrians at the foot of Lasota Hill, where roads leading to and from Krakow, Wieliczka and Kalwaria intersected (see no. 56). It served as the main market square of the Royal Free City of Podgórze until 1915, when the hitherto independent city was swallowed up by Krakow. Within a couple of years trams had arrived in Podgórze and a turning loop was installed where previously merchants from across the Austro-Hungarian Empire had traded. Although the loop was later relocated, the merchants never returned.

These days the square is a peaceful spot, pedestrianised with public seating and lawns for relaxing. It is lined with mostly residential buildings from the 19th century onwards, although visitors should note the pair of 18th century buildings on the north side. The former Pod Czarnym Orłem (Under the Black Eagle) inn at number 13 is where composer Frédéric Chopin (1810–1849) spent a night. Next door at number 14 is Podgórze's original town hall, replaced in 1854 by the neo-Classical structure around the corner at number 1 (abandoned in 1915, it now houses Krakow City Council's Department of Architecture). It was alongside this building on ul. Bolesława Limanowskiego that one of the gates into the Krakow Ghetto once stood (see no. 53).

Presiding over the southern apex of the square is the monumental Church of St. Joseph. Surprisingly it's one of the square's younger buildings having only been completed in 1909 to a design by Lwów-born architect Jan Sas-Zubrzycki (1860–1935). Known for his Gothic Revival red-brick churches, Sas-Zubrzycki created the so-called Vistula Style of which the Church of St. Joseph is a fine example. The decorative brick façade, which is beautifully lit at night, is imposing yet elegant, trimmed with arches, finials and statues in stone. Ranged around the periphery are single-storey chapels, each finished with a tent-shaped copper roof, and towering above the whole, a 262-foot high clock tower reminiscent of the Basilica of St. Mary (Bazylika Mariacka) in Krakow's Old Town. Before entering the church be sure to view the ruins of its modest predecessor to the rear, consecrated in 1832 but later demolished due to a design flaw.

The interior of the church looks like an authentic Gothic cathedral, with its numerous side chapels and altars, lavish sculptural decoration and ornate wooden fittings, all installed to demonstrate the wealth of Old Podgórze. The lovely stained glass was manufactured in the workshop of Stanisław Gabriel Żeleński (1873–1914) (see no. 92). For many years the predominant colour of the walls was red-blue but this was not original. Fortunately between 1978 and 2006, as part of an extensive programme of renovation, the original more modest white-grey colour was reinstated, and the altars, pulpit and pipe organ renovated, too. A stone statue of St. Joseph by renowned local sculptor Zygmunt Langman (1860–1924), which had been removed in the 1950s, was also returned to the main altar.

The Church of St. Joseph (Kościół św. Józefa) in Podgórze

Other locations nearby: 50, 51, 52

50 A Synagogue is Saved

30-535 Kraków (Podgórze), the Starmach Gallery (Galeria Starmach) at ul. Węgierska 5
Tram 6, 8, 10, 13 to Korona; 3, 6, 13, 17, 19, 24 to Limanowskiego (note: ring doorbell for admission)

Before the Second World War, Krakow was home to around 120 synagogues and prayer houses. Many lined the narrow streets of Kazimierz, where the city's flourishing Jewish population had been happily based for centuries (see no. 35). Few reopened, however, after the Nazis deported the congregations that used them. The second greatest concentration lay on the opposite side of the Vistula (Wisła) in Podgórze. Consisting of one synagogue and a dozen prayer houses, these too were desecrated and abandoned during the war. The synagogue, however, has since been reborn as a successful private art gallery.

The brick-built Zucher Synagogue at Węgierska 5 was completed in 1881, at a time when Krakow's Jewish community was thriving, its members living and working harmoniously with their Polish neighbours. Everything changed in August 1940 when German Governor-General Hans Frank (1900–1946) decreed that all Jews except those contributing to the German war effort must leave Krakow. By March of the following year, only 15,000 from an estimated 60,000 Jews remained. Those living in Kazimierz were then rounded up and placed in the Krakow Ghetto in Podgórze (see no. 53).

The Zucher Synagogue was one of four Jewish places of worship that found themselves within the walled Ghetto (the others being prayer houses located at numbers 6 and 7 on the same street and another nearby at ul. Krakusa 7). When the Ghetto was first established, many valuable religious objects retrieved from the synagogues of Kazimierz were safeguarded here despite the fact that the practising of Judaism was outlawed (though inevitably it continued in secret). The objects' security was far from guaranteed though and most were seized once deportations to surrounding concentration camps began in May 1942.

The final liquidation of the Ghetto took place in March 1943 after which the now-empty synagogue was pressed into service as a warehouse and later a factory. After the war, the building fell into dereliction and as with the more famous synagogues of Kazimierz was entirely neglected during the Communist era.

All was not lost though. After the fall of Communism, the unloved building was purchased by local art lovers and historians Andrzej and Teresa Starmach. In 1989, they had established their eponymous Starmach Gallery (Galeria Starmach) on Rynek Główny (Old Town), where for a decade they staged an impressive 55 exhibitions highlighting the best in Polish post-war art. With the synagogue now in their possession, they set about creating a new gallery following restoration of the building's striking red-brick façade and a complete internal conversion. The new Starmach Gallery opened in 1997 and has gone on to become one of Poland's most respected private art spaces, with more than 60 more exhibitions to its name.

The Starmach Gallery (Galeria Starmach) is housed in a former synagogue

Since its relocation to Podgórze, the Starmach has hosted the Nowosielski Foundation Prize for outstanding young artists established by artist and philosopher Jerzy Nowosielski (1923–2011). His distinctive work influenced by Russian iconography and the Byzantine style has long been promoted by the Starmachs. Recipients have included sculptress Mirosław Bałka (b. 1958) and art academic Leon Tarasewicz (b. 1957).

The prayer houses of Podgórze were, as their name suggests, installed within private homes. They included the Rabi Skawiński prayer house at ul. Celna 5, the Anszei Chail prayer house at ul. Rękawka 30, and the Bikur Cholim prayer house at ul. Bolesława Limanowskiego 13. Others existed at ul. Kazimierza Brodzinskiego 8, ul. Stroma 11, Rynek Podgórski 3, and ul. Kalwaryjska 21, 26 and 29. All have reverted to being private residences, shops and workshops, with nothing to suggest their former function.

Other locations nearby: 49, 51, 52

51 Krakow Street Art

33-332 Kraków, (Podgórze), a tour of street art beginning with Ding Dong Dumb at ul. Piwna 3A
Tram 3, 17, 19, 24 to Plac Bohaterów Getta; 6, 8, 10, 13 to Korona; 3, 6, 13, 17, 19, 24 to Limanowskiego

Krakow has a well-deserved reputation for the quality of its street art. Although it lags behind less conservative cities such as Warsaw and Wrocław, its street murals are engaging and entertaining. Unofficial art still comes and goes on many street corners but increasingly graffiti artists are being commissioned by businesses and institutions to adorn their walls. Even the city authorities have begun sponsoring permanent large scale works on otherwise blank architectural spaces.

It's not surprising that Krakow eventually succumbed to street art. After all, Poland has a venerable tradition of graphic art manifested through its expertise in large-scale advertising and poster design. Remarkably this particular art form flourished under Communism and still resonates in the country's graphics today.

Quality street art can be found in several districts of Krakow. A diverse grouping can be found in Podgórze, a former working class industrial district on the south bank of the Vistula (Wisła). To get there from Kazimierz cross the Father Bernatek Footbridge (Kładka Ojca Bernatka) named after a local monk and adorned with cleverly-suspended acrobatic sculptures by Jerzy Kędziora (b. 1947). It has done much to revitalise both sides of the river, for example the popular café-club Drukarnia at ul. Nadwiślańska 1, with its long bar and riverside windows.

Behind Drukarnia on a gable end at ul. Piwna 3A is Italian graffiti artist Blu's *Ding Dong Dumb*. Painted in 2011 and consisting of a huge church bell-shaped megaphone pointing down at an astonished crowd, it is clearly a cynical stab at organised religion. An apartment block at nearby ul. Józefińska 24 sports a pair of gable-end murals. *Lem's Robot* (2011) by Filip Kuźniarz celebrates Polish science fiction writer Stanisław Lem (1921–2006), whilst *Mayamural* (2012) on the other end recalls the Mayan apocalypse that never happened (see no. 100). A couple of streets away at ul. Zamoyskiego 6 is a traditional work celebrating the centenary of Podgórze's incorporation into Krakow in 1915. It features the once-independent city's famous citizens, including Antoni Stawarz (1889–1955), who led the liberation of Krakow in 1918 (see no. 56).

More works can be found in neighbouring Zabłocie, including a Joseph Conrad mural (2017) at ul. Zabłocie 13, *Tolerance* (2014) at the corner with ul. Przemysłowa, in which squeezed tubes of paint become different-coloured holding hands, and *Jedni z Wielu* (One of Many) (2015) at ul. Zabłocie 22, which strives to improve attitudes towards Roma minorities.

Kazimierz is also a fertile hunting ground for quality street art often on a Jewish theme. *Judah* at ul. św Wawrzyńca 16, for example, is by Israeli artist Pil Peled and depicts a Jewish child in a lion's mask showing bravery in the face of adversity. Broken Fingaz' superb gable-end mural at plac Bawół 3 commemorates the Bosaków family that lived here for 400 years before relocating to Israel during the Second World War (see frontispiece). Playful by comparison is the oft-photographed stencil *Singing in the Rain* at ul. Bożego Ciała 18 showing Gene Kelly swinging on a drain pipe.

Ding Dong Dumb is a provocative piece of Krakow street art

Street art elsewhere in Krakow includes an eerie stencil of Jesus in an underpass at the corner of ul. Kopernika and ul. Blich, and another at ul. Strzelecka (both Wesoła), as well as the calamitous *Are You Ready* (2016) by Olaf Cirut at ul. Kolberga 7 (Kleparz). University murals include the colourful Życie to Rozwój (Life is Development) at ul. Reymonta 4 and another courtesy of the University of Science and Technology at ul. Czarnowiejska 50B celebrating technological breakthroughs past, present and future (both Czarna Wieś).

Other locations nearby: 49, 50, 52

52 A Unique Theatrical Experience

30-527 (Podgórze), the Cricoteka – Centre for the Documentation of the Art of Tadeusz Kantor at ul. Nadwiślańska 2–4
Tram 3, 17, 19, 24 to Plac Bohaterów Getta; 6, 8, 10, 13 to Korona; 3, 6, 13, 17, 19, 24 to Limanowskiego

Theatre director Tadeusz Kantor (1915–1990) may be little-known outside Poland but he is ranked among the pioneers of *avant-garde* theatre in 20th century Europe. Devotees remember him for his revolutionary experimental productions both at home and abroad. Those new to Kantor's *oeuvre* can find out more in Krakow's unique Cricoteka arts centre.

Kantor was born in 1915 in the village of Wielopole Skrzyńskie in what at the time was Austro-Hungarian Galicia. He graduated in 1939 from Krakow's Academy of Fine Arts (Akademia Sztuk Pięknych w Krakowie) and despite the Nazi occupation of Poland managed to work alongside *avant-garde* artist Józef Jarema (1900–1974) and his independent CRICOT theatre group (pronounced *cree-co*, the name is an anagram of *Kultura Ruch Inaczej Komedia Oko Teatr* meaning 'Cultural Movement Alternative Comedy Eye Theatre').

After the war, Kantor came into his own as both *avant-garde* director and stage designer. Examples of how he liberated traditional theatre design include the use of thrust stages and handmade props, as well as the juxtaposition of mannequins with live actors. Disenchantment with the gradual institutionalisation of *avant-garde* theatre led him in 1955 to found his own ensemble in Krakow called CRICOT 2. Its main focus was Absurdism – humanity's futile efforts to absolutely define its own existence – with a sprinkling of elements from Jewish theatre (although Kantor was raised Catholic). During the 1960s the group gained a fierce reputation for its 'stage happenings', with innovative takes on playwright Stanisław Ignacy Witkiewicz's *Mątwa* (The Cuttlefish) (1956) and *Kurka Wodna* (The Water Hen) (1969) regarded as highpoints. Later plays were written by Kantor himself, notably *Umarła klasa* (Dead Class) (1975) in which a teacher presides over a class of dead students accompanied by mannequins representing their younger selves. Played like a séance, with words and sounds deformed by the passage of time, this was Kantor's attempt at capturing the collective memory of Polish Jews lost during the Holocaust.

Tadeusz Kantor's *Umarła klasa (Dead Class)* in the Cricoteka

Such works intimately bound to Kantor were difficult to create after his death in 1990, so after performing his last work, *Dziś są moje urodziny* (Today is my Birthday), Cricot 2 disbanded. This would not be the end of the Cricot story though. Since 1980 Kantor had been documenting his theatrical achievements in what he called the Cricoteka. This 'living archive' was initially based at ul. Kanonicza 5 (Okół), where it comprised hundreds of stage artefacts, costumes, drawings, photos and films accumulated as Kantor toured with his ensemble. Whilst much remains there, in 2014 a new Cricoteka opened on the southern bank of the Vistula (Wisła) at ul. Nadwiślańska 2–4 (Podgórze).

The new building is the first art institution in Poland dedicated to an individual artist. Designed by local architects nsMoonStudio, it hangs like a huge rusting bridge over a former municipal power plant, one of the first in Galicia, which once supplied the factories, homes and street lamps of Podgórze. The overall design is based on a drawing by Kantor in which a man carries a table on his shoulders. The new building contains numerous exhibition spaces in which items related to Kantor and Cricot 2 (and inspired by them) are displayed, whilst the old power plant has been converted for use as a theatre. The programme of performances is listed online (www.cricoteka.pl).

Hardcore devotees of Kantor's work can also visit the Tadeusz Kantor Gallery – Studio at ul. Sienna 7/5 (Old Town). A satellite of the Cricoteka organisation, it contains the studio in which Kantor created his final works between 1987 and 1900. Original furniture, letters, drawings and travel souvenirs are displayed.

Other locations nearby: 49, 50, 51

53 Remains of the Krakow Ghetto

30-548 Kraków (Podgórze), a wall from the Krakow Ghetto at ul. Lwowska 25–29
Tram 3, 6, 13, 17, 19, 24 to Limanowskiego; 3, 17, 19, 24 to Plac Bohaterów Getta

In September 1939, Germany and the Soviet Union invaded and divided Poland. Krakow was made headquarters of the Nazi-administered central region known as the General Government. Eager to make it a model of German racial purity, Governor Hans Frank (1900–1946) ordered Jews living in the countryside to move into Krakow, where they were registered and merged with the city's existing Jewish population in Kazimierz. It would be the first step in the Nazis' plan to rid the area completely of Jews.

On 1st August 1940, with the Jews now in one place, Frank decreed that they were to leave unless deemed useful to the German war effort. Many escaped to the Russian occupied zone, whilst others were forcibly resettled in labour camps in the east. In less than a year, Krakow's pre-war Jewish population of almost 60,000 dwindled to just 15,000.

March 13th 1941 was an iniquitous day. Under the terms of Nazi Edict 44/91 the city's remaining Jews were forced from their homes and herded *en masse* across the Silesian Uprisings Bridge (Most Powstańców Śląskich) into Podgórze (the original bridge was rebuilt in 1978). There they were crammed into an area bounded by ul. Piwna, ul. Tragutta, Rynek Podgórski and Lasota Hill that was originally designed for just 3,000 inhabitants. The overcrowded and insanitary conditions in what became known as the Krakow Ghetto meant sickness and starvation were rampant. In the film *Schindler's List*, director Steven Spielberg used the narrow balconied courtyards lining ul. Beera Meiselsa in Kazimierz to recreate the Ghetto's cramped confines (see no. 58).

The systematic deportation of Jews from the Ghetto began in May 1942 as part of an anti-Jewish operation called Aktion Krakau headed by SS-Oberführer Julian Scherner (1895–1945). Thousands were rounded up in plac Zgody and then escorted to the railway station at Prokocim, where waiting trains took them away to various concentration camps. The final liquidation on 13–14 March 1943 was overseen by SS-Untersturmführer Amon Göth (1908–1946), the new comman-

Remains of the Krakow Ghetto wall on ul. Lwowska in Podgórze

dant of Krakow's Płaszów Concentration Camp (see no. 57). His men marched the 6,000 fittest to the camp, transported 3,000 to Auschwitz-Birkenau, and shot 2,000 on the streets.

Despite such harrowing events, the former Ghetto has returned to being a place where people today live and work in peace. Several sights remain, however, to tell the story. They include a 40-foot-long stretch of original perimeter wall at ul. Lwowska 25–29 built by the Jews themselves in the style of the gravestones of their ancestors (where the street joins ul. Bolesława Limanowskiego stood one of the Ghetto's three gates). A longer albeit restored section of wall stands farther south in the school playground at ul. Bolesława Limanowskiego 60–62.

Another of the gates stood in the corner of plac Zgody. Now renamed plac Bohaterów Getta (Ghetto Heroes' Square), it contains a memorial made up of 70 empty metal chairs symbolising the area's emptiness following the deportations (each Sunday after March 14th a remembrance parade sets out from here to the site of the former Płaszów Camp). A plaque at number 6 on the square informs onlookers that this building is where the Jewish Combat Organisation (ŻOB) met to plan acts of resistance outside the Ghetto. The building at number 18 was the Eagle Pharmacy (Apteka pod Orłem) operated by Tadeusz Pankiewicz (1908–1993). He smuggled medicine, food and information to the incarcerated Jews and recorded Nazi brutality in a much-translated book published after the war. The building today is a branch of the Museum of Krakow (Muzeum Krakowa) depicting how life was in the Ghetto.

Other locations nearby: 54, 55, 56

54 On Top of Lasota Hill

33-332 Kraków (Podgórze), a walk over Lasota Hill
Tram 6, 8, 10, 13 to Korona then walk east on Rynek
Podgórski, ul. Rękawka and ul. Parkowa to reach
ul. Porucznika Antoniego Stawarza

Lasota Hill rises up behind the main square of Old Podgórze (Rynek Podgórski) and its red-brick Church of St. Joseph (Kościół św. Józefa) (see no. 49). It can be ascended by leaving the square along ul. Rękawka, turning right onto ul. Parkowa, and then continuing up onto ul. Porucznika Antoniego Stawarza. Here can be found some of Krakow's most sought after private residences. However, if it's history you're after, then walk onwards to reach a large meadow fringed by the Krzemionki cliffs. Here stand two of the city's less well-known architectural treasures.

Sensitives say the meadow has a special feel about it. Perhaps this is to be expected considering the place was once used for pagan worship. More recently, it provided the backdrop for a pivotal scene in the film *Schindler's List*, when Schindler and his wife on horseback witness Nazi troops rounding up Jews in the Ghetto below. Amidst the commotion Schindler spots a young girl in a red coat standing out in the otherwise black-and-white film. For Schindler and many in the audience, the girl's presence makes the horror suddenly personal and her subsequent death all the more painful.

Perched on the limestone cliffs at the northern edge of the meadow is the tiny buttressed Church of St. Benedict (Kościół św. Benedykta). Thought to be one of Krakow's oldest churches (and certainly its smallest) it was probably built during the 11th century by the Benedictine monks of Tyniec Abbey (Opactwo Benedyktynów w Tyńcu) (see no. 105). They were keen to stamp out any persistent pagan practices occurring on Lasota Hill – Pagan 'vampire' burials have been detected beneath the church floor – as well as on the nearby Krakus Mound (Kopiec Krakusa), which can be seen to the south (see no. 106). Saved from demolition by a local priest, the church interior consists only of a nave and chancel, with a painting of namesake Saint Benedict over the pulpit (the church can be visited on St. Benedict's Day (March 31st) and the Tuesday after Easter).

On the cliffs at the southern edge of the meadow stands a very different structure. Fort 31 'St. Benedict' (Fort 31 ' w. Benedykt') was one of a pair of artillery fortresses built hereabouts in the 1850s by

The ancient Church of St. Benedict (Kościół św. Benedykta) crowns Lasota Hill

the occupying Austrians. Part of the broader Fortress Krakow (Twierdza Kraków), their purpose was to protect the Vistula (Wisła) and ul. Wielicka, the road east to Lwów in what is now Ukraine, at a time when partitioned Poland lay only a few miles from the Russian border (see no. 80).

Of the so-called 'Maximillian Tower' type, Fort 31 takes the form of an imposing 16-sided polygon rendered in red-brick. Two storeys high and with a circular internal courtyard, it covers an area of over 16,000 square feet. After relinquishing its original function in the 1890s, the fort served instead as barracks. During the Second World War, it housed French captured prisoners, and in the 1950s was converted into apartments (at the same time Fort 32 'Krzemionki' was demolished to make way for the construction of the television tower that can be seen to the west). Fort 31 currently stands abandoned pending approval from the City of Krakow for some as yet undefined new purpose.

After taking in the expansive views afforded by Lasota Hill, this walk can be extended by continuing eastwards between the church and the fortress to reach the Old Podgórze Cemetery (Stary Cmentarz Podgórski) (see no. 55). It lies opposite a school in whose grounds a stretch of the original Ghetto Wall still stands (see no. 53).

Other locations nearby: 53, 55, 56

55 Cemeteries Old and New

33-332 Kraków (Podgórze), the Old Podgórze Cemetery (Stary Cmentarz Podgórski) at the corner of ul. Bolesława Limanowskiego and al. Powstańców Śląskich
Tram 3, 6, 13, 24 to Podgórze SKA

Travellers who enjoy visiting old cemeteries will not be disappointed by Krakow. The city has half a dozen of them, each worth a visit for their distinctive geography and roster of incumbents (see nos. 36, 76, 100). They include the Old and New Podgórze Cemeteries south of the Vistula (Wisła), where triumph, tragedy and tradition go hand in hand.

The Old Podgórze Cemetery (Stary Cmentarz Podgórski) at the corner of ul. Bolesława Limanowskiego and al. Powstańców Śląskich was the district's main burial ground for more than a century. Laid out in the late 18th century, it is the last resting place of the formerly independent city's great and good (Podgórze became a part of Krakow in 1915).

Despite being near a busy road, the cemetery manages to retain a sense of tranquillity. Indeed from the street its presence is only given away by a tall sculpture of *God the Father*. The arched gateway is set well back and part way up a gentle hill obscured by trees. It is the golden leaves from these trees that make this a special place to visit in the throes of autumn.

Unfortunately the cemetery today is only a fraction of what it once was. After being closed in 1900 having reached capacity, it was allowed to slumber. The Germans then levelled a third of it during the Second World War in order to build the nearby railway. Worse came in the 1970s with the construction of al. Powstańców Śląskich, which claimed even more of it.

Fortunately enough remains of the place to give a sense of its former importance. An important burial is that of independence activist Edward Dembowski (1822–1846), leader of the Krakow Uprising (1846), whose tomb lies just inside the main entrance. He rests here with 28 fellow insurgents shot by the Austrian Army as they attempted to stir agitation among Podgórze's citizens. Nearby stands the crucifix-topped family vault of Wojciech Bednarski (1841–1941), a councillor and educator who did much to improve the lot of Podgórze, including the park that bears his name (Park Bednarskiego). Another local worthy is Emil Serkowski (1822–1900), last mayor of independent Podgórze, whose obelisk-topped mausoleum stands at the top of the cemetery. After 1900, the district's dead were buried in the New Podgórze Cemetery (Nowy Cmentarz Podgórski) a short walk south at ul. Wapienna 13. Occupying a basin between the Krakus Mound (Kopiec Krakusa) and the Liban Quarry (Kamieniołom Liban), it contains much monumental funerary sculpture, with a penchant for angels that reflects the cemetery's original strict Catholic bias (a separate area was designated for Protestants and another for suicides).

Headstone of a local worthy in the Old Podgórze Cemetery (Stary Cmentarz Podgórski)

The architects clearly had in mind a long life for this burial ground because it is large and still very much in use, with the tending of graves a commonplace activity. As such this is the place to come on November 2nd – Dzień Wszystkich Zmarłych (All Souls' Day) – when Catholics visit family graves to place wreathes, light candles and say prayers. As with many Catholic traditions, this one has pagan roots. Established in 998 as a holy day of obligation, it replaced the Slavic tradition of *Dziady* (forefathers), when the living hosted a feast for the departed in the hope they might return to their families. The modern use of candles reflects the pagan use of roadside fires to guide the dead back home. It's certainly a memorable experience for those who have not witnessed such devotion, and the sight of thousands of flickering candles as night descends is eerily beautiful.

Other locations nearby: 53, 54, 56

56 A New Museum for Podgórze

30-553 Kraków (Podgórze), the Podgórze Museum (Muzeum
Podgórza) at al. Powstańców Wielkopolskich 1
Tram 3, 6, 13, 24 to Podgórze SKA

If any district of Krakow deserves its own museum then it's Podgórze.
Despite being absorbed into Krakow in 1915, this once-separate settlement on the south bank of the Vistula (Wisła) has always kept its
own spirit. So much so that its inhabitants have recently helped curate
the new Podgórze Museum (Muzeum Podgórza) at al. Powsta ców
Wielkopolskich 1.

The purpose of the museum, a branch of the Museum of Krakow
(Muzeum Krakowa), is two-fold. Not only is it a place where artefacts
tell a story but it is also a community centre in which present-day
voices can be heard. Additionally there is a strong educational focus,
with a hands-on 'laboratory of the town' for children.

The museum's permanent exhibition is called *In the Shadow of
Krak's Mound* and illustrates the development of Podgórze up to the
present day. This is no dusty old collection of display cabinets though.
Instead a well-defined visitor route passes chronologically through a
series of rooms in which exhibits are brought to life using the latest
graphic design and audio techniques.

The first room deals with the origins of Podgórze, including the
mysterious Krakus Mound (Kopiec Krakusa). The oldest man-made
structure in the area, archaeologists believe it was raised by members
of a Slavic tribe sometime between the 6th and the 10th centuries although its purpose remains unclear (see no. 106). The settlement itself
was established in the Early Middle Ages as a suburban farming settlement at the foot of Lasota Hill (the name Podgórze means 'at the foot
of a hill'). Originally administered by the medieval town of Kazimierz
across the Vistula, which at the time was called Zakazimierką, by the
14th century it had grown thanks to its location on the salt route between Wieliczka and Krakow.

The second room concerns Podgórze during the time of the Polish
Partitions. In the years following the First Partition (1772), when Austria occupied the south bank of the Vistula, Podgórze's development
was facilitated by the Habsburg Emperor Joseph II (1741–1790). In
1784, he established the Royal Free City of Podgórze, a self-governing
city within Austrian Galicia, with a symmetrical Classicist layout centred on a triangular marketplace (Rynek Podgórski). When Krakow

also fell into Austrian hands under the terms of the Third Partition (1795), Podgórze lost its political clout and instead developed as an industrial centre, with factories, warehouses, brickyards and quarries (see no. 58).

The third room covers Podgórze during the late 19th and early 20th centuries. In the 1850s, when partitioned Poland lay only a few miles from the Russian border, the Austrians built Fort 31 St. Benedict (Fort 31 'św. Benedykt') on Lasota Hill as part of their Fortress Krakow (Twierdza Kraków) (see no. 80). By the early 1900s, Podgórze's population had risen to a fifth that of Krakow and in 1915, the town was absorbed into Greater Krakow (Wielki Kraków).

Podgórze's finest hour came on 31st October 1918, when the building containing the museum served as a barracks. It was here (and in another barracks on ul. Kalwaryjska) that Polish officers led

Freedom fighter Lt. Antoni Stawarz remembered in the Podgórze Museum (Muzeum Podgórza)

by Lt. Antoni Stawarz (1889–1955) organised a bloodless rebellion against their Austrian rulers making Podgórze the first place in Poland to regain independence after the Great War.

Podgórze's role in the Second World War is then illustrated, notably the horrors of the Krakow Ghetto and Płaszów Concentration Camp, and the hope provided by Oskar Schindler's famous factory in Zabłocie (see nos. 53, 57, 59). A final room reveals how after being forgotten in the wake of war, Podgórze is now reawakening and its memories preserved for future generations.

Other locations nearby: 53, 54, 55

57 Painful Memories at Płaszów Camp

**30-555 Kraków (Podgórze), the former Płaszów Concentration Camp at the junction of ul. Abrahama and ul. Jerozolimska
Tram 3, 6, 11, 13, 24 to Dworcowa then walk west on ul. Abrahama to reach the former camp entrance**

The name Auschwitz–Birkenau is notorious. The industrialised murder carried out at the former Nazi concentration camp is remembered today in one of the world's most chilling museums (www.auschwitz. org). It is located in Oświęcim, 55 miles from Krakow, and so outside the parameters of this book. Krakow, however, had its own camp and the memories there are no less painful.

Unlike Auschwitz–Birkenau, which retains its ruined barracks, gas chambers and watchtowers, the former Płaszów Concentration Camp is little more than a sparsely-wooded hillside. Retreating before the Red Army, German forces concealed their crimes by demolishing the camp, exhuming and burning the dead, and marching the survivors westwards. There is no museum and instead visitors must use their imaginations, fired by a series of archive photos dotting the site.

Before the Second World War there were almost 60,000 Jews living in Krakow (see no. 35). Following Germany's invasion of Poland in 1939, they faced persecution and deportation. By the time the Krakow Ghetto was established in Podgórze in 1941, the Jewish population had fallen to 15,000 (see no. 53). The initiation in early 1942 of Hitler's 'Final Solution to the Jewish Question' further reduced that number.

It was at this time that the Płaszów Concentration Camp was built south of the Ghetto between an existing labour camp in the Liban Quarry (Kamieniołom Liban) and a railway (see no. 58). Its construction meant the destruction of Podgórze's Jewish Cemeteries, the headstones from which were used to pave the camp roads (see no. 36).

Płaszów functioned as a forced labour camp and killing site. Jews deemed fit were marched daily from the Ghetto to help build barracks, while freight trains brought the young, elderly and infirm for execution and burial in mass graves. With the arrival of brutal camp commandant Amon Göth in early 1943, the Ghetto was liquidated and 6,000 Jews were removed to Płaszów. The rest were transported to Auschwitz–Birkenau or shot.

At its height Płaszów held 25,000 prisoners toiling in the quarry or on-site workshops, with a lucky few permitted to work at Oscar Schindler's factory in Zabłocie (see no. 59). By the time the camp was razed in January 1945, approximately 150,000 prisoners passed through. The incinerated remains of 10,000 of them still lie beneath the grass.

The former camp site covers some 200 acres and is now protected as a branch of the Museum of Krakow (Muzeum Krakowa). The junction of ul. Abrahama and ul. Jerozolimska is where the main gate stood. On the right is the Grey House (Szary Dom) used by the SS as lodgings, with interrogation cells in the basement. Ul. Abrahama continues westwards from here along what was the main road through the camp. On the left is a memorial to 13

The so-called Grey House (Szary Dom) at the entrance to the former Płaszów Concentration Camp

Poles executed in September 1939 before the camp was built; on the right a modern grave memorial to Sara Schenirer (1883–1935), who founded Krakow's first Jewish girls' school. Of Podgórze's Jewish cemeteries only the ruined funerary hall remains (beyond the grave) and the shattered footings of the New Cemetery along a path to the left. Between here and ul. Abrahama can be made out the camp's assembly square around which the prisoners' barracks were once ranged.

South from the camp gate runs ul. Wiktora Heltmana dubbed SS-Strasse by the Nazis (Amon Göth lived in the Red House at number 22). A right turn onto ul. Lecha gives access to a track leading to H Górka, one of the camp's main execution sites. Another, C Dołek, lies farther west and is marked by the camp's monolithic official memorial (see back cover).

58 Spielberg's Abandoned Film Set

30-542 Kraków (Podgórze), Liban Quarry (Kamieniołom Liban) on ul. Za Torem
Tram 3, 6, 13, 24 to Cementarz Podgórski then walk to Krakus Mound (Kopiec Krakusa) and follow the trail beyond leading behind the New Podgórze Cemetery (Nowy Cmentarz Podgórski) and down into the quarry (note: paths through the quarry are unmarked, uneven and overgrown)

Just twenty minutes south of Krakow city centre are the haunted remains of Liban Quarry (Kamieniołom Liban). Located alongside the former Płaszów Concentration Camp, the place has seen its own share of Nazi atrocities. Enclosed and eerily oppressive, it's not surprising that film director Steven Spielberg chose it as a location for his film *Schindler's List* about the destruction of the city's Jewish community.

The limestone quarry was established in 1873 by two local Jewish families named Liban and Ehrenpreis. By the turn of the 20th century they had erected administrative buildings and laid a railway line to remove the quarried materials. Business continued to prosper until late 1939, when Nazi Germany invaded Poland.

In 1942, the Nazis built the Płaszów Concentration Camp on the hillside overlooking the quarry. A year later they populated it with some 6,000 Jews following the liquidation of the Krakow Ghetto (see nos. 53, 57). In its role as a labour camp, Płaszów supplied 800 of its youngest and fittest inmates to toil as slaves in the quarry. A hard-to-find memorial to 21 of them executed on 22nd July 1944 is located at the foot of the rock face at the northern end of the quarry below ul. Za Torem.

Fast forward now to 1993 and Spielberg has arrived in Krakow scouting for locations for *Schindler's List*. Much of the film was to be set in the Płaszów Concentration Camp but that had been razed by the Nazis as the Red Army approached Krakow and was now little more than a grassy hillside. Additionally the incinerated remains known to lie beneath the grass precluded the site's use for filming. Instead Spielberg looked to the abandoned quarry.

Here using original architectural blueprints he set about building an exact replica of the camp replete with 34 barrack blocks, 11 watchtowers, gates and barbed wire fences (to date it remains one of the most expensive set builds in Polish cinema history). Although the buildings were torn down once filming was complete, traces of the set can still be found including parts of the electrified perimeter fence. Most chilling is a path running down the centre of the quarry paved with broken Jewish gravestones. These are, of course, just film props but they are a reminder that the Jews who once really toiled here were forced to lay roads in the camp using headstones removed from nearby Jewish cemeteries (see no. 36).

Another surviving part of the film set can be found on the cliff above the quarry's rusting refinery towers. Reached by a steep flight of dangerously collapsed metal steps are low foundations that once supported a replica of camp commandant Amon Göth's villa. The distinctive curving wall would have supported the balcony from where Göth (played by Ralph Fiennes) is shown taking pot shots at his prisoners. Göth's actual home (the

Remains of the *Schindler's List* film set in the Liban Quarry (Kamieniołom Liban)

so-called Red House) still stands at ul. Wiktora Heltmana 22 near the former camp entrance. The building alongside the foundations doubled as Göth's stables in the film.

Interesting as the site is to film buffs, it should be remembered that the Liban Quarry is first and foremost a place of remembrance for those who suffered here. With this in mind, it seems fitting that the quarry machinery and the film set are being engulfed by vegetation, which in turn is attracting wildlife. In this way life is returning to this former place of torment. There are plans to eventually turn the area into an official green space, with bike paths, climbing walls and an outdoor cinema. It would be a pity if the film set remains were not included, too.

59 The Righteous Oskar Schindler

30-702 Kraków (Zabłocie), Oskar Schindler's Enamel Factory (Fabryka Emalia Oskara Schindlera) at ul. Lipowa 4
Tram 9, 20, 50 to Zabłocie and walk along ul. Tadeusza Romanowicza; 3, 17, 19, 24 to Plac Bohaterów Getta and walk along ul. Kaçik (note: admission only by timed tickets purchased in advance at www.bilety.mhk.pl with last entrance 90 minutes before closing)

Since its formation in 1953, Israel's official Holocaust memorial organisation, Yad Vashem, has been preserving the memory of Jews who fought and died at the hands of the Nazis. It has also sought to recognise non-Jews who at considerable personal risk chose to save Jews from extermination. Recognised as 'Righteous Gentiles', there are 26,973 of them at the time of writing, with the largest number (6,863) coming from Poland. Far fewer hail from Germany (616) and yet one of them, Oskar Schindler (1908–1974), has become the most famous of all.

Schindler was born into a Sudeten German family in Zwittau, Moravia, which at the time was part of Austria-Hungary. Undisciplined and academically disinclined, he worked in his father's farm machinery business and in 1928 married Emilie Pelzl (1907–2001), the daughter of a prosperous Sudeten German farmer. When in 1931 the machinery business became insolvent, Schindler instead began working in a bank. Soon shackled with debts and a drinking problem, he supplemented his income by spying for the *Abwehr*, the intelligence division of the Nazi Party. He became a fully-fledged party member in 1939, travelling regularly to Poland to help prepare for Germany's impending invasion.

Following in the wake of the German occupation, Schindler arrived in Krakow, where in early 1940 he acquired a formerly Jewish-owned enamelware factory at ul. Lipowa 4 in the industrial district of Zabłocie. He renamed it Deutsche Emailwarenfabrik (*Emalia* for short) and used his *Abwehr* connections to secure contracts to supply the Wehrmacht. A year later and motivated purely by profit he took advantage of the creation of the Krakow Ghetto by bribing Nazi officials to allow incarcerated Jews (rather than more expensive Poles) to work for him (see no. 53).

Schindler's motives only changed in 1943, when he witnessed the Nazis' liquidation of the Ghetto during which the city's remaining Jewish population was forcibly removed to Krakow's Płaszów Concentration Camp or else shot (see no. 57). He would later claim that it was seeing a little girl in a red coat being carried along helplessly in the mêlée that provoked his change of heart: "Beyond this day, no thinking person could fail to see what would happen. I was now resolved to do everything in my power to defeat the system."

Rusting plates at Oskar Schindler's Enamel Factory (Fabryka Emalia Oskara Schindlera)

To protect his Jewish workforce, Schindler stepped up his use of bribes, whilst also showering luxury gifts on Płaszów's famously cruel camp commandant, Amon Göth (1908–1946). By late 1944, however, with Germany losing the war, the SS began clearing the easternmost camps, including Płaszów, marching remaining prisoners westwards. Schindler managed to save his workers from certain death by relocating 1,200 of them to another factory in Brünnlitz in what is now the Czech Republic. It was these Jews who were on Schindler's famous list, which in 1993 provided Steven Spielberg with the title for his hugely successful film based on Thomas Keneally's book, *Schindler's Ark* (1982) (see no. 58).

After the war, and with several failed businesses under his belt, Schindler received financial support from the very Jews he had saved. When he died in 1974 they buried him on Mount Zion in Jerusalem, the only member of the Nazi Party honoured in this way. Since 2010, his former factory in Krakow has been a branch of the Museum of Krakow (Muzeum Krakowa), its permanent exhibition *Krakow under Nazi Occupation 1939–1945* telling the story of the city's wartime inhabitants. Little remains of the original factory interior though except for Schindler's office. Don't miss the old machine press and wagons filled with enamelware vessels at the back of the building

Other locations nearby: 60

60 New Trends in Zabłocie

30-702 Kraków (Zabłocie), the Museum of Contemporary Art (Muzeum Sztuki Współczesnej) (MOCAK) at ul. Lipowa 4 Tram 9, 20, 50 to Zabłocie and walk along ul. Tadeusza Romanowicza; 3, 17, 19, 24 to Plac Bohaterów Getta and walk along ul. Kaçik (note: last entrance 30 minutes before closing)

For many years there were few reasons to visit Zabłocie, Podgórze's post-industrial district south of the Vistula (Wisła). Not only did it lack visitor attractions but it was also difficult to get to. That changed in 2010 with the opening of Oskar Schindler's famous factory, the construction of a new tram line and more recently a new railway station (see no. 59). Taking New York, Berlin and Warsaw as their cue, developers have been busy ever since transforming abandoned factories and warehouses into a trend-setting area of cafés, galleries and offices for tech start-ups. Now the area is buzzing with people searching out alternatives to Krakow's traditional cultural scene.

Exhibition posters and concrete bicycles at the Museum of Contemporary Art (Muzeum Sztuki Współczesnej)

In 2011, the Museum of Contemporary Art (Muzeum Sztuki Współczesnej) opened. Called MOCAK for short, it occupies a demolished part of the Schindler factory complex ul. Lipowa 4. The new building designed by the Italy-based Claudio Nardi Architects mimics the sort of factory that once stood here, with its low range of halls and serrated roof line. Where once was noise, grime and gloom, however, is now sleek steel, glass and light, with a single red-brick gable left standing to connect past and present.

The whole building covers almost a hectare of which just over 40,000 square feet is devoted to exhibition space. One floor contains the museum's permanent collection, whilst another is used for temporary exhibitions. Between them they present and support the work of contemporary Polish and international artists working in a range of media. They include the Russian multimedia art collective AES + F (formed 1987), Swiss visual artist Beat Streuli (b. 1957) and Czech sculptor Krištof Kintera (b. 1973). Home-grown creatives include sculptor Robert Kuśmirowski (b. 1973), who uniquely recreates full-size lost landscapes, and visual artist Tomasz Bajer (b. 1971), whose works focus on free culture, social and political issues. There are also recent works by older Polish artists notably Maria Stangret (b. 1929), a former actress of Krakow's Cricot 2 theatre ensemble and wife of its founder, Tadeusz Kantor (1915–1990), urban landscape artist Edward Dwurnik (1943–2018), and Krzysztof Wodiczko (b. 1943), a visual artist concerned with human marginalisation. A highlight is the interactive installation *Live Factory 2* by set designer Krystian Lupa (b. 1943) which was inspired by Andy Warhol's New York City studio. The museum is also home to the Mieczysław Porębski Library and its collection of works on art theory and history.

The fashionable vibe created by MOCAK's presence is also permeating the surrounding area. In the car park immediately behind the gallery is a legal graffiti park consisting of three long walls on which street artists can do whatever they want. And beyond that at ul. Ślusarska 9 (but with a side entrance on ul. Przemysłowa) is BAL, a deservedly popular café-bar inside a converted warehouse. The high ceilings and plain walls form the perfect backdrop to rotating exhibitions of art.

Directly opposite MOCAK is the Lipowa 3 Glass & Ceramics Centre (Centrum Szkła i Ceramiki Lipowa 3) founded in 1931. Up to 500 people were employed here during the time of the Polish People's Republic (Polska Rzeczpospolita Ludowa) (1952–1989) working not only in glass bottle and art production but also scientific research and industrial design. During the 1970s, the works helped Krakow achieve international renown for novel glass forms. Coloured and textured glassware produced here between 1931 and 1998, together with glassblowing tools, make up the permanent exhibition *Glass in Krakow – Industry and Art*. The works are still used for glass research and live glass-blowing demonstrations are staged on the hour.

Other locations nearby: 59

61 Workers Unite!

31-534 Kraków (Grzegórzki), the Monument to the Militant
Proletariat of Krakow (Pomnik Czynu Zbrojnego Proletariatu
Krakowa) on al. Ignacego Daszyńskiego
Tram 3, 19, 24 to Miodowa

Under Communism, public art in Eastern Bloc cities was strictly controlled by Party authorities and mostly rendered in a regime-sanctioned style known as Socialist Realism. The bigger the better, with a penchant for concrete and bronze, these monuments celebrated brave Soviet soldiers, dedicated factory workers and farmers, and proud mothers. Krakow's great example of Socialist Realism is the stand-alone steelworkers' town of Nowa Huta (see no. 74). In central Krakow, however, examples are few and far between including the impressive albeit benign bronze miners and metalworkers flanking the entrance to the University of Science and Technology (Akademia Górniczo Hutnicza) at al. Adama Mickiewicza 30 (Czarna Wieś). For an example of Socialist Realism with an overt political message visit the Monument to the Militant Proletariat of Krakow (Pomnik Czynu Zbrojnego Proletariatu Krakowa) on al. Ignacego Daszyńskiego (Wesoła).

The story behind this monument depicting labourers raising their fists is an interesting and a telling one. It harks back to the mid-1930s, when poverty brought on by economic crisis precipitated a wave of strikes in Krakow's industrial plants. In March 1936, workers downed tools at the *Suchard* Polish-Swiss chocolate factory in Grzegórzki and were quickly followed by fellow workers at the neighbouring *Semperit* Polish-Austrian rubber factory. After a few days, police forcibly removed the strikers, injuring several women in the process and raising tensions across the city.

As a result, the Polish Socialist Party (Polska Partia Socjalistyczna) and its council of trade unions declared a one-day general strike in Krakow. On 23rd March, 10,000 workers congregated in the grounds of the rail workers' union on ul. Warszawska (Kleparz) and began marching towards the main square (Rynek Główny) (Old Town). They didn't get beyond ul. Bastowa, where police started shooting from behind a blockade, killing eight people and wounding many others. Several police were wounded in the skirmish, too. Two days later, with 'order' restored, the victims' coffins were carried through the streets to Rakowicki Cemetery (Cmentarz Rakowicki), attended by workers carrying flaming torches and Socialist banners. The Archbishop of Krakow,

The Monument to the Militant Proletariat of Krakow (Pomnik Czynu Zbrojnego Proletariatu Krakowa)

Adam Stefan Sapieha (1867–1951), a harsh critic of the government, cited unfettered greed and the desire for profit within local industry as the causes of the unrest.

The official line on the incident was rather different. It was said that the use of force was necessary due to the aggressive nature of the crowd, which allegedly contained criminal elements looking for a fight. That this explanation makes no mention of any justified workers' demands explains why the monument on al. Ignacego Daszyńskiego wasn't commissioned at the time. Only 50 years later during the time of the Polish People's Republic (Polska Rzeczpospolita Ludowa) (1952–1989) was it finally erected and then only to glorify the notion of the working class rising up against Capitalist oppression. The names of the dead workers are omitted in favour of a simple inscription giving the date alongside lyrics from *L'Internationale*, a Socialist anthem that was the official hymn of the USSR between 1922 and 1944: *"Ruszymy z posad bryłę świata"* (We will move the world from its foundation).

The message is less than subtle and reflects a period late in Polish Communism, when efforts were still being made to rewrite history and push the party line. After all, it was the authorities that had instructed the police to open fire on the workers and not the other way round. Such ideology was dropped from state policy with the arrival of democracy in 1989 and it is surprising the monument was not removed. Instead it serves as a history lesson in the form of a Communist propaganda poster in concrete.

Other locations nearby: 36, 62

62 The Last Milk Bars

31-537 Kraków (Grzegórzki), a selection of milk bars (bar mleczny) including Bar Targowy at ul. Ignacego Daszyńskiego 19
Tram 1, 17, 19, 22 to Hala Targowa

Communism may be dead and Poland may have joined the EU but some old habits die hard. One endearing relic that Poles seem happy to retain is the milk bar *(bar mleczny)*. These no-frills cafeterias serving cheap traditional fare offer a glimpse into life in Eastern Bloc Poland. What's more, Krakow has the distinction of being the place where they began.

The first milk bar opened on Krakow's main square (Rynek Główny) in 1948. It is no coincidence that this was the same year that the Polish United Workers' Party (Polska Zjednoczona Partia Robotnicza) was established, which governed the Polish People's Republic (Polska Rzeczpospolita Ludowa) until 1989. Indeed the concept of the milk bar was a deliberate attempt by the Party to use Poland's surplus of dairy produce to promote milk-drinking over alcohol thereby maximising workers' productivity.

Originally no hot dishes were available, only milk served in a quarter-litre glass with a straw. However, as the Party nationalised the country's restaurants, so the menu was extended to include affordable dairy-based meals. Thus, in addition to milk, yoghurt and cheese, customers could order omelettes and egg cutlets, as well as flour-based foods such as the ubiquitous *pierogi*. It was not uncommon at the time for milk bar meals to be part of a worker's salary. Times were hard though and some milk bars allegedly chained their cutlery to the table to prevent theft.

Not surprisingly with the fall of Communism and the advent of the free market many milk bars went out of business. Customers remained loyal to the notion of cheap and cheerful food though and with the help of state subsidies several remained in business. The withdrawal of subsidies in 2011 has done little to change this and today suburban Krakow still boasts more than half a dozen classic milk bars.

A fine example is Bar Targowy at ul. Ignacego Daszyńskiego 19 (Wesoła). All the classic features of a milk bar are present here: the modest exterior, the purely-functional interior (with menu board and metal tables), the ladies in white coats staffing the self-service counter, and the hatch, where customers deposit their dirty dishes. The food still includes pierogi, boiled vegetables in sauce and mashed potatoes, with the only real difference being that meat is no longer rationed as it was in the old days. Other milk bars worth a visit include Bar Górnik at ul. Czysta 1 (Piasek), Pod Temidą at ul. Grodzka 43 (Okół) and Pod Filarkami at ul. Starowiślna 29 (Kazimierz); also Bar Południowy at Rynek Podgórski 11 and Bar Krakus at ul. Bolesława Limanowskiego 16 (both in Podgórze). Anyone travelling east to visit Nowa Huta, the Communist-era steelworkers' town, might care to enhance their retro experience by taking lunch at Bar Mleczny Centralny at os. Centrum C 1 on plac Centralny (see no. 74). There is even an example of a *new* milk bar in Krakow, namely Milkbar Tomasza at

Bar Targowy displays the typically modest interior of most milk bars *(bar mleczny)*

ul. św. Tomasza 24 (Old Town), which is a clever fusion of traditional milk bar and 50s-style American diner.

Similar to a milk bar but with table service and English-language menus is U Stasi at ul. Mikołajska 16 (Old Town). This tiny cafeteria takes a bit of tracking down but is worth the effort as it's a Krakow institution. Family-run for over 80 years, it dishes out simple, home-cooked Polish food at very affordable prices. It is perhaps the only place in the Old Town where the clientele includes students and tourists, professors and pensioners! The sweet plum *pierogi* are highly recommended.

Other locations nearby: 61, 63

63 Lost Rivers of Krakow

31-530 Kraków (Grzegórzki), the viaduct and former river bed where ul. Józefa Dietla joins ul. Grzegórzecka
Tram 1, 17, 19, 22 to Hala Targowa

Walking the streets of central Krakow might give the impression that the place has scarcely changed in centuries. Whilst it's true that an impressive number of old buildings are still standing, their surroundings have altered greatly. Cases in point are two not-insignificant rivers that once flowed through the suburbs.

Evidence for the first can be found in Grzegórzki, where ul. Józefa Dietla joins ul. Grzegórzecka. Ul. Józefa Dietla honours Józef Dietl (1804–1878), the city's mayor between 1866 and 1874, whose life spans an important phase in Krakow's history. In 1815 he witnessed the creation of the Republic of Krakow (Rzeczpospolita Krakowska), which despite being controlled by Austria, Russia and Prussia saw the city become a centre of agitation for Polish independence. This prompted Austria to re-annexe it in 1846 and create the Grand Duchy of Krakow (Wielkie Księstwo Krakowskie). In 1867 this in turn became part of the autonomous Kingdom of Galicia and Lodomeria. This last development, and the fact that about 10% of the city had been destroyed during the Krakow Fire of 1850, gave Mayor Dietl the incentive to begin modernising his city.

Dietl is credited with helping establish the first municipal fire brigade, reorganising Krakow's finances, and addressing the city's poor sanitation. In Dietl's day, Krakow was criss-crossed by swampy tributaries of the Vistula (Wisła), which together with stagnant drinking wells, led to frequent outbreaks of cholera. As a respected professor of medicine at the Jagiellonian University (Uniwersytet Jagielloński), Dietl understood the danger of these waterways and was instrumental in their removal.

The largest of them was the Old Vistula (Stara Wisła), which defined the northern shore of the island of Kazimierz. By the 1870s it had become fetid and was infilled to create a more salubrious tree-lined beltway, with part of it named in Dietl's honour (the rest runs along al. Ignacego Daszyńskiego). Some sense of the old riverine landscape can be gained from the railway viaduct at the junction of ul. Józefa Dietla and ul. Grzegórzecka. When first built in 1863 its masonry piers stood not on asphalt but in water, as can be seen in old photographs from the time.

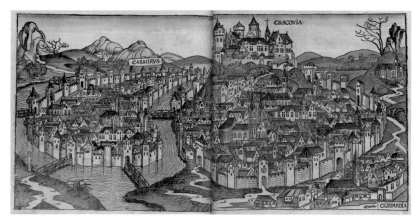

This 15th century woodcut shows clearly the Old Vistula (Stara Wisła) that once made Kazimierz an island

The demise of Krakow's second lost river was also down to Dietl. In the 13th century, a canal was dug to utilise the waters of the Rudawa, a tributary of the Vistula west of the city. Here the king built a series of water mills for tanning and dyeing, recalled in the district of Piasek by the street name ul. Dolnych Młynów (meaning 'Lower Mills'). In 1399, a network of wooden pipes conveyed water from the canal along ul. Adama Asnyka to provide drinking water inside the Old Town. Unfortunately this infrastructure was destroyed in 1665 during the Swedish occupation. Thereafter drinking water could only be gained by digging wells, which again led to outbreaks of disease.

In 1903, Krakow was badly affected by floodwaters from the Rudawa, which arrived via the now-abandoned canal. As a result, it was infilled and the Rudawa's course altered so as to empty into the Vistula at Salwator. Since the 1960s, a linear park called Młynówka Królewska ('royal mills') has marked the canal's former path from ul. Na Błonie in the west all the way to al. Juliusza Słowackiego in Kleparz. Mayor Dietl would undoubtedly have approved.

A fine statue of Józef Dietl can be found in plac Wszystkich Świętych (Old Town). His robe and sceptre are reminders that in 1861 he was made rector of the Jagiellonian University (Uniwersytet Jagielloński).

Other locations nearby: 62, 64

64 The Lantern of the Dead

31-034 Kraków (Wesoła), the Lantern of the Dead outside the Church of St. Nicholas (Kościół św. Mikołaja) at ul. Mikołaja Kopernika 9
Tram 3, 10, 24, 52 to Poczta Główna then walk along Westerplatte onto ul. Mikołaja Kopernika (note: the church interior is only open for Sunday Mass)

With so many historic churches in Krakow's Old Town, it's easy to forget that some equally storied examples lie just outside. The Church of St. Nicholas (Kościół św. Mikołaja) at ul. Mikołaja Kopernika 9 (Wesoła) is a case in point. One of the city's oldest churches, it is a palimpsest of architectural styles, with the bonus of a real rarity in its churchyard.

The church is documented as far back as the early 13th century, when it was erected on what was then an important trade route leading from Krakow to Kiev. The first building was Late Romanesque in style and fragments of this structure can still be detected (the portal from a subsequent Gothic reworking is still in use).

In 1665 during the Swedish occupation (the so-called 'Deluge'), the church was plundered and burned. The ruins were then incorporated into a new structure in the Late Baroque style, completed in 1682. This is the building seen today. The internal furnishings were commissioned by the Academy of Krakow (Akademia Krakowska), as the Jagiellonian University (Uniwersytet Jagielloński) was known originally, whose patronage of the church as a collegiate foundation began in 1465. They include the Academy's coat of arms (a shield with crossed maces) on the backs of the stalls, a high altar carrying an effigy of St. Nicholas, a late Gothic triptych depicting the Coronation of the Virgin, and a Renaissance Madonna and Child, with SS. Adalbert and Stanisław, patron saints of Poland, in attendance.

In the churchyard overlooking the street is something unusual. Taking the form of a sandstone Gothic pinnacle, it is a so-called Lantern of the Dead (Latarnie umarłych). Such lanterns were erected during the Middle Ages, mostly in front of hospitals and cemeteries. They acted as a warning to passers-by that those inside had succumbed to some contagious disease. This example from the 14th century stood originally outside a lepers' hospital in Kleparz. When the church to which the hospital belonged was demolished in the early 19th century, the lantern was relocated, first to plac Słowiański and in 1871 to its current position. There are a handful of other lanterns in Krakow, including one farther along the same street outside the Carmelite convent at number 44, but none are medieval and several most likely served as wayside shrines.

Lanterns of the Dead were once commonplace in Europe, especially during the 14th century, when the region was ravaged by the pandemic infection known as the Black Death. Although Poland was affected, the country escaped relatively unscathed. Theories put forward to explain this have included the country's isolation, sparse population and the significant distance between its settlements. The most likely explanation, however, is that King Casimir III the Great (Kazimierz III Wielki) (1310–1370) wisely quarantined his country's borders forcing merchants' caravans, pilgrims and other travellers to wait outside for a certain time before entering.

Also in St. Nicholas' churchyard is an Armenian cross or *khachar*. Unveiled in 2004, it is a reminder that Armenians have lived and worked in Poland since the 14th century. The cross also commemorates those who suffered

A rare Lantern of the Dead outside the Church of St. Nicholas (Kościół św. Mikołaja)

at the hands of the Ottomans in 1915, Ukrainian Nationalists in 1921, and the Soviets during the Second World War.

It is a little-known fact that in 1910 the Bolshevik revolutionary Feliks Dzierżyński (1877–1926) married his fellow activist Zofia Muszkat in the Church of St. Nicholas, with Sergiusz Bagocki (1879–1953), a friend of Lenin, a witness. Dzerzhinsky, who lived around the corner on ul. Hugona Kołłątaja, later founded the Cheka, the first Soviet secret police organisation.

95 Railway Remains

There was a time when Krakow's Old Main Railway Station (Stary Dworzec Główny) was considered one of the most modern and elegant in Europe. The building dates back to 1847, and the Austrian construction of the Krakow–Upper Silesia Railway (Kolej Krakowsko-Górnośląska) The first service – pulled by a locomotive called *Kraków* – left the station on October 13th bound for Mysłowice, where the borders of the Austrian, German and Russian Empires met during the time of the Third Partition of Poland. A silver miniature of the locomotive is displayed in the nearby Celestat at ul. Lubicz 16 (see no. 66).

From the outside, the station designed by Berlin-born engineer August Rosenbaum resembled a Renaissance palace (Rosenbaum's appointment reflected the fact that the company responsible for building the railway was founded by Prussian entrepreneurs from Wrocław). Inside, however, it was positively futuristic, comprising a glass-roofed booking hall supported on cast iron pillars.

Initially the station functioned as a terminus, with trains departing northwards only. Although a link to Vienna opened in 1853, it only became a through station in 1861, when the Austrians constructed a second line eastwards to Lwów (today Ukraine's Lviv but then capital of the Austrian-ruled province of Galicia). In 1917, to cater for visitors arriving into Krakow by rail, the imposing Hotel Polonia was built across from the station at ul. Basztowa 25.

Like the rest of Krakow, the station remained relatively undamaged during the Second World War. In January 1945, however, when Soviet forces arrived and began arresting Poles loyal to the Polish government-in-exile, as well as those who had served in the Home Army (Armia Krajowa), the station was damaged by artillery. The square in front was subsequently named after Jan Nowak-Jeziorański (1914–2005), who acted as an intermediary between the commanders of the Home Army and the Polish Government-in-exile in London.

After the war the station was reworked into the building seen today. Passengers continued to use the building until 2014, when an entirely new transportation hub connecting the city's train, bus and tram services was built nearby. An underpass leading directly into the nearby Galeria Krakowska now means that visitors arriving by train

An empty platform at Krakow's Old Main Railway Station (Stary Dworzec Główny)

bypass both the old station building and the square in front of it. Abandoned thereafter, the old railway station has only been sporadically reused, its platform now abandoned, with an overall plan for the building's reuse still in the offing.

South of the station there are further historic railway remains. There is a viaduct, for example, over busy ul. Lubicz built in 1898 to relieve congestion previously caused by the railway crossing the road at ground level. Financed by Austria and designed by Polish architect Teodor Talowski (1857–1910) to match the station, it was the city's first transport flyover (see no. 93). Farther south a second viaduct completed in 1863 carries the railway over ul. Józefa Dietla, which at the time was a tributary of the Vistula (Stara Wisła) but has subsequently been drained (see no. 63).

Best of all is the abandoned Płaszów Roundhouse (Lokomotywownia Płaszów) at ul. Kolejowa 25 (Płaszów). Opened in 1908, this is where Krakow's locomotives and rolling stock were maintained, including the *Luxtorpeda* railcar, which in the 1930s transported First Class passengers at over 70 mph to the resort of Zakopane. It still contains several rusting steam engines including a 1950s-era Ty51, Poland's most powerful locomotive. A restored Ty2 from a decade earlier is displayed in the grounds of the University of Science and Technology (Akademia Górniczo Hutnicza) at al. Adama Mickiewicza 30 (Czarna Wieś).

Other locations nearby: 66, 67

The Brotherhood of the Cockerel

31-504 Kraków (Wesoła), the Celestat at ul. Lubicz 16
Tram 2, 4, 10, 14, 20, 44, 52 to Lubicz

One of Krakow's most colourful traditions is performed each year by the city's Brotherhood of the Cockerel (Bractwo Kurkowe). For seven centuries this fraternity of marksmen has celebrated its martial skills in a shooting contest and procession, the culmination of which is the crowning of a new Marksmen King.

Established in the late 13th century, the Brotherhood was originally a paramilitary organisation made up of merchants and artisans. Krakow at that time had defensive walls and each of its 55 city gates and towers was the responsibility of a different trade guild – from bookbinders and blacksmiths to shoemakers and saddlers (see no. 33). The Brotherhood existed as a means of training the various guild members in the shooting and combat skills necessary to defend them.

The Brotherhood's annual tradition has developed over time. Originally it took place on the second Sunday after the Feast of Corpus Christi, when shooters would take aim at a wooden target bird known as the 'Cock'. The winner was deemed the one who could hit the target most accurately. Afterwards the Brotherhood's members attended Mass at the Basilica of St. Mary (Bazylika Mariacka) overlooking the main square (Rynek Główny) then processed to their headquarters – the so-called Celestat (from the German *Zielstätte* meaning shooting range) – which until the late 18th century was located outside St. Nicholas' Gate on ul. Mikolajska. They were accompanied by two expert marshals, an armed royal retinue *(Kozernicy)*, members of various guilds, and representatives of Krakow's City Council. Upon arrival the winner was enthroned as the new Marksmen King and presented with a silver 'Cock' gifted to the Brotherhood by the Council in 1565. The celebrations then finished with a great feast.

In 1837 the Brotherhood relocated the Celestat to its current location at ul. Lubicz 16 (Wesoła). Here in a custom-built neo-Gothic palace, the Marksmen King was elected and dignitaries entertained, including several Polish presidents, Marshal Józef Piłsudski (1867–1935) and even Austrian Emperor Franz Joseph I (1830–1916). Initially the annual procession took place within the attached garden but by the 1930s (by which time Poland had received its independence) the

A cockerel-shaped target at the Celestat

march was incorporated into a broader annual celebration of the city, and once again it took place in the Main Square.

Unfortunately for the duration of the Second World War, the Brotherhood lost control of the Celestat. Instead it was commandeered by the Wehrmacht and served as a barracks and delousing station for German troops returning from the eastern front. At the end of the war it was damaged during the Battle of Krakow.

Only in 1990 was the restored Celestat and its garden finally returned to the Brotherhood. Since 1997 it has been protected as a branch of the Museum of Krakow (Muzeum Krakowa). A permanent exhibition now illustrates the Brotherhood's history and its role in the defence of the city through a variety of artiacts, including rifles, cockerel-shaped targets, portraits and a copy of the 16th century silver 'Cock', which is still presented to the Marksmen King after Corpus Christi each year (usually in June) (the original is stored in the Museum of Krakow's more in Bielany; see no. 104). This has recently been supplemented by an annual archery and art contest whereby local school-children can elect a Little Marksmen King. A fun way of encouraging awareness of this popular Krakow tradition, the winner receives a tiny silver cockerel on a chain.

Other locations nearby: 55, 67

67 An Historic Brewery Reborn

31-503 Kraków (Wesoła), the former Götz-Okocimski Brewery at ul. Lubicz 17
Tram 2, 4, 10, 14, 20, 44, 52 to Lubicz

Krakow has plenty of industrial-era remains, many of which are included in the Museum of Municipal Engineering's Krakow Technology Trail (see no. 41). An unusual example is the former Götz-Okocimski Brewery, which can be found behind an ornate red-brick perimeter wall at ul. Lubicz 17 (Wesoła). Recently converted for use as apartments, offices and leisure facilities, the complex still retains much of its original fabric making a visit worthwhile for those who enjoy industrial archaeology.

The story of the brewery began in 1840, when one Rudolf Jenny purchased a plot of land in Wesoła, a suburb outside Krakow's town walls. At that time, breweries were small concerns, so Jenny's acquisition of 1.67 hectares shows his plans were ambitious. Jenny died in 1853 but by then he had already created the basic infrastructure for commercial brewing. It was left to his son-in-law, Juliusz August John, a merchant from Königsberg, to build on his achievements, which he did with gusto. During the 1850s and 60s not only did he add a new barrel warehouse, cellars, malting plants, ice plants, and stables for draught horses and oxen but also installed steam engines and boilers manufactured at the Zieleniewski Forge in Krakow's Old Town. These improvements ensured that before long the brewery was the region's largest, with an annual production of 15,000 barrels. In 1879, John's sons took over management of the brewery and continued their father's expansion, upgrading the cold stores and ice plants, and converting outmoded cellars into a popular restaurant.

In 1904, the brewery passed to Baron Jan Götz-Okocimski (1864–1931), the hugely wealthy proprietor of the Okocim brewery in Brzesko, the sixth largest brewery in the Habsburg Empire (his philanthropic work includes helping finance the construction of Krakow's magnificent Juliusz Słowacki Theatre). He initiated a modernisation of the factory, building a new production hall, cold store and barrel room, and adding a third steam boiler (he even converted the old restaurant into a 340-seat cinema!). By 1914, the Götz-Okocimski Brewery was one of Krakow's largest industrial concerns producing 3.6 million litres of beer a year.

Only in the 1930s, during the Great Depression, did demand for beer drop prompting a workers' strike and a temporary shut-down in production. The brewery survived though and by 1938 there were three separate facilities operating on the site: the brewery proper (although output had fallen to 1.23 million litres), a malt processing plant producing coffee and candy, and an ice factory.

The brewery remained in the hands of the Götz family until nationalisation in 1946, when further modernisation took place. By 1968, the old steam engines had been replaced by electricity, the ice plants used to cool the beer replaced with refrigeration compressors, the fermentation cellar replaced, and oak barrels discontinued. In this new form, the brewery was eventually merged with the one in Brzesko, and a new bottling line imported from the GDR. Only after privatisation of the brewery in Brzesko in 2001 did new owner Carlsberg decide to discontinue beer production in Krakow bringing to a close an important chapter in the city's manufacturing history.

An old chimney preserved at the former Götz-Okocimski Brewery

It is a chapter that might today be forgotten had not some of the old brewery buildings been preserved for posterity. These include the former brew house, boiler plant with its 121 foot-high chimney, fermentation cellars and a neo-Classical residential building. Each has been cleverly adapted for reuse, interspersed with new-builds that retaining the feel of an early 20th century industrial complex. There is even a restaurant, Browar Lubicz, with its own micro-brewery in the former malt house continuing the site's beer-drinking legacy.

Other locations nearby: 65, 66

68 A Night at the Opera

31-512 Kraków (Wesoła), the Krakow Opera (Opera
Krakowska) at ul. Lubicz 48
Tram 2, 4, 10, 14, 20, 44, 52 to Lubicz

The Krakow Opera (Opera Krakowska) follows a long tradition of musical theatre in the city stretching back several centuries. Remarkably
though Krakow's first tailor-made opera house only opened in 2008.
The striking cube-shaped building at ul. Lubicz 48 (Wesoła) boasts
superb acoustics and vivid red décor that make for a memorable night
at the opera.

Opera in Poland can be traced back to 1625, when the future King
Ladislaus IV Vasa (Władysław IV Waza) (1595–1648) returned from
Florence having been enchanted by Francesca Caccini's *La liberazione
di Ruggiero* (the first opera penned by a woman). Three years later,
Ferdinando Saracinelli's libretto for the opera was published in Krakow
making it the first full Polish-language libretto. The first fully-fledged
operatic performance took place in the city in March 1782.

Since the late-19th century, the Krakow Opera (Opera Krakowska)
has existed under several guises and aliases. In its present incarnation, it was established in 1954 but lacked its own performance space.
Instead the company borrowed the stages of other theatre and concert venues. Chief among these was the neo-Baroque Juliusz Słowacki
Theatre (Teatr im Juliusza Słowackiego) at plac Świętego Ducha
1 (Old Town) (see no. 34). Additionally the company utilised various historical and natural settings, staging *Tosca* in the lee of Wawel
Castle, *Madama Butterfly* in the depths of the Wieliczka Salt Mine,
for example, and *Straszny Dwór* (The Haunted Manor) in the courtyard of Niepołomice Castle. The latter work by Stanisław Moniuszko
(1819–1872) is considered the greatest of 19th century Polish operas,
its strong patriotic undertones making it popular with the Polish public
but unpopular – to the point of being banned – with the Russian authorities, who controlled part of Poland at the time.

The building of the new opera house was not without controversy.
Rising costs resulted in a protracted dispute between Krakow-based
architect Romuald Loegler (b. 1940), who conjured up the building's
Deconstructivist design, and the building contractor, who demanded
additional funds to realise it. Eventually the matter reached the city's
Department of Education and Culture and a special consultant was
appointed to mediate. Although costs eventually rose by 10% and con-

Deconstructivist design at Krakow's new Opera (Opera Krakowska)

struction was delayed by several years, the opera house was eventually completed.

With seats for around 750 opera-goers and a sculpture by Igor Mitoraj (1944–2014) adorning the forecourt, the new opera house has proved a great success. The company stages some 200 performances each year here, including Polish and international operas as well as ballet, operettas and musicals for the young. The average attendance rate is an impressive 98%.

Not surprisingly the Krakow Opera attracts the cream of the opera world from home and abroad. They include renowned Polish singers, conductors and set designers, as well as soloists from the Metropolitan Opera in New York City and La Scala in Milan. They have included the military general-turned-conductor Robert Satanowski (1918–1997), soprano Teresa Żylis-Gara (b. 1935), and theatre visionary Tadeusz Kantor (1915–1990). Additionally, the company's singers regularly accept invitations from abroad to perform.

Here should also be mentioned the Krakow Chamber Opera (Krakowska Opera Kameralna). It was founded in 1991 by a professor from Krakow's Academy of Theatre Arts (Akademia Sztuk Teatraln) at ul. Straszewskiego 21-22 (Nowy Świat), which itself was founded in 1946 by Polish actor Juliusz Osterwa (1885-1947). An independent theatre collective, it has been based since 2000 in a converted town house at ul. Miodowa 15 (Kazimierz), where it specialises in reviving forgotten Polish and international works.

Other locations nearby: 69

69 The Oldest Botanical Garden

31-501 Kraków (Wesoła), the Botanic Garden of the
Jagiellonian University (Ogród Botaniczny Uniwersytetu
Jagiellońskiego) at ul. Kopernika 27
Tram 2, 4, 10, 14, 20, 44, 52 to Rondo Mogilskie (note:
the garden is only open between April and September)

One of Krakow's more serene spots during the summer months is
the Botanic Garden of the Jagiellonian University (Ogród Botaniczny
Uniwersytetu Jagiello skiego). Located since 1783 at ul. Kopernika 27
(Wesoła), it lays claim to being Poland's oldest botanic garden.

Botany had been taught to medical students at the Jagiellonian
University since the late 16th century. However, they lacked a study
garden in which to investigate for themselves the pharmaceutical
value of certain plants. That changed in 1756, when the university's
rector, Dr. Casimir Stepkowskiego, allocated a sum of money for the
creation of a botanic garden.

The chosen location was a suburban estate that originally belonged to the noble Czartoryski family of the Polish-Lithuanian Commonwealth (see no. 32). In 1752, the Jesuits purchased the land but
with their dissolution it was acquired instead by the Commission for
National Education in Poland. So it was that in 1773, Krakow's first astronomical observatory was installed on the roof of the Jesuits' former
residence (itself once the Czartoryski villa), and around it the Botanic
Garden was arranged a decade later.

With natural history professor Jan Jaskiewicz (1749–1809) its first
director, the garden initially covered 2.4 hectares. It took the form of
a French-style Baroque park with geometrical arrangements of both
medicinal and ornamental plants. The first greenhouse was erected in
1787 and is still in place today albeit extensively rebuilt. It is known
as *Victoria* because it contains examples of the water lily *Victoria ama-
zonica*, with leaves famously large enough to support the weight of a
child.

Since then the garden has been expanded several times, acquiring
its present size of 9.6 hectares during the 1960s. Today it is administered as a department of the university's Institute of Botany, whose
staff have subdivided it to reflect their various interests. Thus academ-
ically-minded visitors will find areas devoted to taxonomy (the natural
divisions and relations of the plant kingdom), genetics and variability
(how new species form in nature), flower ecology (pollination and

seed dispersal), and the protection of endangered species, especially those of the Carpathians on Poland's southern border with Slovakia.

Others come simply to wander the garden at random, taking in its myriad colours and forms. There are 9,000 different species to discover encompassing everything from scented herbs and roses to a venerable 250-year-old oak, a remnant of the primeval forest that once covered the entire region. They can also enjoy the *Jubilee* greenhouse, erected in 1964 to mark the 600th anniversary of the founding of the Jagiellonian University, which contains a collection of palms and carnivorous plants (a third greenhouse called *Holenderka* ('Dutch') contains epiphytic plants, orchids and rare plants but is off bounds to the public).

Blossom at the Botanic Garden of the Jagiellonian University (Ogród Botaniczny Uniwersytetu Jagiellońskiego)

Many visitors show an interest in the section on medicinal and other plants useful to mankind, as well as the alpine garden and the arboretum, where geographical and ornamental groupings of trees make for an invigorating atmosphere. They should also look out for the Late Gothic pillars taken from the Collegium Maius and reused as plinths to support plant pots (see no. 24). The garden's didactic function manifests itself in the form of lectures and hands-on workshops not only for university students but also for local schoolchildren.

One final point of interest is the Botanical Museum containing an extensive collection of dried fruits, seeds and fossils. Facing onto ul. Kopernika, it occupies the former astronomical observatory, which relocated to Bielany in 1964 (see no. 103). This explains the astronomical motifs on the façade and the telescope domes on the roof.

Other locations nearby: 68

70 Wings over Krakow

31-864 Kraków (Rakowice), the Polish Aviation Museum (Muzeum Lotnictwa Polskiego) at al. Jana Pawła II 39
Tram 4, 10, 44, 52 from Teatr Słowackiego to Muzeum Lotnictwa

One of Krakow's museums that should be better known is the Polish Aviation Museum (Muzeum Lotnictwa Polskiego). The problem is its location at al. Jana Pawła II 39 in the no-man's land of Rakowice between Krakow's eastern suburbs and Nowa Huta. In other respects, however, the location is perfect since the museum sits on one of Europe's oldest military airfields. Here are displayed aircraft relating not only to Polish but also world aviation history.

Even without the museum this is an historic place. The Rakowice Airfield was built in the late 19th century by the Austrians to house a balloon detachment of the Garrison Artillery 2nd Regiment, one small element in their vast Krakow Fortress (Twierdza Kraków) (see no. 80). Later, in 1912, it became the headquarters of an Austro-Hungarian aviation unit called Flugpark 7. During 1914, aircraft flew from here in defence of Krakow and when a year later the war moved on, the airfield was used instead to train crews and repair damaged aircraft returning from the front.

Immediately after the war, the airfield became a staging post for an airmail service between Vienna, Kiev and Odessa, the first such scheduled service in Europe. Then, in October 1918, a month before before the country declared independence, the Polish military authorities commandeered the airfield and established the country's first aviation unit here. It was called the 1st Combat Squadron.

During the Polish–Soviet War (1919–1921), when the Second Polish Republic fought for control of what is today western Ukraine, the 1st Lower School for Pilots was located at the airfield. Some new aircraft were even built here, a tribute to the skills of the airfield's workshop staff. Such a concentration of talent led to the formation in 1921 of the 2nd Air Regiment (2 Pułk Lotniczy) and by the late 1920s, the airfield was the Polish Air Force's second largest base.

Not surprisingly, the outbreak of the Second World War saw the airfield bombed by the Luftwaffe. Once in German hands, it was extended eastwards into Czyżyny and used to supply the Eastern Front. Near the end of the war, in January 1945, advancing Russian forces overran the airfield and assigned it back to the Polish authorities. The

A fighter-bomber Suchoj Su-22M4 preserved at the Polish Aviation Museum (Muzeum Lotnictwa Polskiego)

subsequent encroachment of commercial and residential development, however, eventually forced the Polish Air Force to relocate ten miles west to Balice, home today to Krakow's John Paul II International Airport (Kraków Airport im. Jana Pawła II). Thereafter the Rakowice–Czyżyny Airfield saw less and less traffic and closed for good in 1963, when the commercial airline LOT departed.

So much for the history of the place. A year after closing, the airfield became home to the newly-formed Krakow Aviation Museum. This extensive collection preserves not only historic aircraft but also helicopters, gliders, engines, and all manner of related artefacts displayed across several distinct areas. A new triple-winged exhibition building is brimming with interactive exhibits, as well as a permanent First World War exhibit, cinema, library and well-stocked museum shop. Elsewhere the airfield's numerous original hangars and outbuildings are full of aircraft, as well as airmen's uniforms, equipment and some fascinating archive photos. And on the tarmac surrounding the buildings are serried ranks of Russian-built fighter jets – the so-called MiG Alley – dating from the time of the Warsaw Pact.

One artefact that shouldn't be missed is the helicopter used by Pope John Paul II on several of his foreign visits. How many visitors recall that his successor, Pope Benedict XVI, held a helicopter pilot's license and occasionally even took the controls himself?

71 An Arena for Everyone

31-571 Kraków (Czyżyny), the TAURON Arena Kraków at ul. Stanisława Lema 7
Tram 4, 10, 44, 52 from Teatr Słowackiego to Tauron Arena Kraków Wieczysta (note: guided tours by appointment only)

The inhabitants of Krakow love their sports, so it's no surprise that the city has its fair share of sporting venues. Undoubtedly the most striking architecturally is the TAURON Arena Kraków. Located a 20-minute tram ride from the city centre, it looks like a flying saucer that has just landed. Superlatives abound since not only is it Poland's largest arena but also running around the outside is the country's largest LED (light-emitting diode) media display.

Three years in the building, the multipurpose indoor arena opened for business in 2014. The architects jettisoned the traditional idea of a rectangular hall in favour of a more versatile disc-shaped one constructed from metal latticework. It contains two halls, the largest of which covers an impressive 660,000 square feet, with 50,000 feet of it taken up by the playing area. The maximum audience capacity for sporting events, with seating spread across three levels, is 20,400 persons. This increases to 22,000 for music concerts. By comparison, the second smaller hall covers an area of just 19,000 square feet, with seats for 300 people. This serves ideally as a training or rehearsal hall, as well as a venue for trade fairs, local sporting and private functions.

The arena has already garnered an impressive performance record for having hosted the Men's European and World Volleyball Championships, the Ice Hockey World Championship and the European Men's Handball Championship. The venue's versatility is demonstrated by the fact that it has also been the venue for badminton, boxing, curling, gymnastics, basketball, figure skating, tennis and even equestrian competitions. As a music venue with excellent acoustics, the arena has hosted world class acts from Jose Carreras and Andre Rieu to Aerosmith and the Foo Fighters.

The LED media display wrapped around the outside of the arena covers an area of 56,000 square feet, with a colossal LED screen mounted over the main entrance that covers an impressive 5,800 square feet. Both were installed by LED specialists Colosseo, whose engineers used 80 tons of aluminium ties and 80,000 screws to secure the display to the building. Colosseo are also responsible for the full HD 360 degree video cube inside the arena.

The impressive TAURON Arena Kraków in Czyżyny

Obviously the best way to experience the arena is by attending an event. However, for those who want to see exactly how a pop concert or a tennis tournament is set up, guided tours are available on Mondays, Tuesdays and Saturdays by appointment (www.tauronarenakrakow.pl). Participants will be taken behind the scenes to witness the arena's elaborate technical infrastructure and extensive visitor facilities, as well as getting the chance to visit the artists' changing rooms and to stand in a glass-fronted VIP 'skybox'.

Krakow's other sporting venues are more traditional in terms of their architecture. Stadion Miejski at ul. Reymonta 22 (Czarna Wieś) is the home ground of Wisła Kraków, Poland's oldest football club, founded in 1906. Built originally in 1914, the rectangular, open-air stadium seen today, with its all-round grandstands, is a 2010 rebuild, with a maximum capacity of 34,000 spectators. It's worth noting that Wisła Kraków currently holds the European football record for consecutive home games without a loss. Farther south, on the opposite side of the Błonia, is the Marshall Jozef Piłsudski Stadium at ul. Józefa Kałuży 1 (Salwator). Of a similar construction, it is the home ground of Cracovia, also founded in 1906. Again a 2010 rebuild (of the team's original stadium built in 1912) it holds just over 15,000 spectators.

72 Wooden Churches of Małopolska

31-979 Kraków (Nowa Huta), a selection of wooden churches including the Church of St. Bartholomew (Kościół św. Bartłomieja) at ul. Klasztorna 11
Tram 10, 70 from Teatr Słowackiego to Klasztorna then a short walk south down ul. Klasztorna (note: the church interior can only be viewed in Spring and Summer)

Those interested in architecture are spoilt for choice in Krakow. The city centre is a vast open air gallery of styles ranging from Romanesque through to Art Nouveau and beyond. There is one style of architecture, however, that most visitors see for few realise that Lesser Poland (Małopolska) – the historical region of which Krakow is capital – is renowned for its historic wooden buildings.

There are no less than 252 old wooden buildings in Lesser Poland, many of them ecclesiastical, which since 2001 have formed the so-called Wooden Architecture Route in Małopolska (Szlak Architektury Drewnianej w Małopolsce). Four wooden churches (including the superb Church of St. Michael the Archangel in Dębno) have made it onto UNESCO's World Heritage List but these are located well outside Krakow. Fortunately there are three other wooden churches within the city limits.

The first is the Church of St. Bartholomew (Kościół św. Bartłomieja) at ul. Klasztorna 11 (Nowa Huta). The oldest of the three, it was constructed back in 1466, as witnessed by the date and the name of master carpenter, Maciej Mączka, carved onto the door. It stands opposite the Cistercian Abbey of Mogiła (Opactwo Cystersów w Mogile), a monastic complex founded by Krakow's bishop Iwo Odrowąż (1160–1229), who brought the order here from Silesia in 1222 (much of the original village was obliterated by the construction of Nowa Huta). The abbey is centred on the magnificent Basilica of the Holy Cross (Bazylika Krzyża Świętego) – so-named because it contains fragments of the true Cross – and its adjoining cloister. Humble by comparison, the wooden church provided accommodation to visiting Catholic laymen. It is noteworthy for its three aisles (a real rarity among sacral wooden architecture), as well as its painted interior and 18th century belfry.

Krakow's second wooden church is also located in Nowa Huta or rather the village Krzesławice, which like Mogiła pre-dates Nowa

Huta. The Church of St. John the Baptist (Kościół św. Jana Chrzciciela) can be reached by heading northwards onto ul. Bulwarowa, turning right along al. Solidarności (passing the Nowa Huta Reservoir (Zalew Nowohucki) on the way), then turning left to reach ul. Wańkowicza 35. It was actually completed in 1648 in the mountain village of Jaworniki on Poland's eastern border with Ukraine. Only when it was threatened with demolition in the 1980s was it brought here, as part of an abortive plan to create an open-air folk museum. Instead a tower was added and the building continued as a place of worship, with services held in the cosy single-aisled interior.

The wooden Church of St. Bartholomew (Kościół św. Bartłomieja) undergoing traditional repair

Krakow's third and final wooden church can be found far away to the west in the leafy suburb of Salwator. The Chapel of St. Margaret (Kaplica św. Małgorzaty) at ul. św. Bronisławy 8 (Salwator) was once part of the nearby Norbertine Monastery (Klasztor norbertanek) and is unique in having an octagonal plan (see no. 99). Originally a cemetery chapel, it has succumbed to fire repeatedly, with the current structure dating from 1690. The Baroque altar inside is on loan from the Church of the Holy Saviour (Kościół Najświętszego Salwatora) across the road.

For a modern take on Małopolska's timber tradition, visit Skansen Smaków at ul. Cholerzyn 424, just outside Krakow in Kryspinów. This traditional inn (Karczma) overlooking a lake near the airport features plenty of wooden timber beams, sheep-skin rugs and hearty country cooking. The experience is rounded out with boisterous folk music on Thursdays and Sundays.

73 A Lot of Rubbish

31-981 Kraków (Nowa Huta), the Waste Thermal Treatment
Plant (Zakład Termicznego Przekształcania Odpadów) at
ul. Jerzego Giedroycia 23
Tram 10, 70 from Teatr Słowackiego to Brama nr. 5 then walk
south along ul. Jerzego Giedroycia (note: guided tours only on
the first Tue of each month at 2pm)

Most visitors won't have rubbish on their mind when they come to Krakow. But all that waste they create whilst exploring the city has to go somewhere and the chances are it goes to Nowa Huta. Out here on a bend in the Vistula (Wisła) can be found Krakow's new Waste Thermal Treatment Plant (Zakład Termicznego Przekształcania Odpadów). With its colourful exterior and state-of-the-art technology, it provides a startling counterpoint to the smoke-blackened chimneys of the Nowa Huta steelworks in the distance.

The ZTP, as the plant is known for short, was inaugurated in 2016 in response to Krakow's growing need for a safe, affordable and ecologically-minded waste management system. With over half the funding coming from the European Union, it meets today's highest environmental and legal standards.

The outside of the building is extraordinary. Other than a solitary chimney poking out of the roof, one would think the funky green, red and white striped structure was a cultural centre or concert venue. Of course it's what goes on inside that really matters. Increasing the public's awareness of ecological waste management is taken seriously here, with guided tours of the plant offered on the first Tuesday of each month at 2pm.

The tour takes visitors through the plant showing them the key elements of the waste treatment process. First they see where trucks loaded with mixed municipal waste arrive from across Krakow and unload into an 85-foot high concrete bunker (the plant is currently processing 220,000 tonnes of waste annually). The waste is stirred to obtain a uniform mixture that will optimise incineration. Cranes with grapple-buckets then move the waste into a series of hoppers from where it falls by gravity into the combustion chamber below.

Next comes the thermal conversion part of the process, which consists of five separate stages: drying, degassing, combustion, gasification (when volatile products are oxidized), and afterburning (when carbon dioxide is reduced and secondary air is supplied for total incin-

Emissions board at the Waste Thermal Treatment Plant (Zakład Termicznego Przekształcania Odpadów)

eration). After that comes the all-important energy recovery process utilising a heat recovery steam generator integrated within the combustion chamber. In principle exhaust gases cooled to a manageable 180°C are used to convert water into superheated steam. This is then used to drive a steam turbine, which converts mechanical energy into electrical energy. This not only powers the plant but also provides electricity for the national grid. In cogeneration mode, the process can also produce heat, which is distributed through Nowa Huta's municipal heating network to local homes and businesses.

The ZTP sees the managing of dangerous gaseous and other airborne residues resulting from incineration as paramount. Various methods are used to achieve this from the obvious (fans, filters and aforementioned smokestack) to the less so (denitrification of exhaust gases through the injection of a special liquid solution). Any slag and ash created during thermal processing is taken away for further processing by authorised outside agents. The exact emissions of the plant on any given day are shown on an LED signboard outside the plant, as well as the operating company's website at www.khk.krakow.pl (click on 'Emission').

Not far from the ZTP is the Kujawy Sewage Treatment Plant (Oczyszczalnia Ścieków Kujawy) at ul. Dymarek 9. In tandem with the Płaszów plant at St. Kosiarzy 3, it services the Krakow by means of a network of pipes measuring over 1,150 miles in length. The city's first modern water treatment plant opened in 1901 at ul. sw. Księcia Józefa 299 (Bielany), where its original ornate red-brick buildings are still used today.

74 A City for Steelworkers

31-932 Kraków (Nowa Huta), a visit to Nowa Huta
Tram 4, 10, 44, 70, 73 from Teatr Słowackiego
to Plac Centralny im Ronalda Reagana

During the late 1940s, the Soviet Union helped the Communist parties of war-ravaged Europe consolidate their power through the construction of model socialist cities built around large-scale industrial concerns. The motive was not only economic (to foster growth through heavy industry) but also ideological (to create a workforce loyal to the party). Several of these factory-cities supported steel plants, Krakow's Nowa Huta being a great example.

Nowa Huta became Krakow's easternmost district in 1951. Consequently trams today run all the way to plac Centralny in the heart of Nowa Huta's residential district. Looking out from here along the apartment-lined streets, it is remarkable to think that a little over 70 years ago this was arable land dotted with ancient villages.

The decision to build Nowa Huta (meaning 'New Steelworks') was approved in 1947 and by 1960 both the works (named in honour of Lenin) and the accommodation for its 20,000 workers (rising to 40,000 during the 1970s) had been completed. From the start, it was intended to be the proletarian antithesis of Krakow, which the Soviets perceived as decadent and bourgeois. Ironically Nowa Huta would be where Solidarity (Solidarność) workers eventually took up arms against Communism in favour of democracy (see no. 75).

Nowa Huta's housing was planned with great care. Its radial street plan fans out from plac Centralny, with greenery breaking up the apartment blocks. That these are human in scale is because the Polish architect Tadeusz Ptaszycki (1908–1980) looked for inspiration not to Moscow but 1920s New York and its concept of self-sufficient 'neighbourhood units'. Nowa Huta's clusters of apartment blocks *(osiedla)* are not overly high and were given shops, restaurants and other facilities at pavement level. Less obviously, and clearly with the Cold War in mind, the wide streets were designed to prevent the spread of fire, the trees to absorb the effects of a bomb blast, and the overall layout designed to facilitate guerrilla defence tactics.

Completed in 1949, plac Centralny is a good example of the Soviet-sanctioned style known as Socialist Realism in which architecture is rendered sufficiently authoritarian and then softened with a limited amount of decoration (note the Renaissance-style arcades). Original

A detail of Nowa Huta's plac Centralny completed in 1949

facilities include the Cepelix shop at os. Centrum B1 and the Centralny milk bar at os. Centrum C 1 (see no. 62). The square would have been entirely closed had plans for a huge theatre marking the southern end of the city's main axis not been abandoned. Instead in 1983 the more modest Nowa Huta Cultural Centre (Nowohuckie Centrum Kultury) was built at al. Jana Pawła II 232 containing a permanent exhibition of paintings by dystopian artist Zdzisław Beksiński (1929–2005).

Not far away at os. Centrum E1 is the Nowa Huta Museum (Dzieje Nowej Huty), a branch of the Museum of Krakow (Muzeum Krakowa). Housed in the former Kino Światowid, it illustrates the life in Nowa Huta past and present. A highlight is a guided tour through the nuclear fallout shelter in the cellar, one of over 250 built across Nowa Huta during the 1950s. Other sights include Kino Studyjne Sfinks at os. Gorali 5 (Nowa Huta's last working cinema), and the nearby Museum of the Armed Act (Muzeum Czynu Zbrojnego) detailing Nazi Germany's occupation of Poland. Teatr Ludowy at os. Teatralne 34 opened in 1955 and is still going strong.

The steelworks that gave Nowa Huta its name ('New Foundry') cannot be visited. However, it's worth taking Tram 21 or 22 out to Kombinat to see the main gate flanked by a pair of remarkable neo-Renaissance administration blocks that can be explored on a guided tour (https://fundacjanh.bookero.pl/).

75 Building the Lord's Ark

**31-831 Kraków (Nowa Huta), the Church of the Lord's Ark
(Kościół Arka Pana) at ul. Obrońców Krzyża 1
Tram 4, 10, 44, 52, 70, 73 from Teatr Słowackiego to Rondo
Czyżyńskie then 1, 5 to Teatr Ludowy and walk north along
ul. Obrońców Krzyża (note: no visits during Mass)**

Nowa Huta was created in 1949 as a separate city east of Krakow. Populated with workers from the Vladimir Lenin Steelworks, the utopian planned settlement served as a colossal advertisement for Soviet social engineering (see no. 74). It also took a deliberate swipe at the cultural values held dear by the city's middle classes, who opposed their country's post-1945 Socialist government.

Ironically Nowa Huta eventually became a focus for anti-Communist activity and played a large part in the Solidarity (Solidarność) strikes of the early 1980s that heralded Polish democracy. But before that, its residents fought another battle to build a church. Not surprisingly, the one type of building omitted from the original plan for Nowa Huta was a Catholic place of worship. From the start, Nowa Huta's workers campaigned peacefully but unsuccessfully to build one. Permission was finally granted in 1956 but when this was rescinded without explanation it lead to protests. The erection of a simple wooden Cross without a permit saw the riot police sent in. Local sentiment remained steadfast though, with support from the Auxiliary Bishop of Krakow, Karol Wojtyła (1920–2005) (later Pope John Paul II), who on Christmas Eve 1959 celebrated Nowa Huta's first ever Mass outdoors.

In 1960, Nowa Huta's residents began lobbying again to build their church. This time they were successful and in 1967 permission was re-granted, with Wojtyła in attendance to lay the foundation stone. Building the Church of Our Lady Queen of Poland (Kościół Matki Bożej Królowej Polski) was not straightforward though. Whilst the government granted building consent, they refused to provide any materials or tools. This was a significant problem in a state-run economy, so instead Nowa Huta's Catholics banded together and built the church themselves! They made their own bricks, mixed their own concrete, and gathered some two million river pebbles to clad the building's façade. Despite a Second World War ammunition dump being found along the way, Wojtyła consecrated the finished church in 1977.

The church was designed by architect Wojciech Pietrzyk (b. 1930) to resemble Noah's Ark resting on Mount Ararat after the Biblical flood

The workers of Nowa Huta built the Church of the Lord's Ark (Kościół Arka Pana) by hand

(it features a 246 foot-high mast-shaped crucifix rising from its deck-like roof). This has given rise to the building's popular name of the Lord's Ark (Kościół Arka Pana). It shouldn't be forgotten that at the time of its construction, the church represented a lone Catholic vessel navigating the hitherto godless waters of Nowa Huta. Its completion represented the people's victory over totalitarianism.

The church contains some remarkable treasures, including a rock brought back from the Moon by Apollo 11 embedded in the tabernacle, a huge figure of Christ breaking free from his crucifix by Bronisław Chromy (1925–2017), a fragment of St. Peter's tomb in Rome in the Chapel of Our Lady of Fatima, and a statue in the Chapel of Reconciliation dedicated to *Our Lady the Armoured* made from shrapnel removed from Polish troops at the Battle of Monte Cassino (1944).

Inevitably the church became a focal point during anti-Communist protests in Nowa Huta in the early 1980s. Notably it provided shelter from government militia and celebrated monthly Masses for Poland through the violent period of Martial Law (1981–1983). A monument outside the church commemorates the spot where one activist, Bogdan Włosik (1962–1982), was fatally wounded.

A decade after the completion of the Lord's Ark work began on another Catholic church in Nowa Huta. The Church of Our Lady of Częstochowa in Krakow (Kościół Matki Boskiej Częstochowskiej w Krakowie), with its striking crystal-shaped roof, was born out of the same demand for freedom to worship.

76 Life and Death at Rakowicki

31-510 Kraków (Warszawskie), Rakowicki Cemetery (Cmentarz Rakowicki) at ul. Rakowicka 26
Tram 2 from Teatr Słowackiego to Cmentarz Rakowicki
(note: a useful map of the cemetery is displayed just inside the main entrance)

On January 15th 1803, according to local lore, the first burial took place at Krakow's Rakowicki Cemetery (Cmentarz Rakowicki). It was that of an 18-year-old local girl, Apolonia Bursikowa, who had succumbed to tuberculosis. Since then Krakow's first municipal cemetery has grown to become the city's largest burial ground, where ordinary citizens rest peacefully alongside artists and musicians, scientists, political figures and war heroes.

Until the late 18th century, Krakow's dead had been buried in increasingly overcrowded Old Town churchyards (examples include plac Szczepański and plac Wszyskich Świętych). Their closure by the Austrians for health reasons and subsequent paving over prompted the opening of Rakowicki. The new cemetery located well outside the city limits on land purchased from a monastery was named after a nearby village. It is best visited on All Souls' Day (November 2nd), when the graves are aglow with candles lit by families, friends and fans of the deceased.

The oldest part of the cemetery faces onto ul. Rakowicka. It consists of a grid plan of burial zones *(kwatera)* identified alphabetically, its main axis leading to a funerary chapel; the zones beyond radiate outwards in semicircles. The oldest gravestones line the wall just inside the main entrance on the left, whilst to the right can be found the grave of revered artist Józef Mehoffer (1869–1946) (see no. 84). Also hereabouts are the graves of philosopher Roman Ingarden (1893–1970) and Romantic painter Piotr Michałowski (1800–1855), as well as monuments to those killed during various national revolts, including the November Uprising (1830), Krakow Uprising (1846) and January Uprising (1863). The cemetery was subsequently enlarged to the west and north, and divided into zones using numerals.

Continuing westwards along the main axis are the graves of Mayor Józef Dietl (1804–1878), who did so much to modernise Krakow, Jan Matejko (1838–1893), Poland's 'national painter', and internationally renowned actress Helena Modjeska (1840–1909) (see nos. 30, 63). Also here are some outstanding funerary sculptures, including the sword-wielding *Anioł Zemsty* (Angel of Vengeance) (1913) commemorating the victims of the Austrian siege of Krakow (1848). Where the axis reaches the cemetery's back wall, a clutch of memorials recall the victims of Nazi concentration camps, and resistance fighters who perished fighting for Poland during the Second World War. Ranged around the perimeter wall are graves of soldiers from various Polish legions conscripted into the Austrian, Russian and Prussian armies during the First World War.

All manner of monuments in the Rakowicki Cemetery (Cmentarz Rakowicki)

More celebrity graves can be found in the cemetery's northern extension, including that of theatre visionary Tadeusz Kantor (1915–1990) (see no. 52). Nearby in zone LXIX is the so-called Aleja Zasłużonych (Avenue of the Distinguished) containing the graves of the Piwnica Pod Baranami cabaret founder Piotr Skrzynecki (1930–1997), singer-songwriter Marek Grechuta (1945–2006) and religious artist Jerzy Nowosielski (1923–2011) (see no. 25).

Across ul. Biskupa Jana Prandoty (the road marking Rakowicki's northern limit) is a separate Military Cemetery (Cmentarz wojskowy) opened in 1920. A flower-strewn statue of Pope John Paul II at the entrance is a reminder that his parents and brother also rest here. Specially designated plots contain all manner of war memorials. They recall the country's Home Army (Armia Krajowa) that fought for Polish freedom throughout the Second World War, Allied pilots shot down over Poland, Russian soldiers who died liberating Krakow in January 1945, and even German SS and Wehrmacht troops (see no. 77). Another commemorates Poles who died in Galicia between 1945 and 1948 at the hands of the Ukrainian Insurgent Army, an extreme nationalist group bent on re-establishing a mono-ethnic Ukrainian national state.

77 Poland's Brave Home Army

31-511 Kraków (Warszawskie), the Home Army Museum (Muzeum Armii Krajowej) at ul. Wita Stwosza 12 Tram 2 from Teatr Słowackiego to Uniwersytet Ekonomiczny then walk along ul. Wita Stwosza (note: guided tours in English are recommended (www.muzeum-ak.pl), last entry one hour before closing)

In September 1939, the invasion of Poland by Nazi Germany triggered the Second World War. The Soviet Union followed suit, and the country was divided into occupied zones. Far from breaking the will of the Polish people, however, plans were already in place for the formation of an underground Home Army (Armia Krajowa) that would commence the fight for freedom. The Home Army Museum (Muzeum Armii Krajowej) at ul. Wita Stwosza 12 (Warszawskie) tells its story.

The idea for the museum was mooted in 1990 in the wake of the collapse of Communism. Over the next decade, historical items relating to the Home Army were collected and in 2000 the museum opened inside a three-storey former railway building. Comprising some 7,000 artefacts, including uniforms, weapons, maps and insignia, the museum illustrates the activities of the Home Army across three distinct time periods.

The first period covers the years 1939–1941 and the army's establishment in Warsaw, just before the surrender, when a covert resistance movement called Służba Zwycięstwu Polski (SPZ) (Service for Poland's Victory) was established under General Michał Karaszewicz-Tokarzewski (1893–1964). It operated under the auspices of the Polish Government-in-exile in France, which comprised the Polish Socialist Party, the Peasant Party (Partia Ludowa) and the National Party. The movement quickly morphed into the more aggressive Zwišzek Walki Zbrojnej (ZWZ) (Union for Armed Struggle), with the aim of creating centres of national armed resistance inside Poland. In 1940, following the fall of France, the Polish Government relocated to London from where it orchestrated the ZWZ's various propaganda, reconnaissance and sabotage campaigns. The greatest successes at the time occurred in and around Krakow, which lay far enough away from direct German, Soviet and pro-German Ukrainian military activity.

The second period encompasses the years 1942–1943. In 1942, the Polish Prime Minister-in-exile General Władysław Sikorski (1881–1943) changed the ZWZ into the Armia Krajowa (AK) (Home Army), with

A pistol used by members of the Polish Home Army at the Home Army Museum (Muzeum Armii Krajowej)

General Stefan Rowecki (1895–1944) as its commander. With various other partisan groups under its wing, including the paramilitary Polish Scouting Organisation known as the Gray Ranks (Szare Szeregi), the Home Army now numbered 300,000 members. Secret training schools and weapons' factories were established, and plans for an uprising were prepared. Meanwhile, German resupply lines to the Russian front were disrupted and guerrilla operations targeted attempts to settle Polish lands with German farmers. Unfortunately in 1943 there were significant losses, too, notably the capture of General Rowecki, who was replaced by General Tadeusz Bór-Komorowski (1895–1966), and the death of General Sikorski in an air crash.

The final period covers 1944 and 1945. In order to tackle German troops now retreating in the East, the Polish Government-in-exile instructed Home Army units to reveal themselves to the advancing Soviets (the code name given to the operation was *Burza* meaning 'Tempest'). The Soviets, however, proved hostile and after commandeering a particular area simply arrested any Home Army troops they found and imprisoned them. With the Soviets rapidly approaching Warsaw, it was decided that Polish soldiers should free the city from German hands. On August 1st 1944, the Home Army struck and for a while made great progress. Victory was short-lived though and with the Soviets looking on, the Home Army surrendered to the Germans on October 2nd 1944, with 20,000 of its soldiers taken prisoner.

Home Army troops elsewhere in Poland soldiered on until January 1945, when their last commander, General Leopold Okulicki (1898–1946), ordered their disbandment. This brought an end to the Home Army's brave story.

78 Shopping the Old Fashioned Way

30-962 Kraków (Kleparz), the Stary Kleparz market
at Rynek Kleparski 20
Tram 2, 4, 14, 18, 20, 24, 44 to Stary Kleparz

Krakow is rightly proud of its market tradition. After all, the city's Rynek Główny laid out in 1257 is Europe's largest medieval market square. These days, however, it's more cafés and shops than market stalls that attract visitors there (see no. 13). So if it's fresh local produce you're after, head instead to the suburbs, where several markets still encourage shopping the old fashioned way.

During medieval times, the presence of a market made a place. That was certainly true of the three separate towns comprising medieval Krakow: Old Town, Kazimierz and Kleparz. In the Old Town, a Brotherhood of Merchants was founded in the 15th century in the Church of St. Barbara (Kościół św. Barbary) at Mały Rynek 8 (Old Town), where services are still held for the city's merchants. In Kazimierz, the main marketplace was plac Wolnica. Laid out in 1335 and used to trade amber, salt and furs, its name reflects the fact that trading was exempt *(wolne)* from the rents imposed at Rynek Główny to protect trade. Despite once being equal in stature to Rynek Główny, it is today much reduced and pedestrianised.

That leaves Kleparz and its still-bustling marketplace at Rynek Kleparski 20. Known as Stary Kleparz (Old Kleparz), this covered market was established in the mid-14th century just outside the Floriańska Gate and is Krakow's oldest market still in operation. Grain, cattle and horses were originally traded here. When business waned following the collapse of Communism, the market was leased by the newly-formed Guild of Stary Kleparz Merchants, which set about modernising it. Today, some 200 traders sell everything from fresh vegetables, fruit, local cheeses and smoked meats to cut flowers, clothing and crafts. They have also forged strong relations with the local community, helping to support its needy, as well as the local authorities, who recognise the market's worth as a cultural asset. Anyone wishing to shop further should travel a couple of stops north on Tram 18 to Nowy Kleparz (New Kleparz). This large farmers' market located on the corner of ul. Długa and al. Słowackiego opened in 1925.

Not quite so old is plac Targowy Unitarg at ul. Grzegórzecka 3

(Grzegórzki). It is known locally as Hala Targowa (meaning 'market hall') after the covered market erected just before the Second World War. Trading at this location, however, goes back to the late-14th century, when Grzegórzki was a village on an arm of the Vistula (Stara Wisła), which served as a customs' boundary (vegetables were sold on the north bank, manufactured goods on the south). The area was industrialised during the second half of the 19th century and in the 1870s the river infilled to become a road (see no. 63).

As with Stary Kleparz, a merchant's association was formed here in the 1990s to ensure the market's survival. Called UNITARG, it too has reinvigorated trading and engaged successfully with the local community. A food and clothing market takes place here between Monday and Saturday, and on Sundays there is a huge flea market offering everything from war-time memorabilia to vinyl records. And don't miss the street food, which includes the best grilled sausage *(kiełbasa)* sold each evening (except Sunday) from the blue Kiełbaski z Niebieskiej Nyski van.

Fresh home-grown cucumbers for sale at the Stary Kleparz market

Krakow's other active markets include plac Nowy (the old Jewish marketplace in Kazimierz) and Rynek Dębnicki (originally part of the former village of Dębnicki) (see no. 39). The 18th century Rynek Podgórski hasn't seen traders for years whereas plac na Stawach is relatively occupying the site of a former monastic pond (see nos. 49, 99).

Other locations nearby: 33

79 Behind Bars at Montelupich

31-155 Kraków (Kleparz), the Montelupich Prison (Areszt Śledczy w Krakowieon) at ul. Montelupich 7 Tram 18 from Stary Kleparz to Nowy Kleparz then walk along al. Juliusza Słowackiego turning left onto ul. Kamienna and ul. Montelupich (note: the prison is only open to authorised visitors)

A prison might seem like an unusual visitor attraction but Krakow's Montelupich Prison (Areszt Śledczy w Krakowieon) has an important story to tell. Standing ominously at ul. Montelupich 7 (Kleparz), it acts as a reminder of the bravery of those unfairly incarcerated, tortured and murdered here under the Nazi and Soviet regimes.

Curiously for a prison, Montelupich began as a grand house. The so-called Kamienica Montelupich was the Krakow home of the wealthy Italian Montelupi family, who decorated it in the Renaissance style. It was Sebastian Montelupi who in 1569 took up the position of Royal Postmaster, dispatching royal and private mail to Venice from his office at Rynek Głowny 7 (Old Town) (see no. 13).

As a prison, Montelupich opened in the early 20th century, with its darkest chapter occurring during the Second World War. In 1939 it served as a detention centre for professors from the Jagiellonian University (Uniwersytet Jagielloński) arrested during Sonderaktion Krakau, an operation designed to eliminate Polish intelligentsia. Then in March 1941 it was commandeered by the Gestapo and overseen by Nazi official Ludwig Hahn (1908–1986), who was later involved in the liquidation of the Warsaw Ghetto. Montelupich quickly became one of the worst prisons in occupied Poland.

Those detained during this time were mostly Polish political prisoners rounded up during Gestapo street raids. Additionally there were Jews, British and Soviet spies, captured Allied airmen, regular convicts, and even German deserters. It is estimated that during the war some 50,000 political prisoners were processed at Montelupich, with many enduring brutal interrogation methods before being killed. A notable inmate was Jewish activist Gusta Dawidson Draenger (1917–1943) (code name 'Justyna'), whose prison memoirs scribbled on toilet paper were published in English in 1996 as *Justyna's Narrative*.

Atrocities associated with Montelupich were commonplace. In January 1944, for example, 232 random prisoners were executed by firing squad followed by another hundred in retaliation for an unsuccessful

High security at the Montelupich Prison (Areszt Śledczy w Krakowieon)

attempt on the life of Hans Frank (1900–1946), Governor General of the Occupied Polish Territories. After the liberation of Krakow by the Red Army in January 1945, Montelupich became a Soviet prison. Twenty one Nazis were held here pending death sentences given out at the First Auschwitz Trial. They included Amon Göth (1908–1946), the barbarous commandant of the Krakow-Płaszów concentration camp, who was hung here on 13th September 1946. Atrocities still occurred though, notably the torture and murder of resistance fighters from the Polish Home Army (Armia Krajowa) by the Soviet NKVD and Urząd Bezpieczeństwa security organisations (see no. 77). Among those who survived was decorated resistance fighter Witold Kieżun (b. 1922), who endured deportation to a Soviet gulag before eventually becoming a respected economist.

Montelupich today, whilst being recognised both as an historic monument and a place of martyrdom, continues to serve as a detention and correctional facility. Administered by the Polish Prison Administration (Służba Więzienna), it has 158 cells and a hospital. The last death sentence in Poland was carried out here in 1988.

Unfortunately Montelupich's grim reputation still persists as witnessed in 2008 by the case of a young Romanian detainee, Claudiu Crulic (1975–2008). In protest against what he saw as an unnecessarily aggressive investigation for theft, Crulic went on hunger strike and died after being ignored by the prison's doctors and the Romanian consul. The incident was condemned by human rights groups and became the subject of the award-winning film *Crulic – Drumul spre dincolo* (Crulic: The Path to Beyond) (2011).

Other locations nearby: 80

80 Fortress Krakow

30-001 Kraków (Kleparz), Fort 'Kleparz' at ul. Kamienna 2–4
Tram 18 from Stary Kleparz to Nowy Kleparz

Krakow's medieval city wall was demolished during the early 19th century and replaced by the Planty Park (see no. 33). Later in the same century, however, a more ambitious system of fortifications was constructed in the suburbs. Known as Fortress Krakow (Twierdza Kraków), its significant remains make for an exciting thematic tour.

These later fortifications find their origins in the 18th century, when the political affairs of the Polish–Lithuanian Commonwealth were in the hands of the Great Sejm (1788–1792), a powerful parliamentary body dominated by aristocratic nobles. The abolition of their far-reaching rights of veto under Poland's 3rd May Constitution (1791) enfranchised the country's bourgeoisie and is arguably the reason why Austria, Russia and Prussia decided to partition the country.

The Russian army entered Commonwealth territory in 1792. Together with Prussia they seized two thirds of the land under the terms of the Second Partition of Poland (1793); Austria already occupied the right bank of the Vistula (Wisła) under the First Partition (1772). The Third Partition (1795) banished Poland from the map altogether and made Krakow part of Austria.

With Krakow now just four miles from the Russian border, the Austrians set about protecting 'their' city. Initially the work comprised an inner ring of forts built in the 1850s–60s, a mile or so beyond the line of the old medieval wall. A good example is Fort 'Kleparz' at ul. Kamienna 2–4 (Kleparz), known also as Bastion III. Sturdily built of red-brick, the self-contained, horseshoe-shaped redoubt was strategically placed so as to allow troops to sally forth and retreat safely in defence of this part of the city. Protected by a series of defensive ditches and embankments (and serviced by its own railway that ran along al. Juliusza Słowackiego), it functions today as a music venue with a 200-person concert hall. Another redoubt, Fort 'Luneta Warszawska' (Bastion IVa), stands at the other end of the same street and is currently abandoned except for a ceramic studio.

The inner ring also contained two specialised types of fort. Fort 31 'St. Benedict' on Lasota Hill (Podgórze) is a 16-sided 'Maximilian Tower' built to guard over the Vistula (see no. 54). Fort 2 'Ko ciuszko' is unique in being built around the pre-existing Ko ciuszko Mound (Zwierzyniec) (see no. 106). It subsequently saw action in both World

Wars and today contains an extensive exhibition about the fortification of Krakow.

The invention of longer range artillery soon rendered much of the inner ring defences obsolete. As a result, from the late 1860s onwards a new outer ring was constructed, which by 1914 comprised 32 armoured forts of different types. Built on both sides of the river, they stretched from Mogiła in the east all the way to Bielany in the west.

More than half of these forts are still standing, some abandoned and others adapted for reuse (Fort 38 'Skała', for example, now contains an astronomical observatory and Fort 45 'Zielonki' is a hotel) (see no. 103). It is possible to see many of them by following the communication routes that once connected them, marked today by yellow-and-black signs. A good example is

Fort 'Kleparz' on ul. Kamienna is one of many that make up Fortress Krakow

Fort 47a 'Węgrzce' in the village of the same name on the road north to Kielce. Consisting of an angled, two-storey range with attendant earthworks, it was reused by the *Wehrmacht* in January 1945 during the defence of Krakow against the Red Army and now houses a transport company. Its southern counterpart, Fort 52a 'Łapianka' on the road to Lwów, saw action during the Battle of Krakow in 1914 and is now a museum of scouting.

Other locations nearby: 79

81 The Horrors of Reichsstrasse

30-039 Kraków (Nowa Wieś), the Ulica Pomorska Museum
at ul. Pomorska 2
Tram 4, 8, 13, 14, 24, 44 to Plac Inwalidów then walk along
ul. Królewska

During the Second World War, Krakow's ulica Królewska (Nowa Wieś) was renamed Reichsstrasse by the Nazis. It was on a side street here – ul. Pomorska – that the regime's Secret State Police (Geheime Staatspolizei, abbreviated *Gestapo*) had their headquarters and detention cells. Here they interrogated and tortured prisoners with impunity.

Following the joint invasion of Poland by Nazi Germany and the Soviet Union in September 1939, Poland was split into three zones: the German General Government in the centre, areas annexed by Nazi Germany in the west, and others annexed by the Soviet Union in the east. Krakow fell inside the General Government ruled by Governor-General Hans Frank (1900–1946), who ensconced himself in the former royal palace on Wawel Hill.

A month later, Krakow became Distrikt Krakau, one of four administrative districts within the General Government. The Nazis envisioned a complete Germanisation of the city through the removal of all Poles and Jews, the German renaming of streets and a propaganda programme that would repaint Krakow as a historically German city. The *Gestapo*, of course, had a significant role to play in all this. It was their job to round up political dissidents, anti-German agitators and anyone they deemed might get in the way. Intelligence was everything, and to gather it they established themselves in a building known as the Silesian House (Dom Śląski) at ul. Pomorska 2 (built in the late 1930s, it had originally housed students from the Silesian region).

The building today contains the Ulica Pomorska Museum, a branch of the Museum of Krakow (Muzeum Krakowska) detailing the inhuman activities that occurred in what is otherwise an innocent-looking building. It consists of two separate exhibits, the first of which is entered by means of a staircase in the corner of the courtyard. Called *People of Krakow in Times of Terror 1939–1945–1956*, it details chronologically the atrocities committed in Krakow by both the Nazi and Stalinist regimes. Photos, documents, artefacts and audio recordings depict everything from the first victims executed by the Nazis to the Communist show trials of the mid-1950s. During the late 1940s and early 50s, the building was used by the Soviet secret police (NKVD).

Villains and victims at the Ulica Pomorska Museum

An extensive electronic database enables visitors and relatives to delve deeper into the lives of individual victims.

The second exhibit, which is even more affecting, comprises the former Gestapo detention cells in the basement of the building. Hundreds of inscriptions scratched onto the walls by prisoners awaiting their fate provide sobering and poignant evidence of those incarcerated here during the Nazi occupation.

The Ulica Pomorska Museum is one of three branches of the Museum of Krakow (Muzeum Krakowa) comprising the so-called Museum Remembrance Route: the others are Oscar Schindler's Enamel Factory (Fabryka Emalia Oskara Schindlera) and the Eagle Pharmacy (Apteka pod Orłem) (see nos. 53, 59).

The Nazis had plans to convert the Błonia meadow into a vast housing estate but only ever managed to build residential architecture along ul. Królewska. This explains the air raid shelters built for those loyal to the regime at ul. Królewska 30 and in the park opposite plac Inwalidów 8 (the former can be visited by appointment). Other buildings in Krakow associated with the Nazis include the former headquarters of Distrikt Krakau at Rynek Główny 28 (Old Town), the former Hitler Youth headquarters at ul. Szlak 71 (Kleparz), the Hotel Royal at ul. šw. Gertrudy 26–29 (Okół), once popular with *Wehrmacht* officers, and the Montelupich Prison (Kleparz) (see no. 79).

82 Religious Relics, Miraculous Icons

31-131 Kraków, (Piasek), the Church of the Visitation of the Blessed Virgin Mary (Kościół Nawiedzenia Najświętszej Maryi Panny) at ul. Karmelicka 19
Tram 2, 4, 8, 13, 14, 18, 20, 24, 44 to Teatr Bagatela

Krakow's Catholic churches are repositories for all manner of religious relics and miraculous icons. They recall a time when the possession of such things brought a ruler political power and a town considerable wealth by attracting pilgrims. Still popular with believers today, they help keep congregations buoyant and remain a feature of the city's newest churches.

Relics take many forms – from a stone soaked with the blood of Saint Stanislaus at the Skałka Sanctuary (Sanktuarium Skałka) in Kazimierz to fragments of the true Cross in the Abbey of Mogiła in Nowa Huta (see nos. 44, 72). Icons often have miracles attributed to them and a good example (together with an unusual relic in the form of a footprint) can be found at the Church of the Visitation of the Blessed Virgin Mary (Kościół Nawiedzenia Najświętszej Maryi Panny) at ul. Karmelicka 19 (Piasek).

According to legend, the earliest church on ul. Karmelicka was founded in the 11th century by Duke Ladislaus I Herman (Władysław I Herman) (c. 1044–1102). Suffering from disfiguring scurvy, he was visited by the Virgin Mary and instructed to go to Krakow's marshy outskirts and find an unusually dry, sandy spot where violets bloomed. These he rubbed into his sores and was immediately cured. The miracle warranted the construction of a church, which bore the alternative name of the Church on the Sand (Kościół Na Piasku).

In reality, the first church on ul. Karmelicka was not built until 1395 on the initiative of King Ladislaus II Jagiello (Władysław II Jagiełło) (c. 1352–1434) and his wife, Jadwiga (1374–1399). Legend still finds a place here though. Attached to the outside wall at the corner with ul. Gabarska is an iron grille protecting a block of sandstone. The oval impression on its surface is said to be Jadwiga's footprint, left here when the visiting queen bent down to bestow a gold shoe buckle upon a poor stonemason.

Two years later the church passed to the Carmelite Order, which the monarchs had recently invited to Krakow from Prague. Badly damaged in the mid-17th century during the Swedish occupation (the so-called 'Deluge'), the Gothic building was rebuilt in the Baroque style and re-consecrated in 1679.

A survivor from the original building is an icon known as the Madonna of the Sands. Painted around 1500, and originally displayed on an outside wall, it is said to have been miraculously completed after being left unfinished by its painter. Having survived the depredations of the Swedes, it was given its own chapel on the south side of the nave. Renowned for mercies obtained through the intercession of the Virgin Mary, King John III Sobieski (Jan III Sobieski) (1629–1696) believed that his victory over the Ottomans at the Battle of Vienna (1683) was made possible by praying before the icon (the gold crowns known as canonical coronations were added later). A clutch of devout worshippers will usually be seen praying here.

Jadwiga's footprint is on this wall at the Church of the Visitation of the Blessed Virgin Mary (Kościół Nawiedzenia Najświętszej Maryi Panny)

Other miraculous icons in Krakow include a 16th century image of Our Lady of the Redemption of Slaves in the Church of SS. John the Baptist and John the Evangelist (Kościół św. Jana Chrzciciela i Jana Ewangelisty) at ul. św. Jana 7 (Old Town), a 17th century image of Saint Joseph in the Church of the Immaculate Conception of the Blessed Virgin Mary (Kościół Matki Bozej Nieustajacej Pomocy) at ul. Rakowicka 18 (Warszawskie), and a copy of a 15th century image of the Virgin Mary in the Church of Our Lady of Perpetual Help (Kościół pw. Matki Bożej Nieustającej Pomocy) at ul. Jana Zamoyskiego 56 (Podgórze).

Other locations nearby: 26, 27, 83

83 A Young Cultural Hub

31-124 Kraków (Piasek), the Małopolska Garden of the Arts (Małopolski Ogród Sztuki) at ul. Rajska 12
Tram 2, 4, 8, 13, 14, 18, 20, 24, 44 to Teatr Bagatela

In 2012, Krakow's cultural scene received a youthful injection. In deliberate contrast to the Old Town's venerable Juliusz Słowacki Theatre (Teatr im Juliusza Słowackiego), the Małopolska Garden of the Arts (Małopolski Ogród Sztuki) in Piasek opened as an arts' hub aimed squarely at the young. With its award-winning modern architecture and daily calendar of events, it is already proving a popular addition to the city's media landscape.

The Małopolska Garden of the Arts (Małopolski Ogród Sztuki) was originally a stable block

Far from competing with the old venue, it is the dream of theatre director Krzysztof Orzechowski (b. 1947) that the MOS (as the new venue is known locally) should serve as a means of getting the performing arts to the masses. The MOS couldn't be structurally more different though (see no. 34). The location chosen for the building was a former 19th century Austrian stable block used previously by the theatre for storage. Around it the Wrocław-born architect Krzysztof Ingarden (b. 1957) has wrapped an eye-catching, L-shaped structure containing a variety of different facilities. Externally two features make this new structure particularly appealing. On the one hand, the façade is clad with variably-spaced, vertical ceramic elements known as 'razor blades', which give dynamic interest. On the other, the structure's height has been variously adapted so as to help it integrate harmoniously with existing neighbouring buildings. The result is a structure that is both exciting and inviting, especially the main entrance, where the architect has extended the building's design elements out over a small garden so as to reach potential visitors walking past on the pavement.

The programme of events staged at the MOS is clearly designed to appeal to a younger demographic, as well as to those prevented from previously enjoying Krakow's cultural offerings because of limited means, mobility or language. There is something happening here for everyone, every day of the week, from theatrical presentations and dance performances to film screenings, symposia, fashion shows and workshops. These are all hosted in the main wing on ul. Rajska, which contains a multipurpose hall with retractable stages that can variously be used as a theatre, concert hall, cinema and conference room.

By contrast the wing on ul. Józefa Szujskiego has a more literary and visual purpose in the form of the two-storey Arteteka art and media library. A branch of the public library across the road, it loans out books, films and music, with public computers available on which to watch films and play games. Other facilities include the Pauza In Garden Café, which offers its own calendar of cultural events. The café is an outpost of the renowned Pauza Bar and Gallery at ul. Stolarska 5/3 (Old Town), where drinkers relax beneath framed contemporary photos.

The architect Krzysztof Ingarden is responsible for several of Krakow's more striking postmodern buildings, including the Wyspiański Pavilion (Pawilon Wyspiański) and parts of the Manggha Museum of Japanese Art and Technology (Muzeum Sztuki i Techniki Japońskiej Manggha) (see nos. 45, 92). However, his most ambitious design thus far has undoubtedly been for the ICE Krakow Congress Centre (Centrum Kongresowe ICE Kraków) at ul. Marii Konopnickiej 17 (Dębniki). Opened in 2014, this state-of-the-art venue has a sleek exterior and a multi-functional interior containing three main halls for conferences, concerts and other events. The acronym ICE (International Conferencing and Entertainment) inspired Ingarden to create a building resembling a melting slab of ice, which is best appreciated in the striking glazed foyer overlooking the Vistula (Wisła), with Wawel Hill beyond.

Other locations nearby: 82, 84, 85, 86

84 An Artist's Home and Garden

31-123 Kraków (Piasek), the Józef Mehoffer House
(Dom Józefa Mehoffera) at ul. Krupnicza 26
Tram 2, 4, 8, 13, 14, 18, 20, 24, 44 to Teatr Bagatela

It is one thing to see an artist's work hanging on a wall and quite another to see how that artist lived. The two come together nicely in Polish painter and decorative artist Józef Mehoffer (1869–1946). One of the country's great all-round creatives during the late 19th and early 20th centuries, his Krakow home and garden have been preserved for posterity and are a joy to visit.

Mehoffer was born in Ropczyce in south-eastern Poland, a Galician county capital where his father was *starosta* (mayor). Like fellow artist Jan Matejko (1838–1893), he studied at Krakow's Academy of Fine Arts (Akademia Sztuk Pięknych w Krakowie) under renowned historical painter Władysław Łuszczkiewicz (1828–1900), and later at the Academy of Fine Arts in Vienna and the Académie Colarossi in Paris. During this time he mostly painted portraits of historical characters.

Around the turn of the century Mehoffer began expanding his repertoire to include a variety of applied arts, notably stained glass, medieval-style murals and textiles (he also dabbled in theatre set design, furniture and book illustration). It was the time of Young Poland (Młoda Polska), an artistic movement that sought to revive Polish national spirits in the face of foreign occupation by championing bohemian decadence, symbolism, Impressionism and the craze for Art Nouveau (see no. 31). Mehoffer turned out to be one of its leading lights.

Mehoffer received many predominantly ecclesiastical commissions from across Galicia and beyond. In Krakow he collaborated with fellow artist Stanisław Wyspiański (1869–1907) on the installation of glass and polychrome murals in numerous medieval church interiors. These include the Basilica of St. Mary (Bazylika Mariacka) at plac Mariacki 5 (Old Town) and the Basilica of St. Francis (Bazylika šw. Francoszia) at plac Wszystkich Świętych 5 (Okół) (see nos. 12, 18, 90, 92). One of his notable secular commissions was the Art Nouveau interior of the Café Noworolski inside the Cloth Hall (Sukiennice) at Rynek Główny 3 (Old Town) (see no. 87).

Mehoffer's passions and private life come alive in his former home, the Józef Mehoffer House (Dom Józefa Mehoffera) at ul. Krupnicza 26 (Piasek). A branch of the National Museum in Krakow (Muzeum Narodowe w Krakowie), its elegantly-furnished rooms with their chandeliers, furniture and fittings would still be recognised by Mehoffer, as well as by his fellow Young Poland colleagues, who often congregated in the drawing room. Of particular interest are the various sketches and decorative designs that attest to Mehoffer's broad-ranging talents, and some superb examples of his stained glass work (for example *Vita Somnium Breve* and *Caritas*). Also displayed are some superb portraits, including *Portret żony, tzw. florencki* (The Florentine Portrait of the Artist's Wife) and *Róża Saronu – Portret Zofii Minderowej* (Rose of Sharon – Portrait of Zofia Minderowa), as well as landscapes such as *Wisła pod Niepołomicami* (The Vistula near Niepołomice).

Mehoffer's house is perfectly complemented by the adjoining garden, which was lovingly restored in 2003 in line with Mehoffer's original design (his painting *Czerwona Parasolka* (Red Parasol) depicts the garden in its original form).

Roses in bloom at the Józef Mehoffer House (Dom Józefa Mehoffera)

In the warmer months between April and October it is pleasant to relax among the roses and fruit trees, with a drink from the Meho Café.

The mural on the side of the Józef Mehoffer House provides quite a contrast to Mehoffer's work. Created as part of the ArtBoom Festival in 2012, it is the work of Gdynia-born street artist Mariusz 'M-City' Waras (b. 1978) and is simply called *Mural no. 658*. It depicts an armoured paddle steamer with an inverted city suspended beneath it, threatened on all sides by fish-shaped torpedoes. Make of it what you will.

Other locations nearby: 83, 85, 86, 87

85 The Cappuccino Church

31-114 Kraków (Piasek), the Church of the Annunciation (Kościół Zwiastowania Najświętszej Maryi Panny) at ul. Loretańska 11
Tram 20 to Uniwersytet Jagielloński; Tram 2, 4, 8, 13, 14, 18, 20, 24, 44 to Teatr Bagatela

Serious coffee drinkers probably know the origin of the word *cappuccino*. It is the diminutive form of the Italian *cappuccio*, meaning 'hood', which in turn derives from the Latin *caputium*. One might therefore assume that the frothy topping of a *cappuccino* resembles a hood. In reality, however, the beverage takes its name from the Capuchin friars (an offshoot of the Franciscans), whose Krakow headquarters can be found just outside the Planty park in Piasek.

The Capuchin order emerged in Italy in 1525, when Matteo da Bascio (1495–1552), a strong-willed Franciscan, sought to return to the ascetic way of life practiced by Francis of Assisi. Persecuted for his deviancy, da Bascio and his followers were given refuge by the Camaldolese Fathers, in gratitude for which they adopted the white hood (or *cappucio*) worn by that particular order (see no. 102). Later the Capuchins coloured their hooded robes a distinctive red-brown, so as to distinguish themselves from other orders. It is this red-brown – rather than the hoods *per se* – that inspired the name of today's *cappuccino* coffee.

The Capuchins were brought to Poland in 1695 by King John III Sobieski (Jan III Sobieski) (1629–1696). By 1700 their monastery and Church of the Annunciation (Kościół Zwiastowania Najświętszej Maryi Panny) had been built at ul. Loretańska 11 by devotee Wojciech Dembliński, whose portrait and sarcophagus can be found here. On a summer's day, the modest stuccoed buildings have a vaguely Tuscan air about them, which seems fitting considering the origins of the Order.

It is also appropriate that the interior of the monastery buildings are modestly appointed in line with the Capuchin principle of poverty. Other than a few sculptures and paintings, the whitewashed walls are only broken up by memorials honouring military men, including General Józef Wodzicki (1750–1794), whose imposing monument is flanked with stone cannon. They reflect the fact that from the time of the abortive Kościuszko Uprising (1794) until the outbreak of the First World War, the Capuchins served as chaplains to those fighting for

Polish independence. Related artefacts include a cannonball from the time of the Bar Confederation (1768–1772), an uprising which led to the First Partition of the Polish–Lithuanian Commonwealth, and a tomb in front of the church containing the remains of several confederates.

Adjoining the church is a so-called Loreto House, a chapel completed in 1719 and dedicated to the Virgin Mary. It is modelled after the Santa Casa in Loreto, Italy, which the faithful believe was the Virgin's original home, flown by

The Loreto House at the Church of the Annunciation (Kościół Zwiastowania Najświętszej Maryi Panny)

angels from Nazareth in the 13th century to prevent its destruction by Saracens. During the time of the Polish Partitions (1772–1918), it served as a patriotic sanctuary for those who wished to see their country freed from the yoke of foreign rule. They included national hero Tadeusz Kościuszko (1746–1817) and his officers, who attended Mass here on the morning of March 24th 1794 and had their sabres blessed (see no. 106). After declaring an oath of loyalty to their homeland they proceeded to Krakow's main square (Rynek Główny) (Old Town) and declared the start of the Kościuszko Uprising (a commemorative plaque marks the spot). It was not enough though and in 1795 Poland was partitioned between Austria, Russia and Prussia. For the next two decades Krakow served as a provincial outpost of the Austro-Hungarian Empire.

The church also contains a traditional herbal pharmacy (Sklepik Klasztorny) and during Christmas an elaborate nativity scene is erected outside.

Other locations nearby; 83, 84, 85

86 Tobacco, Tytano and Beyond

31-124 Kraków (Piasek), the former Tytano cultural complex at ul. Dolnych Młynów 10
Tram 4, 8, 13, 14, 24, 44 to Batorego; Tram 2, 4, 8, 13, 14, 18, 20, 24, 44 to Teatr Bagatela

Krakow has a good track record when it comes to converting industrial-era buildings to new uses. Examples include a brewery that is now apartments, a power plant that's become an arts centre, and a tram depot containing a beer hall (see nos. 41, 52, 67). Another successful conversion was until recently the Tytano cultural complex on ul. Dolnych Młynów (Piasek), which rose from the ashes of a former cigarette factory.

The story of how this abandoned factory briefly became one of Krakow's most popular social venues is worth telling here. It began in 1876, when the factory opened as the *Cesarski i Królewski Rządowa Fabryka Tytoniu* (Imperial and Royal Government Tobacco Factory). The name reflected the fact that Krakow was at the time part of Austro-Hungarian Galicia wherein all government enterprises had to show their allegiance to Emperor Franz Joseph I (1830–1916) (the corresponding name in German was *Kaiserliche und Königliche Tabakfabrik*).

Remarkably the factory remained in operation for 125 years surviving World Wars, Communism and the country's eventual transition to democracy. For a while in the early 1900s it was Krakow's biggest factory, employing over a thousand workers, 90% of whom were female. By the time the factory closed in 2002, it was operated by the American tobacco giant Philip Morris, producing not only *Gwarant*-brand cigarettes for the local market but also *Marlboro* cigarettes, cigars and chewing tobacco.

After the workforce was laid off, the huge empty factory – the largest uniformly-designed industrial complex left in the central Krakow – was sold to a Spanish property company. Fortunately for devotees of industrial design, their plan to create a hotel and apartment complex on the site fell through. Instead, after a decade of lying dormant, the old factory was reborn as a much-needed space for urban creativity.

Certainly the time was right for such a project. Eager to find spaces to express themselves, Krakow's young urbanites had been flocking to the abandoned *Miraculum* cosmetics' factory in Zabłocie, which had become a magnet for studios, start-ups and social venues. When that was demolished, the empty cigarette factory seemed an ideal replacement. Covering an impressive 160,000 square feet and encompassing six large buildings, its potential was obvious.

So it was that two local entrepreneurs established the Tytano Foundation with the intention of transforming the factory into what they envisioned as an 'Urban Ecosystem of Ideas' (derived from the Polish word for tobacco, the name 'Tytano' recalls the factory's original function). After renting the entire space from the Spanish property company, they set about building a self-contained community, one where business and community initiatives in food, culture and nightlife could thrive. The response was overwhelming, with dozens of young, novel businesses setting up shop there.

The post-industrial aesthetics lent themselves well to Tytano's multicultural restaurants, shabby chic bars and clubs. Highlights included Weźże Krafta, the first bar to open at Tytano, Hala Główna purveying craft ales with the added bonus of urban art and DJs, and the live music venue Zet Pe Te inside one of the factory's former cavernous warehouses. The latter's name (like that of Tytano) reflected the

Until recently Krakow's former Imperial and Royal Tobacco Factory played host to the Tytano cultural complex

factory's former function, being short for *Zakład Przetwórstwa Tytoniowego* (Tobacco Processing Plant).

Unfortunately, whilst Tytano was a huge success, its days were always numbered. The lease negotiated between the Tytano Foundation and the Spanish owners of the site only ever ran to 2020 and at the time of writing it has not been extended. So the historic site looks set to become the hotel and apartment complex originally slated for it and Krakow's urbanites will now have to look elsewhere to get their kicks.

Other locations nearby: 83, 84, 87

87 Coffeehouse Culture

31-120 Kraków (Piasek), a selection of cafés including
Pojnarówka Art & Coffee Bar at al. Adama Mickiewicza 21b
Tram 4, 8, 13, 14, 24, 44 to Batorego; Tram 2, 4, 8, 13, 14, 18,
20, 24, 44 to Teatr Bagatela

The European coffeehouse tradition was born in Vienna, where some claim a Polish nobleman, Jerzy Franciszek Kulczycki (1640–1694), opened the first coffeehouse in 1683 using coffee beans left behind by the retreating Ottomans. In truth that honour goes to an Armenian trader, Johannes Theodat (1640–1725), but the story evinces the longevity of Poland's own coffeehouse tradition.

The country's first coffeehouse *(Kawiarnia)* was opened in 1724 in Warsaw by a courtier of King Augustus II (August II Mocny) (1670–1733) and was patronised by men from the royal court. Krakow followed suit in 1775, when a coffeehouse opened on Rynek Główny (Old Town). Business only really took off later though when Italian pastry chefs introduced confectionery. Following the admission of women and the introduction of gas lighting, the classic 19th century coffeehouse landscape was born.

Whilst coffee drinking seems more popular today than ever, the traditional role of the coffeehouse has changed. Until the Second World War, it was a place where loners browsed newspapers and academics read books, where struggling artists sought respite from their chilly garrets, and where activists met to discuss politics and plan uprisings. Each coffeehouse had its own clientele and by purchasing a single drink they were allowed to stay all day.

That's all gone now although a whiff of the old days persists in a few Old Town cafés. On Rynek Główny a dozen traditional establishments still operate, their tables spilling out into the square during the summer months. A classic is Café Noworolski inside the Cloth Hall (Sukiennice) (see no. 15). Opened in 1910 and still retaining its Art Nouveau interiors by renowned artist Józef Mehoffer (1869–1946), this is where Lenin came to read the papers, where Nazi officials chinwagged during the Second World War, and where Communist authorities scrutinised people's affairs (see no. 84). Others include Café Restaurant Europejska at Rynek Główny 35, where patrons hide in wainscoted booths, and Café Jama Michalika farther north at Floriańska 45, where the Young Poland (Młoda Polska) movement was born (see no. 31). Such charms naturally attract the tourists, so for something

The Pojnarówka Art & Coffee Bar was formerly a university greenhouse

more intimate try Café Zakątek at ul. Grodzka 2, its walls smothered with pictures, Café Philo at ul. św. Tomasza 30, with its books and blues concerts, and the literature-inspired Nowa Prowincja at ul. Bracka 3–5.

Krakow's café scene is alive in the suburbs, too. One of them is Café Szafé at ul. Felicjanek 10 (Nowy Świat). Old photographs show that the entrance here has scarcely changed in a century. Inside the stencilled walls and quirky furniture lure not only coffee drinkers but also barflies. It should be remembered that alcohol is frequently served in Polish cafés, a throwback to when the morning drink of choice for many was wine or beer broth. The café's back room plays host to concerts, exhibitions and film screenings.

Elsewhere in the city it's good to know that the coffeehouse is being reinvented. The Pojnarówka Art & Coffee Bar at al. Adama Mickiewicza 21b (Piasek) is a case in point. This unusual café-cum-art space is housed inside a one-hundred-year-old former greenhouse belonging to the surrounding University of Agriculture (Uniwersytet Rolniczy). Being concealed inside a courtyard means there is a refreshingly unhurried air about the place. The Metaforma Design Café at ul. Powiśle 11 (Nowy Świat) doubles as a showcase for contemporary Polish artists and designers, while Palarnia Kawy at Karmelicka 17 (Piasek) boasts its own roaster. Most novel of all is the Frania Café at ul. Stradomska 19 (Kazimierz), where the funky fittings include a row of washing machines making it Krakow's only laundromat café!

Other locations nearby: 84, 85, 86

88 Wojtek the Soldier Bear

30-062 Kraków (Czarna Wieś), the statue of Wojtek in Park
im Henryka Jordana on al. 3 Maja
Tram 20 to Park Jordana

There are lots of memorials in Krakow's Park im Henryka Jordana (Czarna Wieś) but perhaps the greatest is the park itself. It honours the Polish physician and philanthropist Henryk Jordan (1842–1907), who pioneered the concept of physical education in Poland and created the country's first children's playground here in 1889.

Jordan pioneered his children's playground concept whilst Professor of Obstetrics at the Krakow's Jagiellonian University (Uniwersytet Jagielloński). Accordingly he interspersed the usual specimen trees, flower beds and pleasure pavilions with sports fields, a swimming pool, exercise equipment and designated play areas. The idea quickly caught on and so-called 'Jordan Parks' were soon opened in other cities, including Warsaw and Lwów (today Ukraine's Lviv).

In 1914 to mark the park's 25th anniversary a bust of Jordan was erected on the main tree-lined avenue. There it was joined by a growing number of busts of famous Poles – scholars, writers, musicians and priests – which today total more than fifty. More recently, however, another memorial has appeared and it's one that is very different since it celebrates the life of a six-foot tall Syrian brown bear!

The statue of Wojtek the soldier bear stands in the northern reaches of the park towards ul. Władysława Reymonta. Erected in 2014 and funded entirely by private donations, the life-sized bronze effigy by local sculptor Wojciech Batko has quickly become the park's star attraction thanks to the real Wojtek's irresistible story.

Wojtek was bought as a homeless cub in 1943 at a railway station in Hamadan, Iran by soldiers of the co-called Anders' Army, the Polish Armed Forces in the East led by General Władysław Anders (1892–1970), which was being evacuated from the Soviet Union to Palestine. After spending three months in a refugee camp near Teheran, the cub was given to the 2nd Transport Company (later the 22nd Artillery Supply Company), which christened him Wojtek, a diminutive of the old Slavic name *Wojciech* meaning 'happy warrior'. It is said the little bear was weaned on condensed milk from an old vodka bottle.

In 1944, Wojtek moved with the 22nd Company through Iraq, Syria, Palestine, and on to Egypt. By this time he was working and sleeping alongside his fellow soldiers. From there the 22nd Company sailed as

Wojtek the bear memorialised in Park im Henryka Jordana

part of the Polish II Corps to fight alongside the British Eighth Army in the Italian campaign. So as not to be separated, and to circumvent the fact that animal mascots were not allowed on British transport ships, Wojtek was officially enlisted as a private in the Polish Army.

During the Battle of Monte Cassino, Wojtek proved himself invaluable in moving live shells and crates of ammunition to Allied artillery positions. Subsisting on a diet of fruit, marmalade and honey he had by this time assumed various human traits, including saluting visiting generals and wrestling with his fellow soldiers. He had also developed a love of beer and cigarettes, which he was given as a reward for a good day's work. Wojtek's role in the battle earned him his promotion to the rank of corporal.

At the end of the war, Wojtek was redeployed with the rest of the 22nd Company to Berwickshire in Scotland. Demobilization followed in November 1947 after which Wojtek was placed in the care of Edinburgh Zoo. His celebrity status preceded him ensuring a steady stream of visitors, journalists and former Polish soldiers. Despite his death in 1963 at the age of 21, the story of Wojtek the soldier bear lives on thanks to various memorials not only in Krakow but also Edinburgh and elsewhere.

Other locations nearby: 87

89 Shooting Rifles and Photos

30-218 Kraków (Wola Justowska), the former Garrison Shooting Range (Strzelnica Garnizonowa) at ul. Królowej Jadwigi 220
Bus 134, 152, 192, 252 from Muzeum Narodowe to Strzelnica

Until recently, an architectural gem lay forgotten in Krakow's western suburbs. The former Garrison Shooting Range (Strzelnica Garnizonowa) at ul. Królowej Jadwigi 220 (Wola Justowska) is an unusual example of late-19th century martial architecture. Associated with one of Poland's great patriots and now adapted for new uses, it has become an unconventional visitor attraction.

The Garrison Shooting Range was built in the late 1880s as part of the supporting infrastructure of Fortress Krakow (Twierdza Kraków), the system of fortifications erected by the occupying Austrians (see no. 80). It should be remembered that following the Third Partition of Poland (1795), Krakow lay less than five miles from the Russian border. Located between two fortresses – Fort 2 'Kościuszko' and Fort 4 'Błonia' – the range was used by Austrian riflemen for target practice.

Still preserved much as it was, it consists of a long, timber-framed, glazed pavilion facing southwards over an elongated open space in which targets would have been placed at varying distances. Although this has now partially been built over, its parameters can still be made out between ul. Koło Strzelnicy and ul. Pod Sikornikiem.

After the First World War and the emergence of an independent Poland, the range was used by members of Piłsudski's Polish Legions (Legiony Polskie). One of the most revered figures in Polish history, Józef Piłsudski (1867–1935) was born in Imperial Russia but from an early age a supporter of Polish independence. At the start of the First World War, he established the Polish Legions, which supported the Central Powers against Russia. Realising Polish independence could not be guaranteed, however, the Legions switched to the Entente – and the winning side. As a result on 11th November 1918, Piłsudski became head of the Second Polish Republic after 123 years of partition. As Chief-of-State and First Marshall, he led several campaigns in an effort to re-establish Poland's rightful boundaries, notably the Polish–Soviet War (1919–1921), when he turned the Russian Army back from Warsaw. He is buried in the crypt of Wawel Cathedral (Katedra Wawelska) and memorialised with a mound not far from the shooting range, as well as a statue on ul. Piłsudski (Piasek) (see nos. 4, 106).

The superbly restored former Garrison Shooting Range (Strzelnica Garnizonowa) in Wola Justowska

The range remained the property of the Polish Army and in use right up until 1993, when it was transferred to the State and listed as an historic monument. Following much-needed restoration, it is now home to the Projekt Strzelnica Restaurant and a temporary gallery of the Museum of Photography (Muzeum Fotografii) illustrating the history of photographic portraits from the first cameras through to the modern craze for 'selfies'. The museum plans to relocate in 2020 to an entirely new building at ul. Rakowicka 22 (Warszawskie).

Another interesting building associated with Józef Piłsudski stands at the corner of ul. Długa and ul. Pędzichów (Kleparz). Completed in 1885, it is known as the Turkish House (Dom Turecki) for its three minarets. The building was owned by Artur Teodor Rayski, a veteran of the January Uprising (1863) against Imperial Russia, who afterwards became an officer in the Ottoman Army. Following his return to Poland in 1890, his wife commissioned the minarets as a reminder of where he'd served. A plaque attached to the front of the building commemorates Rayski's son, Ludomił Rayski (1892–1977), who in 1914 joined Piłsudski's Polish Legions. Having inherited his father's Turkish citizenship, however, he was soon obliged to join the Ottoman Army instead, where he trained as a pilot. In 1919, after being demobilised, he returned to Poland and eventually rose to Commander of the Polish Air Force.

90 Bullet Holes and Beautiful Things

**30-062 Kraków (Czarna Wieś), the Main Building
(Gmach Głowny) of the National Museum in Krakow
(Muzeum Narodowe w Krakowie) at al. 3 Maja 1
Tram 20 to Muzeum Narodowe**

The Main Building (Gmach Głowny) of the National Museum in Krakow (Muzeum Narodowe w Krakowie) contains Poland's largest collection of decorative arts encompassing everything from medieval fabrics to Art Nouveau glass. By contrast, it also houses a collection of weapons, and the building itself bears the scars of war. This collision of beauty and brutality is apposite given the last 800 years of Polish history during which the country scaled great artistic heights, whilst also being invaded and partitioned.

As Poland's first national museum, it was founded in 1879, when the country had long been divided and Krakow was under Austrian occupation. The first acquisition was the large-scale painting *Nero's Torches* by Polish artist Henryk Siemiradzki (1843–1902). He donated it on condition it form part of a public gallery of national art. This duly opened in 1883 in the Cloth Hall (Sukiennice) in Krakow's famous main square (Rynek Główny), where it functioned as a much-needed symbol of national pride. The gallery remained the country's only large public museum until Poland regained its sovereignty in 1918.

Today the National Museum comprises eleven separate branches across Krakow. The Cloth Hall is now dedicated to 19th century Polish art (including Siemiradzki's epic work), with other branches in various artists' homes and historic structures (see no. 15). The Main Building (Gmach Głowny) at al. 3 Maja 1 is more recent having been largely completed in 1939 in a monumental Socialist Classical style. The Jagiellonian Library (Biblioteka Jagiellońska) alongside it exhibits the same 1930s penchant for authoritarian functionalism.

The museum's military collection is extensive and includes room after room of crossbows, pikes, swords and suits of armour, as well as uniforms and decorations. Of related interest albeit later in date are the bullet holes around the museum's main door, which most visitors miss. They are the result of heavy fighting between German and Soviet forces in January 1945 by which time German troops had looted the building (to this day a thousand or more artefacts are still missing).

Quite different is the Main Building's collection of decorative arts. Displayed in period wooden cabinets across multiple rooms, it reveals Polish craftsmanship across a huge array of media, from Renaissance cutlery and porcelain snuff boxes to ornate clocks and ladies' silk bodices. The oldest exhibit is a 14th century stole from the Benedictine Abbey in Tyniec (Opactwo Benedyktynów w Tyńcu), the most recent being distinctive examples of 21st century Polish painting (see no. 105).

The entrance to the Main Building (Gmach Główny) of the National Museum in Krakow (Muzeum Narodowe w Krakowie)

The most important part of the collection relates to Stanisław Wyspiański (1869–1907). Not only an artist but also a playwright and poet, Krakow-born Wyspiański was a key member of the Young Poland (Młoda Polska) movement, which adapted the tenets of French Art Nouveau to create a wholly native variant (see no. 31, 34). The sheer range of Wyspiański-related material held by the museum is testament to his versatility. On display are pastel portraits and landscapes, typographic and scenographic sketches, custom-made furniture, and intricate designs for the stained glass and polychrome murals he deployed to such stunning effect in several Krakow churches (see nos. 12, 84, 92). The large memorial dominating the museum forecourt leaves visitors in no doubt about his importance, and like his contemporaries Klimt, Gaudí and Mucha, his oeuvre is still considered influential today.

The newest branch of the National Museum is the Europeum Centre for European Culture (Ośrodek Kultury Europejskiej Europeum) at plac Sikorskiego 6 (Old Town). Occupying a former 17th century granary, it contains such works as Rembrandt's *Landscape with the Good Samaritan* (1638) and Lorenzo Lotto's *The Adoration of the Infant Jesus* (1507).

Other locations nearby: 91, 92, 93, 94

91 The Hotel Cracovia

**30-111 Kraków (Salwator), the Hotel Cracovia
at al. Marsz. F. Focha 1
Tram 20 to Muzeum Narodowe**

The former Hotel Cracovia appears like a cruise liner moored at the eastern tip of Błonia Park, Europe's largest urban green space. Despite being closed in 2011 and loathed by some for its Communist-era connotations, the hotel is admired by fans of Modernist architecture. Fortunately for them, it has been acquired by the National Museum in Krakow (Muzeum Narodowe w Krakowie), with plans to transform the building into a design museum and store.

It was built between 1960 and 1965 to a design by local architect Witold C ckiewicz (b. 1924) (see no. 48). Although at first glance it resembles the contemporary panel-built apartment blocks of East Germany, the Cracovia is rather different. Cęckiewicz looked for inspiration to 1950s Paris, where housing estates of a lighter, airier construction were being built on the edge of the city. So the Cracovia features a Modernist glass and aluminium façade that makes the building seemingly float when compared with the hefty Socialist Classical architecture of the National Museum opposite (see no. 90).

At the time of its opening, the Cracovia offered facilities unheard of in Polish hotels, namely 422 rooms fitted with bathrooms, telephones, radios and specially commissioned décor. Additionally there was a hair salon, florist and a café with cream cakes so revered that Prime Minister Józef Cyrankiewicz (1911–1989) had them sent to his office in Warsaw! Guests also had access to the neighbouring Kino Kijów Centrum again designed by Cęckiewicz, which boasted the city's largest screen. Western visitors and well-off party dignitaries made up the clientele, and they enjoyed luxuries here that most citizens of the Polish People's Republic (Polska Rzeczpospolita Ludowa) could only dream of. It is said that government-appointed receptionists ensured that anyone considered suspicious was placed in a bugged bedroom and monitored.

Although the old hotel is currently off-limits, there are several shops on the ground floor that impart a flavour of the place. They include Forum Designu, a vast showcase for Polish interior design, Forum Mody, which offers cutting-edge Polish fashion and jewellery, and the Dydo Poster Gallery. An offshoot of the Cracow Poster Gallery (Galeria Plakatu w Krakowie) at ul. Stolarska 8–10 (Old Town), it is a

The former Hotel Cracovia is admired by fans of Modernist architecture

reminder of Poland's long tradition of graphic art, which notably flourished under Communism (see no. 51).

Krakow's other great Communist-era hotel is the Forum Hotel at ul. Marii Konopnickiej 28 (Dębniki). This concrete leviathan was constructed between 1978 and 1988 to a Brutalist design by Janusz Ingarden (1923–2005). It lacks the finesse of the Cracovia though and instead relies on its sheer mass and futuristic stilted form. It, too, was advanced for its time, with 278 air-conditioned rooms, swimming pool, casino, tennis court and even an outdoor clock showing the temperature. Closed in 2003, it today pays its way as Poland's longest billboard and has a go-cart track in the car park. Parts of the interior have found new uses, too, with a night club in the basement and a sauna (Termy Krakowskie Forum) on the ground floor. The old foyer is now home to Forum Przestrzenie, one of the city's trendiest bars, which spills out onto the huge, graffiti-adorned riverside terrace during the summer months.

Błonia Park is a river meadow covering an impressive 50 hectares. When the Hotel Cracovia opened in 1965, developers moved to ban the ancient right of cattle grazing on the meadow but were thwarted by a still-binding 14th century decree attributed to Queen Jadwiga (1373–1379). An unexpected sight so near the city centre, it is still farmed and also used to host large-scale outdoor events.

Other locations nearby: 90, 92, 93, 94

92 Stunning Stained Glass

31-111 Kraków (Nowy Świat), the Stained Glass Museum
(Muzeum Witrażu) at al. Krasińskiego 23
Tram 20 to Muzeum Narodowe (note: guided tours in English
on the hour for two or more people are highly recommended)

One of Krakow's major artistic achievements is its stunning stained glass. Some of the best was produced in the early 20th century, when the city's artists were at the vanguard of the Polish Art Nouveau (Młoda Polska). Remarkably the studio that produced it is still in business, offering an insight into the manufacture of this most intricate art form.

Stained glass manufacture finds its origins in medieval church architecture and there are some fine examples in Krakow, including Wawel Cathedral (Katedra Wawelska). More interesting though is the 14th century Basilica of St. Mary (Bazylika Mariacka) at plac Mariacki 5 (Old Town), where it is accompanied by some striking modern glass installed as part of a late-19th century makeover led by artist Jan Matejko (1838–1893) (see nos. 18, 30). The new glass, which adorns the chancel, was designed by the city's two great Art Nouveau practitioners, Stanisław Wyspiański (1869–1907) and Józef Mehoffer (1869–1946), who undertook a similar medieval-modern fusion in the Basilica of St. Francis (Bazylika šw. Francoszia) at plac Wszystkich Świętych 5 (Okół) (see nos. 12, 84, 90).

This new stained glass was manufactured at the workshop of Stanisław Gabriel Żeleński (1873–1914), brother of Polish writer and critic, Tadeusz Boy-Żeleński (1874–1941). Opened in 1902, the workshop quickly attracted the great artists of the day, with Wyspiański and Mehoffer its leading lights. That the pair was not averse to new-build churches is evidenced by windows in the early 20th century Church of St. Joseph (Kościół św. Józefa) at ul. Zamojskiego 2 (Podgórze) (see no. 49). And the commissions didn't only come from churches. Wyspiański and Mehoffer took secular commissions, too, including the Medical Society House (Towarzystwo Lekarskie Krakowskie) at ul. Radziwiłłowska 4 (Wesoła), where a marvellous window called *Apollo: the Copernican Solar System* illuminates the stairwell.

Exactly how all this glorious glass was made can be understood by visiting the Stained Glass Museum (Muzeum Witrażu) at al. Krasińskiego 23 (Nowy Świat). The name, however, is a misnomer since despite being housed inside Żelenski's historic workshop, the 'museum' is very much a living one. Guided tours of what is today

Poland's largest stained glass studio reveal all the various stages of producing large-scale stained glass windows. It will be seen how initial sketches are sized up, how variously coloured pieces of glass are carefully selected and cut to shape, and how they are then leaded into place and wired for solidity. Most interesting is the way in which figurative glass is created, especially the clever way in which skin tones are rendered on human faces.

The result of the studio's more recent endeavours can be seen both in the workshop and in Krakow's contemporary buildings. Notable is the Herbewo Office Complex at ul. Lubelska 29 (Kleparz) completed in 2001. The six-storey staircase here features abstract designs at every level, which when viewed from the building's glass elevator form Poland's largest non-ecclesiastical stained glass window. Another example is the Wyspiański Pavilion (Pawilon Wyspiański) featuring a triptych of windows designed by Wyspiański for Wawel Cathedral but not manufactured until 2007, when they were installed instead in a custom-made building at plac Wszystkich Świętych 2 (Old Town). Wyspiański's disturbing portrayals of St. Stanisław, King Casimir III the Great (Kazimierz III Wielki) and Henryk Pobożny were deemed unsuitable at the time.

Anyone wishing to take away a sample of Krakow-made stained glass can do so at the museum shop. All of the pieces on sale were made in the workshop using the same time-honoured techniques employed in the city for centuries.

Other locations nearby: 90, 91, 93, 94

93 An Eclectic Architect

**31-108 Kraków (Nowy Świat), a tour of houses
by Teodor Talowski beginning at ul. Retoryka 1
Tram 20 to Uniwersytet Jagielloński or Muzeum Narodowe**

Surely Krakow's most eccentric architect was Teodor Talowski (1857–1910). Embracing both backwards-looking Historicism and adventurous Art Nouveau, his buildings cherry-pick a variety of architectural styles to which he added his own quirky details. Whimsical beasts, Latin aphorisms and invented histories all played a part in his work. Talowski was born in the village of Zasów in south-east Poland. After attending school in Krakow he spent time in Lwów, where he finished his Masters in architecture. Returning to Krakow in 1881, he became a professor at the city's University of Technology and Industry (Wyższa Szkoła Techniczno-Przemysłowa), where over the next 20 years he designed many of his career-defining works.

Talowski was a prolific and successful architect designing churches, public buildings and houses across the Austro-Hungarian province of Galicia. In Krakow these included the Hospital of the Bonifratrów Order (Szpital Zakonu Bonifratrów) at ul. Trynitarska 11 (Kazimierz), the Sokół Gymnastics Association at ul. Piłsudskiego 27 (Piasek) and the railway bridge over ul. Lubicz (Wesoła) (see no. 65). Talowski's *oeuvre* is best represented though by his apartment houses. A cluster of them stand on and around ul. Retoryka (Nowy Świat), where it can be seen how freely he drew on Gothic, Renaissance and Art Nouveau design. Unable to categorise this habit, commentators have categorised it as Eclecticism.

The house at ul. Retoryka 1 displays several classic Talowski traits, namely deliberate asymmetry, quirky ornamentation, decorative stone stripes and the use of clinker bricks. Completed in 1890 as a music school, Talowski worked bars of music into the façade alongside a ukulele-playing frog referencing the Rudawa, a tributary of the Vistula (Wisła) that once flowed here. Consequently the building is known as the House under the Singing Frog (Pod śpiewającą żabą) (this use of a memorable moniker dates back to the Middle Ages, when illiteracy and a lack of house numbers forced architects into identifying buildings figuratively instead). Next door at number 3 (1891) is a house by Talowski with a highly ornate roof gable.

Now bypass number 5 to reach number 7, Talowski's earliest work in Krakow. Completed in 1887, it reveals another Talowski trait, namely the use of inscriptions. Here he uses two in Latin: *Festina lente* (Hurry slowly) and *Ars longa vita brevis* (Life is short but art endures). Note also the incorporation of stones in the brickwork giving the fanciful impression that some older building once stood here. This house was later sold by Talowski's family to buy a Bugatti racing car for his grandson Jan Ripper (1903–1987), Poland's first internationally successful race driver.

Another inscription adorns number 9 (1891): *Faber est suae quisque fortunae* (Everyone is the architect of their own fate). The carved mule's head accounts for it being called the House under the Ass (Pod Osłem). The tour concludes around the corner at

Architect Teodor Talowski designed his own house on ul. Karmelicka

ul. Smoleńsk 18–20 (1887), which Talowski adorned with a bronze dragon – hence the name House under the Dragon (Pod Smokiem) – and a *sgraffitoed* gable end.

Talowski's own house stands at ul. Karmelicka 35 (Piasek). Built in 1899, the flamboyant building again features signature brickwork, which in this case gives the impression of it having been repaired after a siege (note the cannonballs embedded here and there) A rooftop porthole contains a bronze spider's web hence the building being known as the House under the Spider (Pod pająkiem).

Talowski returned to Lwów in 1901, where he worked at the city's Polytechnic. He died there, too, but was interred in his family mausoleum back in Krakow's Rakowicki Cemetery (Cmentarz Rakowicki), which he designed in the form of a sphinx (see no. 76).

Other locations nearby: 92, 94, 95, 96

94 The Czapski Palace and Pavilion

31-109 Kraków (Nowy Świat), the Czapski Museum (Muzeum Czapskich) and Czapski Pavilion (Pawilon Czapskiego) at ul. Marszałka Józefa Piłsudskiego 12
Tram 20 to Uniwersytet Jagielloński, 2, 8, 13, 18, 20 to Filharmonia or Teatr Bagatela (note: entry tickets cover both venues)

Few visitors to Krakow will have heard of the Czapskis. To find out more about this influential Polish family they should visit a pair of collections at ul. Marszałka Józefa Piłsudskiego 12 (Nowy Świat). Both branches of the National Museum in Krakow (Muzeum Narodowe w Krakowie), they illustrate some easily overlooked aspects of Polish history.

The oldest collection, the Czapski Museum (Muzeum Czapskich), is housed in a neo-Renaissance palace once owned by Emeryk Hutten-Czapski (1828–1896). A Polish count, scholar and collector, he was born near Minsk, in what at the time was the Lithuanian part of Partitioned Poland. His grandfather had been the last governor of Chełm during the Polish-Lithuanian Commonwealth, otherwise known as the First Polish Republic (1569–1795). Thanks to his aristocratic background, Emeryk spoke several languages, studied in St. Petersburg and entered the Russian civil service. He excelled and in 1865 became Deputy Governor of St. Petersburg, where the Tsarist authorities revived for him the title of *Hutten* (Count) previously held by his ancestors.

After leaving the civil service in 1879, Emeryk settled at his estate in Stanków in south-eastern Poland. There he assembled a superb collection of Russian and Polish coins, banknotes and medals, mostly acquired from his fellow nobles. He relocated to Krakow in 1894 moving into the palace on ul. Piłsudskiego, where he commissioned a special wing to house his treasures. It carries the inscription *Monumentis Patriae Naufragio Ereptis* (Treasures of the Fatherland Saved from Destruction) and is protected by a sculpture of the mythical Greek chimera. After his death in 1903, his widow donated the palace and its collections to the City since when it's functioned as a museum.

The garden of the palace is a lovely place to wander, its statues and sculptural fragments salvaged from various city renovations. It also provides access to the second collection, namely the Czapski Pavilion

(Pawilon Czapskiego). Opened in 2016, this houses a permanent exhibit about Emeryk's grandson, the patriot Józef Czapski(1896–1993), as well as temporary art exhibitions. Józef was born in Prague and like Emeryk also studied in St. Petersburg – but there their paths diverge. Józef graduated in Law and in 1917 joined briefly a Polish cavalry unit formed in Russia. Following the Russian Revolution, he moved to the newly-liberated Poland and in 1918 entered the Academy of Fine Arts in Warsaw. He only stayed a couple of years though before volunteering for the Polish Army.

Józef had an on-off relationship with the military. A pacifist, he was gladly sent back into Russia to locate officers of his former unit, who had

A chimera stands guard outside the Czapski Museum (Muzeum Czapskich)

been taken prisoner by the Bolsheviks. Upon returning to Poland he fought as an NCO in the Polish-Soviet War receiving Poland's highest decoration in the process.

In 1921, he entered the Academy of Fine Arts in Krakow (Akademia Sztuk Pięknych w Krakowie) then moved to Paris, where he painted under the influence of the French Post-Impressionists. Returning to Poland he again enlisted and was captured by the Russians during the 1939 Defensive War (Wojna obronna 1939 roku). He was among the very few officers to survive the infamous Katyń massacre of 1940. Józef spent the rest of the war searching for missing Polish officers in Russia and afterwards remained exiled in Paris, where he co-founded the Polish émigré literary journal, *Kultura*.

The exhibition in the Czapski Pavilion uses Józef's personal effects, as well as archival material, to demonstrate his role as a key witness to history during a tumultuous period in European history.

Other locations nearby: 92, 93, 95, 96

95 A New Baroque Concert Hall

31-103 Kraków (Nowy Świat), the Krakow Philharmonic (Filharmonia Krakowska) at ul. Zwierzyniecka 1
Tram 1, 2, 6, 8, 13, 18 to Filharmonia

The Krakow Philharmonic (Filharmonia Krakowska) stands squarely just outside the Old Town at ul. Zwierzyniecka 1 (Nowy wiat). The city's primary concert hall for the best part of a century, its splendid neo-Baroque interior has played host to much glorious classical music and is still going strong.

The earliest attempts at creating a resident symphony orchestra in Krakow date back to the 18th century. Only in 1909, however, did they become reality under the leadership of composer Feliks Nowowiejski (1877–1946). Born in East Prussia during the time of the Polish Partitions, he is remembered for leading the citizens of Krakow in a rousing chorus of *Rota*, a patriotic poem protesting against Germanisation, scored to mark the 500th Anniversary of the Battle of Grunwald (1410). It is interesting to note that this early incarnation of Krakow's Philharmonic Orchestra also administered the Polish Professional Musicians Trade Union, which safeguarded the welfare and artistic integrity of its members. These were not only orchestra members but also performers working the city's cafés and silent film theatres.

The orchestra performed regularly until the invasion of Poland in September 1939. Thereafter, a new German-only orchestra called the General Government Symphony Orchestra was formed at the behest of Nazi Governor-General Hans Frank (1900–1946). Only in February 1945 was the Krakow Philharmonic Orchestra able to regroup. The first professional symphony orchestra in post-war Poland, it was led by Professor Zygmunt Latoszewski (1902–1995).

The Krakow Philharmonic concert hall was completed in 1931 to a design by Józef Pokutynski (1859–1929), a Polish architect responsible for several public buildings in the city during the late 19th and early 20th centuries. It comprises a main 693-seat hall for orchestral performances plus two smaller venues – the Golden Hall and Blue Hall – used by the chamber music ensemble Capella Cracoviensis. It was in the Blue Hall on the 15th of October 1938 that the young Karol Wojtyła (1920–2005), later Pope John Paul II, first read his poetry in public. He had arrived in Krakow that same year to study philology and languages at the Jagiellonian University (Uniwersytet Jagielloński) (see no. 10).

The interior features neo-Baroque design elements inspired by the

The Art Deco organ at the Krakow Philharmonic (Filharmonia Krakowska)

Maison du Peuple in Brussels. Since 1996, a magnificent new organ has taken centre stage in the main hall, replacing an older one that was destroyed by fire. With 50 silver pipes set into a stupendous Art Deco-style frame, it was built by Orgelbau Klais, a Bonn-based family firm that has been building organs since 1882 (more recently they installed organs in Cologne Cathedral and Hamburg's Elbphilharmonie).

Among the renowned composers, conductors and directors associated with the Krakow Philharmonic is Krzysztof Penderecki (b. 1933), who is considered Poland's greatest living practitioner. In 1997, his wife Elżbieta Penderecka (b. 1947) inaugurated an annual Ludwig van Beethoven Easter Festival, which takes place in various venues around the city. The Philharmonic's renowned visiting soloists include everyone from Yehudi Menuhin (1916–1999) and Arthur Rubinstein (1887–1982) to Nigel Kennedy (b. 1956) and Yo-Yo Ma (b. 1955).

Another classical music venue is the Florianka concert hall at the Academy of Music (Akademia Muzyczna w Krakowie) at ul. św. Tomasza 43 (Old Town). The roof-top Metrum Restobistro has two patios offering unrivalled views across the city. Classical concerts are also performed in Wawel Castle, the Ceremonial Hall of the Jagiellonian University (Uniwersytet Jagielloński), the Cloth Hall (Sukiennice), and a host of city churches.

Other locations nearby: 12, 93, 94, 96

96 Krakow for Bookworms

**31-104 Kraków (Nowy Świat), Massolit Books & Café
at ul. Felicjanek 4
Tram 1, 2, 6, 8, 13, 18 to Filharmonia; Tram 20 to Uniwersytet
Jagielloński**

In 2013, Krakow became the seventh UNESCO City of Literature. Several historical reasons supported the designation, notably that the city is home to the Jagiellonian University (Uniwersytet Jagielloński), Poland's oldest university founded in 1364, and that it boasts a thriving publishing tradition stretching back to the 16th century (see no. 24). This helps explain why Krakow has long been at the heart of Polish language and literature, and why it has fostered two Nobel Prize winners for literature, namely Henryk Sienkiewicz (1846–1916) and Wisława Szymborska (1923–2012). Krakow was also the birthplace of Polish literary modernism, which gave rise to the poetic *avant-garde* that remains the city's dominant literary form to this day.

Several modern reasons were given, too. For a start, Krakow plays host to the country's most important literary festivals, including the Miłosz Festival in May and the Conrad Festival in November. Poet Czesław Miłosz (1911–2004), another Nobel Prize recipient, and the internationally famous novelist Józef Konrad Korzeniowski (1857–1924) both spent time in Krakow. Additionally several prestigious literary prizes and scholarships are presented annually in the city, which is home to 20 or so institutes of higher education and is the seat of the Polish Writers' Union. It should also be mentioned that in 2011 Krakow joined the International Cities of Refuge Network to help provide persecuted writers with a safe haven to live and work.

Another facet of Krakow's literary scene is its bookshops. Indeed it is claimed that Europe's oldest bookshop was opened in the city in 1610. A wall plaque at Rynek Główny 23 (Old Town) marks the spot, where a bookshop still operates today run by the Empik company.

One of the best English-language bookshops can be found at ul. Felicjanek 4 (Nowy Świat). Massolit Books & Café has an extensive general stock, with good holdings of Polish, East European and Jewish literature. Remainder books are also available and used copies can be part exchanged. Part of its popularity is unquestionably its cosy café, where English-language magazines can be perused for free (more coffee and cake is available at the Massolit Bakery & Café around the corner at ul. Smoleńsk 17). English-language books can also be found at the American Bookstore at ul. Sławkowska 24a (Old Town), which specialises in bestsellers, and Jak Wam Się Podoba at ul. Stradomska 10 (Stradom), with its shelves of Central European literature in translation.

Krakow's other café-bookshops include De Revolutionibus at Bracka 14 (Old Town) and Lokator at Mostowa 1 (Kazimierz). Also in Kazimierz is Kawiarnia Literacka at ul. Krakowska 41, which offers bookshelves and sofas ranged over several different levels. Italophiles should head for the Italian-language bookshop Italicus at ul. Kremerowska 11 (Piasek).

Of Krakow's specialist bookshops, Sklep Podróżnika at ul. Jagiellońska 6 (Old Town) is a must for outdoor enthusiasts as it sells maps and guides in a number of languages. Kurant at Rynek Główny 36 (Old Town) is a music

A cosy corner at Massolit Books & Café on ul. Felicjanek

bookshop with a great view over the square. Jarden at ul. Szeroka 2 (Kazimierz) is a combined Jewish bookshop and tourist agency offering everything from history to cookbooks. Antykwariat Rara Avis at ul. Szpitalna 11 (Old Town) is an antiquarian bookshop that offers not only old tomes but also antique maps, film posters and old postcards, as does Krakowski Antykwariat Naukowy several city blocks away at ul. Sławkowska 19. And don't miss Antykwariat Abecadło at ul. Tadeusza Kościuszki 18/U3 (Salwator), which occupies a perfectly-preserved late 19th-century pharmacy.

Other locations nearby: 92, 93, 94, 95

97 The Communist Department Store

31-111 Kraków (Nowy Świat), the Jubilat Department Store (Handlowa Spółdzielnia Jubilat) at al. Zygmunta Krasińskiego 1
Tram 1, 2, 6 to Jubilat

One of Krakow's great Communist-era relics is the Jubilat Department Store (Handlowa Spółdzielnia Jubilat) at al. Zygmunta Krasińskiego 1 (Nowy Świat). It may not have been the city's first modern department store – that accolade goes to the Art Nouveau Czynciel House (Kamienica Czyncielów) opened in 1908 at Rynek Główny 4 (Old Town) – but its defiantly 1960s architecture makes it no less of a landmark.

The origins of the Jubilat Department Store can be traced back to 1908, with the founding of the *Społem* co-operative movement by Socialist activists from the Workers' Association of Food. Meaning 'jointly', *Społem* established general stores that were owned and run by its members, who shared the profits and benefits. Their first store opened that same year at ul. Wiślna 8 (Old Town).

The development of *Społem* into the *Spółdzielczości Spożywców* (Grocers' Co-Operative Movement) occurred after the Second World War. In 1948, Polish authorities merged Krakow's 34 co-operatives into a single organisation, with its headquarters at plac Jana Matejki 8 (Kleparz). It was the 10th anniversary of this event in 1958, and the 50th anniversary of the founding of *Społem*, that prompted the idea of building the Jubilat ('Jubilee') Department Store.

The award-winning Warsaw architect, Henryk Jerzy Marconi (1927–2011), was commissioned to design the seven-storey building. Known for his industrial designs, including a textile factory and a cement plant, it is not surprising that despite subsequent softening by a female architect, Jadwiga Sanicka, the building still appears distinctly functional. Opened in 1969, it consists of over 73,000 square feet of retail space spread across the lower three storeys, two of which have windows for walls. Additional space in the upper storeys was earmarked for administration, whilst on the roof, alongside a terrace café that must originally have seemed unimaginably glamorous, is the huge Jubilat logo, a black-on-gold stylisation of the winged cap of Mercury, Roman god of commerce.

In 2008, the Jubilat Department Store celebrated its 100th anniver-

The roofline of the Jubilat Department Store (Handlowa Spółdzielnia Jubilat)

sary together with various other grocery stores and milk bars *(Mleczny)* still in operation (see no. 62). By that point the original fur coats displayed on alluring mannequins and the pyramidal stacks of cocoa tins had long been replaced by affordable clothes, furniture and electronics, alongside modern department store staples such as cosmetics and key cutters, and a sprawling 24-hour food and drink department on the ground floor. Other than the original brown-tinted glass being replaced with blue glass in 2014, the exterior of the building remains much as it did when first opened.

The Jubilat Department Store remains a popular with Krakow's shoppers but the *Społem* concept is waning in the face of modern supermarket chains. Co-operative stores are increasingly relegated to smaller towns without commercial supermarkets, where older customers are happy to be served by older staff still proud of their Socialist credentials. For a rare taste of old fashioned shopping protocol visit the grocer Vitaminka ul. Szpitalna 11 (Old Town), where the goods are all beautifully displayed and service always comes with a smile.

Poland's first newspaper, *Merkuryusz Polski Ordynaryiny* (Polish Mercury Ordinary), was published in Krakow in 1661. Over two centuries later the Workers' Association of Food helped launch *Naprzód* (Forwards), Poland's first Socialist daily newspaper. The official organ of the Galician Social Democratic Party (Galicyjska Partia Socjaldemokratyczna), it ran from 1892 until 1948 promoting Left wing issues such as workers' rights and the independence efforts of Józef Piłsudski (1867–1935). Two years later the equally influential Socialist paper *Robotnik* (The Worker) was inaugurated by the Polish Socialist Party (Polska Partia Socjalistyczna).

Other locations nearby: 91, 92, 93, 96

98 Hotels Ancient and Modern

30-114 Kraków (Salwator), a selection of hotels including the Niebieski Art Hotel & Spa at ul. Flisacka 3
Tram 1, 2, 6 to Salwator

When it comes to accommodating visitors, Krakow offers myriad places to stay. There is something for all tastes and budgets here from modest hostels to luxury historic house hotels. What follows is a taster of the more unusual ones.

At the top end is the Copernicus, which occupies a former 15th century canon's house at ul. Kanonicza 16 (Okół), arguably the city's prettiest street (see no. 8). It is named after the famous astronomer Nicolaus Copernicus (Mikołaj Kopernik) (1473–1543), who resided here during visits to Krakow whilst Canon of the Archbishopric of Warmia. Guests fortunate enough to stay here sleep in rooms with original beamed ceilings and wall frescoes, and can swim in a pool installed in the vaulted medieval cellar.

An equally historic hotel stands nearby. The Kanonicza a few doors away at number 22 offers just three huge apartments, each occupying the entire floor of another former canon's house. The Royal Suite on the first floor features late 17th century murals and a carved wooden ceiling.

Elsewhere in the Old Town are more hotels in old properties. Well known among the city's *grande dame* hotels is the Grand at ul. Słakowska 5/7 (Old Town. Opened in 1887 in the former Czartoryski Palace, it still retains a privileged air. The hotel's elegant café was traditionally popular with the city's artistic and academic communities, and its stunning glass-roofed dining room is a sight to behold. The Stary at ul. Szczepańska 5 (Old Town) also occupies a once aristocratic residence, with a rooftop bar offering views over Rynek Główny. Like the Copernicus, it too boasts a swimming pool in the cellar.

On Rynek Główny itself, at number 42, is the Pałac Bonerowski. Housed inside a 16th century building, its original Gothic columns provide a contrast to the sweeping 19th century staircase. Notice, too, the lovely black and white *sgraffito* work on the façade. Krakow's oldest hotel is the Pod Różą at ul. Floriańska 14, a medieval building that later served as an inn, where Tsar Alexander I (1777–1825) stayed whilst Russian King of partitioned Poland. The Latin inscription above the Renaissance portal reads "May this building stand until an ant drinks the ocean, and a tortoise circles the earth".

Two custom-built hotels complete this Old Town survey. The Francuski, which opened in 1912 at ul. Pijarska 13, revels in its Art Deco interiors and French flair, whilst the Pollera at ul. Szpitalna 30 features a beautiful stairwell window by revered Polish artist, Stanisław Wyspiański (1869–1907).

Krakow's modern hotels of note tend to be in the suburbs. They include the Good Bye Lenin Revolution Hostel at ul. Dolnych Młynów 9 (Piasek) just around the corner from trendy ul. Krupnicza. The Lenin-themed decoration here forms a backdrop to the dormitory-style sleeping areas. A second branch at ul. Joselewicza 23 (Kazimierz) has a similar retro vibe and feel.

The Niebieski Art Hotel and Spa in Salwator

Also in the suburbs is a well-regarded eco residence. The Niebieski Art Hotel & Spa at ul. Flisacka 3 (Salwator) may offer five-star pampering but it is designed to be environmentally friendly, too. This explains why the building has its own water treatment plant, a Building Management System that minimises energy consumption, and a wavy frontage that harmonises with neighbouring buildings and mimics the nearby river. This green approach extends inside, too, where the bedrooms feature soothing colours and harmonious artworks designed to promote well-being. Additionally there is a rooftop restaurant serving meals made from certified organic ingredients with a sweeping vista of Wawel Hill. A spa offers footsore sightseers a range of holistic treatments.

Other locations nearby: 99, 100

99 An Ancient Fortified Monastery

30-114 Kraków (Salwator), the Monastery of the Norbertine Sisters of Krakow (Klasztor Sióstr Norbertanek w Krakowie) at ul. Kościuszki 88
Tram 1, 2, 6 to Salwator Pętla (Terminus) (note: all three churches are only open for Sunday Mass)

The fortified Norbertine Monastery (Klasztor norbertanek) in Salwator is Krakow's most extensive sacral complex. Known more fully as the Monastery of the Norbertine Sisters of Krakow (Klasztor Sióstr Norbertanek w Krakowie), it stands as if on its own island, bounded by the Vistula (Wisła), its tributary the Rudawa, and ul. Tadeusza Kościuszki. It is a place where history and legend collide.

The monastery has ancient origins having been founded in 1148 by the Premonstratensian Sisters of St. Norbert. They were the first female religious order in Poland and once held considerable sway over the area. Since that time the monastery has been destroyed numerous times, notably at the hands of marauding Tatars, but always rebuilt.

Much of the monastery's present fabric, including its crenelated walls and numerous courtyards, was built around 1700, with interiors completed during the 18th century. This includes the magnificent Baroque monastery Church of SS. Augustine and John the Baptist (Kościół św. Augustyna i św. Jana Chrzciciela), which can be entered from the outer courtyard or else through an older, 13th century portal under the tower (the church, which is open for Mass on Sundays, is the only part of the monastery accessible to the public).

Until as recently as 1910, when Krakow's mayor incorporated the area into the city, the Norbertine Sisters owned all of Salwator and surrounding Zwierzyniec (their fishponds, for example, lay half a mile away in what is now plac na Stawach). In addition to the monastery church, their realm also included two other churches at the foot of St. Bronisława's Hill. One of them on the monastery side of ul. św. Bronisławy is the wooden Chapel of St. Margaret (Kaplica św. Małgorzaty). Built in 1690, it originally served as chapel for the cemetery across the street (see no. 72). There stand the second church, dedicated to the Holy Saviour (Kościół Najświętszego Salwatora), which sits atop an early Slavic temple dating back to the 10th century. This makes it the oldest Catholic site in Poland. First documented in 1148, and repeatedly burned and rebuilt, the present structure is 17th century and contains some precious frescoes. The cemetery itself contains a tomb for the Sisters and a gravedigger's cottage.

Another measure of the monastery's importance is the fact that two Norbertine Sisters have been canonised: Blessed Bronisława (c.1203–1259) and Emilia Podoska (1845–1889). Additionally two of Krakow's most important customs are connected with the monastery, one of which is the Emmaus Festival, which has been staged here each Monday after Easter since the 12th century. The other is the Lajkonik procession on the first Thursday after Corpus Christi (in May or June), when a local

The Monastery of the Norbertine Sisters of Krakow (Klasztor Sióstr Norbertanek w Krakowie)

man on a wooden hobby horse sets out from the monastery to poke fun at Tatar raiders, who tried but failed to take the city in the 13th century (see no. 23).

Several other Tatar-related legends are associated with the Norbertine Monastery. The first concerns Saint Bronisława, who having been visited by the Holy Spirit and warned of an imminent raid was able to rally the Sisters to safety on the hill that now bears her name. The second is more downbeat and relates how during another raid, a storm destroyed a local ferry crossing causing the fleeing merchants of Zwierzyniec to drown in the Wisła. Only one made it across and in thanks he commissioned a bell for the ravaged monastery. When the Tatars returned they hurled it into the river, where each St. John's Night (June 23rd) its mournful toll can still be heard.

Other locations nearby: 98, 100

100 Where Lem Lies Dreaming

30-114 Kraków (Salwator), Salwator Cemetery (Cmentarz na Salwatorze) at al. Jerzego Waszyngtona 1 Tram 1, 2, 6 to Salwator Pętla (Terminus) then walk along ul. św. Bronisławy, ul. Gontyna and al. Jerzego Waszyngtona

Krakow's most charming yet unsung suburb is leafy Salwator. Spread across St. Bronisława's Hill, it is home to the Salwator Cemetery (Cmentarz na Salwatorze), where famous Polish sci-fi author Stanisław Lem (1921–2006) lies forever dreaming of future worlds.

To find the cemetery, alight the tram at the Salwator terminus, where the Vistula (Wisła) joins its tributary the Rudawa. Turn right off the main road onto ul. św. Bronisławy, passing on the way the area's original cemetery surrounding the Church of the Holy Saviour (Kościół Najświętszego Salwatora) (see no. 99). Then turn left onto ul. Gontyna, a curving street lined with lovely villas built for a 1910 design competition. They represent the original enclave of Salwator, a name that has recently been extended to include parts of surrounding Zwierzyniec.

At the end of the street turn left onto al. Jerzego Waszyngtona, which continues up St. Bronisława's Hill to the Salwator Cemetery. Inaugurated in 1865, it is considered by many to be Krakow's most beautiful burial ground. Not only is the hillside setting tranquil but the sacral art is impressive, ranging from sombre guardian angels to a sleek Chapel of All Saints (Kaplica Wszystkich Świętych) by local architect Witold Cęckiewicz (b. 1924). Remarkably the graves and grounds are not included in the city's list of heritage sites and so are maintained instead by volunteer parishioners.

The cemetery has its fair share of resting Polish luminaries, including film and theatre director Andrzej Wajda (1926–2016), psychiatrist Antoni Kępiński (1918–1972), artist Andrzej Wróblewski (1927–1957), social philosopher Feliks Koneczny (1862–1949), decorated Polish Air Force pilot Janusz Meissner (1901–1978), and geographer Eugeniusz Romer (1871–1954).

Another famous incumbent is the philosophical science fiction writer Stanisław Lem (1921–2006), whose plain sandstone grave can be found outside the funerary chapel on the right-hand side. Born in Lwów in what is now Ukraine, he studied medicine during the Nazi occupation, while his family, which had Jewish roots, avoided imprisonment thanks to having false papers. Resettled in Krakow after the war, he resumed his studies but failed to sit finals so as to avoid military service obligatory for graduates.

Against this turbulent backdrop Lem made his literary debut in 1946 with the science fiction novel *Człowiek z Marsa* (The Man from Mars). Works such as *Astronauci* (The Astronauts) and *Obłok Magellana* (The Magellanic Cloud) followed, with many more published after 1956, when de-Stalinisation brought Poland greater freedom of speech. *Dzienniki gwiazdowe* in translation as *The Star Diaries* (1957) is a good starting point for anyone interested in Lem's work.

Stanisław Lem's grave at the Salwator Cemetery (Cmentarz na Salwatorze)

Lem's most successful work, *Solaris*, was published in 1961 and subsequently filmed to great acclaim by Russian director Andrei Tarkovsky (1932–1986). It embraces one of Lem's recurring themes, namely the impossibility of human communication with aliens. In the book all attempts by the crew of a research vessel studying an alien ocean are thwarted and instead the seemingly intelligent ocean delves into the minds of the crew. Ranked alongside the works of H. G. Wells, *Solaris* and Lem's other works have sold 28 million copies in over 40 languages making him the only Polish-language writer to gain significant popularity outside the Slavic world.

Youngsters interested in science will enjoy the Stanisław Lem Science Garden (Ogród Doświadczeń im. Stanisława Lema) at al. Pokoju 68 (Czyżyny), a family-friendly interactive science park with interactive displays demonstrating scientific concepts.

To discover more about Zwierzyniec, the district surrounding Salwator, visit the Zwierzyniecki House (Dom Zwierzyniecki) at ul. Królowej Jadwigi 41, where Lenin lived when he came to Krakow in 1912. It now houses a small museum.

Other locations nearby: 98, 99, 100

101 Safari in Las Wolski

30-232 Kraków (Zwierzyniec), the Krakow Zoo (Ogród
Zoologiczny w Krakowie) at ul. Kasy Oszczędności Miasta
Krakowa 14 (note: last entry one hour before closing)
Tram 20 from Uniwersytet Jagielloński to Cichy Kaçik then
Bus 134 to Zoo

Just five miles west of Krakow's city centre is the wild and peaceful Wolski Forest (Las Wolski). Animal enthusiasts come here to spot indigenous species such as deer, badgers, foxes and hares. They also come to see more exotic creatures since the forest is home to the Krakow Zoo (Ogród Zoologiczny w Krakowie).

The protected Wolski Forest sprawls across several hills. Declared a municipal park in 1917 and encompassing 422 hectares, it includes 22 miles of marked hiking paths, as well as cycle, horse riding and cross-country skiing trails. Krakow Zoo at ul. Kasy Oszczędności Miasta Krakowa 14 (Zwierzyniec) is one of several visitor attractions within its

Saharan Addax antelopes at the Krakow Zoo (Ogród Zoologiczny w Krakowie)

confines. Opened in 1929 as a small menagerie, it has since grown into a medium-sized zoo covering 17 hectares. What sets it apart from other zoos is that the 1,400 or so creatures living here are exhibited against the natural backdrop of the forest. Around 270 distinct species are represented. Many are well-known and still relatively common in the wild, including giraffes, camels, elephants, sea lions and penguins. Others are decidedly rarer, with 88 species classed as officially endangered and 32 on the verge of extinction. Among the rarities are pygmy hippos from West Africa and Przewalski's horses from the central Asian steppe, the elusive Siberian or Amur tiger, Saharan Addax and Bongo antelopes, and the Somali wild ass There are also ruffed lemurs, Chinese Père David's deer, South American tapirs, and the Indian barasingha or swamp deer.

The zoo has had considerable success with its captive breeding programme. Species that have benefitted include the Andean condor, Asian snow leopard, desert fennec fox, caracal lynx, black crested mangabey, Lar gibbon, and the ground cuscus, a marsupial from New Guinea. The zoo also boasts regular hatches of steppe eagles, white (or umbrella) cockatoo, blue-and-yellow macaw and the African grey parrot.

Be sure not to miss the Reptile House, with its dwarf caimans, turtles, snakes and exotic fish. And if you plan your journey right, there are various feeding sessions, including sea lions (9.30am and 2pm), penguins (10am), and elephants (1pm), all much to the great delight of younger visitors.

Two grand houses stand within a few miles of the zoo. To the north at ul. 28 Lipca 1943 17a is the Villa Decius (Willa Decjusza). This Renaissance palace was built in the early 16th century for Alsatian diplomat Justus Ludwik Decjusz (1485–1545), who served as finance minister and secretary to King Sigismund I the Old (Zygmunt I Stary) (1467–1548). A literary salon was established here in the second half of the 16th century, which despite the palace later serving as a boarding school and tuberculosis hospital was revived in 1995 in the form of a cultural centre under the auspices of the Villa Decius Association. The building also houses the Willa Decjusza restaurant in a series of brick-vaulted chambers.

To the south at ul Jodłowa 13 is Przegorzały Castle (Pałac w Przegorzałach) built in the 1920s for a local architect. Seized by the Nazis during the Second World War, it became a country seat for Baron Otto von Wächter (1901–1949), Nazi Governor (Gauleiter) of Krakow, who established the Krakow Ghetto in Pogórze and orchestrated the mass murder of Polish Jews across Galicia. When he was relocated to Lviv, the castle instead became a sanatorium for Waffen-SS and Luftwaffe veterans. It today houses the U Ziyada café and restaurant, which offers sweeping views of the Vistula (Wisła) and Tatra Mountains beyond.

102 Retreat to Silver Mountain

30-248 Kraków (Zwierzyniec), the Monastery of the Camaldolese Fathers in Bielany (Klasztor Ojców Kamedułów na Bielanach) at al. Konarowa 1
Tram 1, 2, 6 from Filharmonia to Salwator then Bus 109 to Bielany Szkoła and walk up al Wędrowników (note: women are only permitted 12 days a year, including Easter Sunday, and photography is prohibited inside)

When city life gets too much, why not retreat westwards into the Wolski Forest (Las Wolski). Crowning a densely wooded hill is the Monastery of the Camaldolese Fathers in Bielany (Klasztor Ojców Kamedułów na Bielanach), where seclusion and limited access keep it a place apart.

To reach the monastery, take Bus 109 to Bielany Szkoła then follow the steep signposted path. The 1,040-foot-high hill is called Srebrna Góra (Silver Mountain) and is one of several peaks in the Sowińca Range. The climb gives visitors the feeling of making a real pilgrimage but before doing so note the monastery's strict opening times. Whilst men are admitted daily between 10 and 11.30am and 3.30 and 4.30pm, women are unfortunately only permitted entry on a dozen days a year (February 7th, the Annunciation, Easter Sunday, Pentecost Sunday, Pentecost Monday, May 31st, first Sunday after June 19th, June 24th, August 15th (Assumption of Mary), September 8th (Nativity of Mary), December 8th and 25th).

The Camaldolites – part of the Benedictine family of monastic orders – trace their origins to Italian monk Saint Romuald (c. 950–c. 1025), who strove to renew the ancient hermetic tradition of monastic life and to integrate it within the more modern cenobitic (communal) practice (this is reflected in their emblem of two doves drinking from the same chalice). Their name is derived from the Holy Hermitage of Camaldoli, high in the Tuscan hills, which Romuald founded in 1012.

Krakow's Camaldolites were invited to Srebrna Góra in 1603, when their founder Grand Court Marshal Mikołaj Wolski (1553–1630) acquired the land from a Polish-Lithuanian nobleman (the surrounding forest was subsequently named in Wolski's honour). After the original monastery succumbed to fire it was rebuilt in 1814. This is the building seen today and it is regarded as one of the finest examples of Late Baroque architecture in Europe.

Not surprisingly, the walled monastic complex gives rise to speculation as to how the monks spend their days. Visitors fortunate enough

The mysterious Monastery of the Camaldolese Fathers in Bielany (Klasztor Ojców Kamedułów na Bielanach) in Bielany

to gain access will be made privy to an essentially medieval way of life. Having renounced worldly possessions and pledged their lives to God, the half dozen monks live a solitary and ascetic life. Clad in their characteristic hooded white habits known as *Bielany* (after which the surrounding area is known), they follow the principles of *Ora et labora* (Pray and work) and *Memento Mori* (Remember you must die). They usually remain silent, with short verbal exchanges permitted only three times a week, and enjoy neither holiday leave nor family visits. Between prayer and work, the monks eat simple vegetarian meals alone in their cells, which contain little decoration.

Despite such restrictions, the monastery church is a grand affair. It features two towers each 165-feet high, eight ornate Baroque chapels, an impressive main altar, and a multi-storied crypt. The richly-decorated interior was undertaken by the Milanese artist Giovanni Battista Falconi (1600–1660), with a painting in the presbytery by Michał Stachowicz (1768–1825) depicting the Assumption of the Blessed Virgin Mary, to whom the church is dedicated.

Today's pilgrims follow in some famous footsteps including those of King John III Sobieski (Jan III Sobieski) (1629–1696), who visited before setting out to relieve Vienna from the Ottomans in 1683, and Pope Saint John Paul II (1920–2005) during his pilgrimage to Poland in 2002.

In 2009, the monastery consented to leasing some of its land for use as a vineyard. Winnica Srebrna Góra is now the second largest vineyard in Poland.

Other locations nearby: 103, 104

103 Where to Watch the Stars

30-244 Kraków (Bielany), the Astronomical Observatory at Fort Skała (Obserwatorium Astronomiczne Fort Skała) at ul. Orla 171
Tram 20 from Uniwersytet Jagielloński to Cichy Kącik then Bus 102 to Obserwatorium; Tram 1, 2, 6 from Filharmonia to Salwator then Bus 109 to Bielany Szkoła and Bus 102 to Obserwatorium (note: guided tours by appointment only)

Poland's reputation for astronomy rests squarely on the shoulders of Nicolaus Copernicus (Mikołaj Kopernik) (1473–1543). A Renaissance-era mathematician and astronomer, he studied both disciplines during the 1490s at the Academy of Krakow (Akademia Krakowska), as the Jagiellonian University (Uniwersytet Jagielloński) was originally known (see no. 24). His formulation in 1510 of a universe centred on the Sun rather than the Earth was a major milestone in scientific history.

Remarkably, the heliocentric theory of Copernicus was dismissed in Krakow, where the traditional geocentric theory of Ptolemy remained compulsory until 1750. Any thought of constructing an astronomical observatory in the city during this time therefore fell on deaf ears. The situation only changed in the early 1770s, when the Commission for National Education in Poland was established under Hugo Kołłątaj (1750–1812), one of the great figures of the Polish Enlightenment. Experimental sciences, including astronomy, now gained a more prominent role in the curriculum and the demand for an observatory grew.

Conveniently around the same time, the Jesuit Order in Krakow was abolished. Their former residence at ul. Mikołaja Kopernika 27 (Wesoła) was acquired by the Commission and reworked as an observatory by Stanisław Zawadzki (1743–1806), court architect to King Stanislaus II Augustus (Stanisław II Augustus) (1732–1798). Opened in 1792, with Polish astronomer Jan Śniadecki (1756–1830) its first director, the neo-Classical building had telescopes on the roof and astronomical symbols adorning its façade.

Many directors followed in the footsteps of Śniadecki, each improving the observatory's facilities. This continued throughout the 19th and early 20th centuries. Krakow's growth, however, created increased levels of light pollution making accurate astronomical observations difficult. Several failed attempts to build a new out-of-town observatory followed until in 1953 an abandoned 19th century Austrian fort was acquired at ul. Orla 171 (Bielany) (see no. 80). Retrofitted as the Astronomical Observatory at Fort Skała (Obserwatorium Astronomiczne Fort Skała), it opened in 1964 as part of the celebrations marking the 600th anniversary of the founding of the Jagiellonian University. Thereafter the old observatory in Wesoła became the museum of the Botanic Garden of the Jagiellonian University (Ogród Botaniczny Uniwersytetu Jagiellońskiego) (see no. 69).

One of several telescopes at the Astronomical Observatory at Fort Skała (Obserwatorium Astronomiczne Fort Skała)

The new observatory comprises five telescope domes used by two separate departments, one for stellar and extragalactic astronomy, the other for radio astronomy and space physics. Over the years the 40-strong staff of scientists has observed the positions of the Sun, Moon and Jupiter satellites, with a focus today on daily radio observations of the Sun using an eight-meter-wide, polar mounted parabolic antenna (the solar flux is recorded every 11 seconds). Much work is also carried out on the physics of galaxies. The observations made here together with those taken at the old observatory have provided Poland with its longest sequence of unbroken meteorological observations.

Guided tours of the observatory are available between September and June by appointment only, (www.oa.uj.edu.pl).

Of Poland's other modern observatories, probably the best known is the Mount Suhora Observatory (Obserwatorium astronomiczne na Suhorze) located in the Gorce Mountains, 30 miles south of Krakow. Taking full advantage of the favourable climatic conditions offered by a mountainous region, it opened in 1987 under the auspices of the Astronomy Department of the Pedagogical University of Krakow (Uniwersytet Pedagogiczny w Krakowie). Since 1991, Mount Suhora has been part of a world-wide network of observatories called the Whole Earth Telescope, which carry out simultaneous observations of stars around the clock. This research is focussed primarily on high density, compact stars known as white dwarfs.

Other locations nearby: 102, 104

104 Thesaurus Cracoviensis

30-243 Kraków (Bielany), the Thesaurus Cracoviensis –
Artefacts Interpretation Centre (Thesaurus Cracoviensis –
Centrum Interpretacji Artefaktów) at ul. Księcia
Józefa 337
Tram 1, 2, 6 from Filharmonia to Salwator then Bus
109 to Bielany Szkoła and walk on to ul. Wincentego
Oszustowskiego (note: visits each Saturday by
reservation only)

A problem encountered by many museums today is lack of space. Since their primary objective is the accumulation of historic artefacts, it follows that sooner or later they will need more room to display them. The Museum of Krakow (Muzeum Krakowa) has found a novel solution to the problem that has created a new visitor attraction in its own right.

The main branch of the museum is at Rynek Główny 35 (Old Town), with a further 18 satellite museums dotted around the city. Until recently an estimated 200,000 artefacts remained off limits to visitors, who were thus robbed of any educational potential they might offer.

The situation changed in late 2007, when the museum acquired an unfinished wing of a primary school at ul. Księcia Józefa 337 (Bielany). The architectural firm PLAN-PROJEKT-ART was commissioned to complete the structure as a museum storage facility providing over 21,000 square feet of much-needed space, as well as conservation workshops and a photographic laboratory.

Of course such storage spaces are common in many larger museums but few offer visitor access). The museum wanted to be one of those that did and so taking the Jewish Museum in Vienna among others as its cue, invited the Polish design studio ARCHISSIMA to create a bespoke interior. The brief was that it should be not only functional but also visitor friendly, with a reception area, clearly marked visitor route, multimedia zone, and even a café. The result is the Thesaurus Cracoviensis – Artefacts Interpretation Centre (Thesaurus Cracoviensis – Centrum Interpretacji Artefaktów), which opened in 2017.

Making the trip out to Bielany to explore the Thesaurus Cracoviensis is worthwhile both for museum fans and design students (visits are possible each Saturday by reservation www.muzeumkrakowa.pl). During the guided tour it is possible to get up close to the thousands of artefacts thanks to the custom-made, partially-glazed cabinets and drawers lining the visitor route. The main storage area can be found in the basement, where everything from carpets and cribs to furniture and suits of armour can be found. The multimedia room is also here, where visitors can view many of the artefacts online as part of the museum's ongoing Digital Thesaurus programme. There is a meeting room, too, that is suitable for workshops and presentations.

Artworks innovatively stored at the Thesaurus Cracoviensis – Artefacts Interpretation Centre (Thesaurus Cracoviensis – Centrum Interpretacji Artefaktów)

On the ground floor, the tour takes in collections of coins, weapons and graphic arts, whilst up on the first floor there are paintings and textiles. The connecting staircase is interesting in that it contains a collection of 'Leniniana' acquired by the museum in 1990 when Krakow's Lenin Museum closed (it is bolstered by objects pertaining to the Polish United Workers' Party).

To escape the dryness sometimes associated with museum labelling, each section has been given a popular name, for example 'Treasury' for the numismatics, 'Arsenal' for the weapons' store, and 'Grandma's Wardrobe' for the textiles' area. This deliberate theatricality is designed to better engage the visitor, and is reinforced by the wall coverings unique to each themed area. Thus a backdrop of red-bricks accompanies the Arsenal and one of embroidery accompanies Grandma's Wardrobe. Particularly fascinating is the glazed hallway on the second floor through which visitors can observe workshop operatives conserving and restoring artefacts using their highly prized skills and some very specialised equipment.

Visitors can also participate in the various information-based educational programmes on offer. Available to all ages, these include curated encounters with specific museum collections. It is this rare combination of sensory experience and professional interpretative education that makes the Thesaurus Cracoviensis a museum for today.

Other locations nearby: 102, 103

105 Prayer and Natural Products

30-398 Kraków (Tyniec), the Benedictine Abbey
in Tyniec (Opactwo Benedyktynów w Tyńcu) at
ul. Benedyktyńska 37
Tram 18 from Filharmonia or 17, 22, 52 from Starowiślna to
Rondo Grunwaldzki then Bus 112 to Tyniec and walk along
ul. Benedyktyńska; alternatively by boat on Saturdays
and Sundays until early September from ul. Flisacka
(Salwator)

All sorts of traditional products can be purchased in Krakow. One location where this is especially true is the Benedictine Abbey in Tyniec (Opactwo Benedyktynów w Tyńcu). Here for centuries a community of monks have busied themselves not only praying but also producing natural products the time honoured way.

Although medieval Tyniec sits just inside Krakow's city boundary (it was absorbed in 1973), the limestone crags and dense woodland give the place a wild aspect. The abbey perches on one of the crags overlooking a bend in the Vistula (Wisła), as well as the old amber trade route that ran from the Baltic to the Adriatic. One of Poland's oldest religious foundations, the abbey is thought to have been established in 1044 by Casimir I the Restorer (Kazimierz I Odnowiciel) (1016–1058), who invited the Benedictines to help reinstate order after a pagan revolt and to cement the position of State and Church.

The order has been there on and off ever since surviving numerous upheavals along the way. The original complex of Romanesque buildings was destroyed during a Czech raid in the 14th century. Rebuilt in the Gothic style, it was remodelled in the 17th and 18th centuries in the Baroque and Rococo styles respectively. Further damage was sustained in 1665 during the Swedish occupation (the so-called 'Deluge') and again in 1768 during the Bar Confederation, when Polish nobles used the abbey as a fortress. Eventually in 1816 the Austrians closed the abbey, which then burned in 1844. Only in 1939 did eleven Belgian Benedictines return to initiate yet another rebuilding. Remarkably they survived the Second World War and Communism unscathed, and in 1968 the monastery reclaimed the rank of abbey.

It is entered through a sturdy archway reflecting the defensive nature of the hilltop complex. Inside is a courtyard surrounded by the abbey church, cloisters and other buildings. The most impressive element is undoubtedly the oft-rebuilt Church of SS. Peter and Paul (Ko ciół w.

Beers for sale at the Benedictine Abbey in Tyniec (Opactwo Benedyktynów w Tyńcu)

Piotra i św. Pawła), with its Baroque nave and Gothic chancel, where the monks chant in Latin. It is impossible to miss the remarkable pulpit in the form of a gilded ship's prow.

Several visitor facilities help humanise the abbey. One is the museum at the back of the courtyard, which offers interactive presentations illustrating the lives of present-day Benedictines, and their gregarious outlook compared with other monastic orders. Another is the modest guesthouse and restaurant serving simple, homemade food. Before leaving don't forget the abbey shop – Produkty Benedyktyńskie – where the monks show off their manufacturing and commercial skills. A large selection of products is on sale, all derived from traditional Benedictine recipes, including cheeses, preserves, honey, herbal teas, wines, beers, dried fruit and natural cosmetics. More products are on sale in the tiny gatehouse shop run by nuns from the Benedictine monastery of Staniątki.

Krakow's retailers offer a wealth of other traditionally-manufactured products. They include the confectioner Wawel at Rynek Główny 33 (Old Town) selling chocolate, candies and wrapped sweets since 1898, the Galician delicatessen Krakowski Kredens in the Galeria Krakowska at ul. Pawia 5 (Wesoła), old fashioned gingerbread from Kopernik at ul. Grodzka 14 (Old Town), Polish vodka and craft beer from Regionalne Alkohole at ul. Miodowa 28A (Kazimierz), and honey mead from Szambelan at ul. Bracka 9 (Old Town). Traditional non-comestibles include Baltic amber jewellery from Schubert's World of Amber at ul. Grodzka 38 (Okół), Bolesławiec-brand folk pottery from Kobalt Pottery at ul. Grodzka 62 (Okół), and bespoke headwear from Chorąży Caps & Hats at ul. Krakowska 35A (Kazimierz).

106 Mysterious Mounds, Memorial Mountains

30-204 Kraków (Zwierzyniec), the Kościuszko Mound
(Kopiec Kościuszki) at al. Jerzego Waszyngtona 1
Tram 1, 2, 6 to Salwator Pętla (Terminus) then walk
up ul. šw. Bronisława or take Bus 100 (note: last entry
30 minutes before closing)

Four great earthen mounds stand in Krakow's suburbs. Raised by human hands, two of them are ancient and two are modern. Locals and visitors have long been drawn to them, eager to scale their summits and discover their purpose.

Of the two ancient mounds, the best known is the Krakus Mound (Kopiec Krakusa) on ul. Franciszka Maryewskiego in Podgórze. Not only is it Krakow's oldest man-made structure but at 52 feet in height it also forms its highest geographical point. The mound's name reflects the traditional belief that it contains the body of Krakow's mythical founder, the shadowy 12th century King Krak (or Krakus). Although archaeological work conducted in the 1930s failed to find his burial, it did reveal artefacts dating even further back to the 8th century.

Historians now believe that the Krakus Mound was created by members of a Slavic tribe (probably Avars or Vistulans) sometime between the 6th and the 10th centuries, although its purpose is still unclear. The fact that there were once four smaller mounds around its base suggest this was some sort of cult site. The place still retains an ancient and alluring aura especially on the Tuesday after Easter, when locals climb it in celebration of the pagan Rękawka festival. The name, meaning 'sleeves', recalls how according to legend the earth used to create the mound was transported to the site in the builders' sleeves.

Krakow's other ancient mound is Wanda's Mound (Kopiec Wandy) near the junction of ul. Ujastek Mogilski and ul. Bardosa (Nowa Huta). It seems fitting that this mound stands near what remains of the ancient village of Mogiła, which has been inhabited since around 5000BC. Historians theorise that like the Krakus Mound, Slavs built it during the early Middle Ages. As to its purpose, legend insists that King Krak's daughter, Princess Wanda, is buried here (although again no evidence for a burial has been found). She famously resisted the advances of a German suitor – both amorous and military – thereby keeping Poland out of foreign hands. A statue of Wanda that once

The ancient Krakus Mound (Kopiec Krakusa) in Podgórze

topped the mound has been replaced by a stone eagle carved by artist Jan Matejko (1838–1893), who lived nearby (see no. 30).

Both mounds offer sweeping views raising the possibility that they perhaps served some defensive, observational or signalling purpose. More attractive, however, is the likelihood of a calendric function. Though seemingly unrelated within the modern landscape, the mounds become magically connected at certain times of year. Climb the Krakus Mound at dawn on May 1st (the Celtic sun feast of Beltane) and the sun will be seen rising directly over Wanda's Mound six miles away to the east; then climb Wanda's Mound at dusk on the summer solstice to see the sun setting directly over the Krakus Mound. This seemingly intentional alignment supports the theory that both mounds are Celtic in origin and part of some vast landscape calendar that helped divide the year into seasons and perhaps dictated the dates of farming activities and festivals.

During the 19th century, Krakow's two ancient mounds inspired the raising of two modern ones to commemorate contemporary military heroes. The first, the Kościuszko Mound (Kopiec Kościuszki), was constructed in the 1820s at al. Jerzego Waszyngtona 1 on St. Bronisława's Hill (Zwierzyniec). It honours Tadeusz Kościuszko (1746-1817), who fought in vain against the partition of Poland during the Kościuszko Uprising (1794) (see nos. 4, 85). He had previously fought with distinction in the American War of Independence and was described by Thomas Jefferson as "the purest son of liberty that I have ever known".

The tallest of Krakow's mounds, it is 110 feet high and was made using earth brought from battlefields where Kościuszko fought, including Racławice, Maciejowice and Dubienka. During the 1840s, a wind-

The towering Kościuszko Mound (Kopiec Kościuszki) in Zwierzyniec

ing path to the top was added, where later a commemorative stone was placed. A decade later the Austrians fortified the mound as part of their ambitious plans to make Krakow an impregnable fortress (see no. 80). In deference to Krakow's ancient mounds and their seemingly deliberate alignment, the sun when seen from the Kościuszko Mound on 1st November (Celtic New Year) rises directly over the Krakus Mound.

Krakow's other modern mound is Piłsudski's Mound (Kopiec Piłsudskiego). Standing farther west on al. Do Kopca in the Wolski Forest (Las Wolski), it was completed in 1937 to honour the revered Polish statesman, Józef Piłsudski (1867–1935). A key architect of Poland's bid for independence after 123 years of partition, he became head of the Second Republic on 11th November 1918 (see no. 89). Not surprisingly the Nazi regime earmarked the mound for demolition and the Communists used tanks to topple a huge granite cross that once stood on the summit. Despite all this, it still stands as an enduring icon of Polish independence and on a clear day offers views reaching as far as the Tatra Mountains.

A fifth mound once existed in Krakow. The Esterka Mound (Kopiec Esterki) stood on ul. Głowacki in Łobzów and according to legend was raised during the 14th century to honour Esterka, the Jewish mistress of King Casimir III the Great (Kazimierz III Wielki) (1310–1370). Just 20 feet in height and obscure in purpose, it was levelled in the mid-20th century to make way for a sports ground. Yet another mound, the Grunwald Mound (Kopies Grunwaldzki), lies farther afield in the town of Niepołomice. It was completed in 1915 to mark the 500th anniversary of the Battle of Grunwald (1410) at which Polish–Lithuanian forces defeated those of the Teutonic Order thus gaining access to Baltic trade.

Other locations nearby: 100

Opening Times

Correct at time of going to press but may be subject to change. All branches of the National Museum in Krakow (Muzeum Narodowe w Krakowie) are free on Sundays and closed on Mondays.

Alchemia (Kazimierz), ul. Estery 5, Mon 10am–4am, Tue–Sun 9am–4am
Ambasada Śledzia (Old Town), ul. Stolarska 8,
American Bookstore (Old Town), ul. Sławkowska 24a, Mon–Fri 10am–8pm, Sat & Sun 10am–7pm
Antykwariat Abecadło (Salwator), ul. Tadeusza Kościuszki 18/U3, Mon–Fri 10am–6pm, Sat 11am–5pm
Antykwariat Rara Avis (Old Town), ul. Szpitalna 11, Mon–Fri 10am–6pm, Sat 10am–4pm
Archaeological Museum in Krakow (Muzeum Archeologiczne w Krakowie) (Okół), ul. Poselska 3, Jan–Jun, Sep–Dec Mon, Wed & Fri 9am–3pm, Tue & Thu 9am–6pm, Sun 11am–6pm, Jul & Aug Mon–Fri 10am–5pm, Sun 10am–3pm (last entrance 30 minutes before closing)
Archdiocesan Museum of Cardinal Karol Wojtyła (Muzeum Archidiecezjalne Kardynała Karola Wojtyły) (Okół), ul. Kanonicza 19–21, Tue–Fri 10am–4pm, Sat & Sun 10am–3pm
Ariel (Kazimierz), ul. Szeroka 18, daily 10am–midnight
Astronomical Observatory at Fort Skała (Obserwatorium Astronomiczne Fort Skała) (Bielany), ul. Orla 171, guided tours Sep–Jun Mon & Wed 10am–2pm by appointment only www.oa.uj.edu.pl
Auschwitz–Birkenau (Oświęcim), ul. Więźniów Oświęcimia 2, Jan & Nov 7.30am–3pm, Feb 7.30am–4pm, Mar & Oct 7.30am–5pm, Apr, May & Sep 7.30am–6pm, Jun–Aug 7 30am–7pm, Dec 7.30am–2pm
BAL (Zabłocie), ul. Ślusarska 9, Mon & Sun 9am–9pm, Tue–Fri 8am–10pm, Sat 9am–10pm
Bar Górnik (Piasek), ul. Czysta 1, Mon–Fri 8am–6pm, Sat 8am–4pm
Bar Krakus (Podgórze), ul. Limanowskiego 16, Mon–Fri 8am–7pm, Sat & Sun 9am–4pm
Bar Mleczny Centralny (Nowa Huta), Osiedle Centrum C1, plac Centralny, Mon–Fri 7am–7pm, Sat Apr, Aug & Dec 8am–5pm, Sat & Sun Feb, Jun & Oct 8am–3pm
Bar Południowy (Podgórze), Rynek Podgórski 11, Mon–Fri 7am–7pm, Sat & Sun 7am–3pm
Bar Smak (Piasek), ul. Karmelicka 10 (Piasek), daily 11am–10pm
Bar Targowy (Grzegórzki), ul. Ignacego Daszyńskiego 19, Mon–Fri 7am–6pm, Sat & Sun 8am–4pm

Barbican (Barbakan) (Old Town), Museum of Krakow (Muzeum Krakowa), ul. Basztowa, Apr–Oct daily 10.30am–6pm (closed 2nd Mon each month)
Barka (Kazimierz), Bulwar Kurlandzki, Sun Thu noon–11pm, Fri & Sat noon–1am
Basilica of Corpus Christi (Bazylika Bożego Ciała) (Kazimierz), ul. Bożego Ciała 26, daily 9am–noon, 1–7pm, no visits during Mass
Basilica of SS. Michael the Archangel and Bishop Stanislaus the Martyr (Bazylika św. Michała Archanioła i św. Stanisława Biskupa i Męczennika), see Skałka Sanctuary (Sanktuarium Skałka)
Basilica of St. Francis (Bazylika św. Francoszia) (Old Town), plac Wszystkich Świętych 5, Mon–Sat 10am–4pm, Sun 1–3pm, no visits during Mass; Italian Mass Sun 3.30pm, Spanish Mass Oct–Jun every 3rd Sun 2.30pm
Basilica of St. Mary (Bazylika Mariacka) (Old Town), plac Mariacki 5, Mon–Sat 11.30am–6pm, Sun 2–6pm; Bugle Tower guided tours only Apr–Oct Tue–Sat every 30 minutes 9.10–11.30am, 1.10–5.30pm, Sun 1.10–5.30pm, Nov, Dec & Mar Thu, Fri & Sat every 30 minutes 9.10–11.30am, 1.10–5.30pm; Bell Tower guided tours only Apr–Oct Tue–Fri 10am–4pm
Basilica of the Holy Cross (Bazylika Krzyża Świętego) (Nowa Huta), ul. Klasztorna 11, open by appointment only www.mogila.cystersi.pl
Basilica of the Holy Trinity (Bazylika św. Trójcy) (Old Town), ul. Stolarska 12, Mon–Sat 9.30–11.30am, 1.30–4.30pm
Basilica of the Sacred Heart of Jesus (Bazylika Najświętszego Serca Pana Jezusa) (Wesoła), ul. Kopernika 26, Sun Mass 6, 7.30, 9 & 11am, 12.30, 3.30 & 6pm
Benedictine Abbey in Tyniec (Opactwo Benedyktynów w Tyńcu) (Tyniec), ul. Benedyktyńska 37, guided tours Mon–Fri 9am–noon, 2pm & 3pm, Sat May–Sun 10.15am, noon–3pm (extra tours from Apr onwards 4pm & 5pm); Church of SS. Peter and Paul (Kościół św. Piotra i św. Pawła), Mon–Sat 1–8.30pm, Sun all day but no visits during Mass; Museum (Muzeum), daily 10am–4pm; Produkty Benedyktyńskie (Benedictine Products) shop daily 9.30am–6pm
Bishop's Palace (Pałac Biskupi) (Old Town), ul. Franciszkańska 3, courtyard only open daily until dusk
Bochnia Salt Mine (Kopalnia soli Bochnia) (Bochnia), Campi 15, Mon–Fri 8am–6pm, Sat & Sun 10.15am–4.15pm
Botanic Garden of the Jagiellonian University (Ogród Botaniczny Uniwersytetu Jagiellońskiego) (Wesoła), ul. Kopernika 27 Apr–Sep daily 9am–7pm, greenhouses Sun–Thu 10am–6pm, Botanical Museum Thu & Fri 10am–2pm, Sun 11am–3pm

Browar Lubicz Restauracya (Wesoła), ul. Lubicz 17, Mon–Thu noon–midnight, Fri noon–1am, Sat 1pm–1am, Sun 1–10pm
Café Jama Michalika (Old Town), Floriańska 45, Mon–Thu 9am–10pm, Fri, Sat & Sun 9am–11pm; folk dancing Jun–Dec Wed and Sat 7pm
Café Noworolski (Old Town), Rynek Główny 1 (Sukiennice), daily 8am–10pm
Café Philo (Old Town), ul. św. Tomasza 30, daily all hours
Café Restaurant Europejska (Old Town), Rynek Główny 35, daily 8am–midnight
Café Szafé (Nowy Świat), ul. Felicjanek 10, Mon–Fri 9am–2am, Sat & Sun 10am–2am
Café Szał (Old Town), Rynek Główny 3 (Sukiennice), daily 10am–12.30am
Café Zakątek (Old Town), ul. Grodzka 2, Mon & Sun 10am–11pm, Tue–Sat 9am–11pm
Camelot (Old Town), ul. św. Tomasza 17, daily 9am–midnight
Celestat (Wesoła), Museum of Krakow (Muzeum Krakowa), ul. Lubicz 16, Tue–Sat 10.30am–6pm
Centre for Nature Education (Centrum Edukacji Przyrodniczej) (Dębniki), ul. Gronostajowa 5, tours by appointment only www.cep.uj.edu.pl
Chapel of St. Margaret (Kaplica św. Małgorzaty) (Salwator), ul. św. Bronisławy 8, Jul & Aug Mass first and third Sun each month at 11.15am
Chata (Kleparz), ul. Krowoderska 21 (Kleparz), Sun–Thu 1pm–1pm, Fri & Sat 1pm–11pm
Cheder (Kazimierz), ul. Józefa 38, daily 10am–10pm
Chimera (Old Town), ul. św. Anny 3, Tue–Sat noon–10pm, Sun noon–8pm
Chorąży Caps & Hats (Kazimierz), ul. Krakowska 35A, Mon–Fri 10am–5pm
Church of Our Lady of Częstochowa in Krakow (Kościół Matki Boskiej Częstochowskiej w Krakowie) (Nowa Huta), os. Szklane Domy 7, daily for Mass
Church of Our Lady of Perpetual Help (Kościół pw. Matki Boskiej Nieustającej Pomocy) (Podgórze), ul. Jana Zamoyskiego 56, Sun Mass 7.30, 9, 10.30am, noon
Church of SS. John the Baptist and John the Evangelist (Kościół św. Jana Chrzciciela i Jana Ewangelisty) (Old Town), ul. św. Jana 7, Sun Mass 8am, 2.30 & 6pm
Church of SS. Peter and Paul (Kościół św. Piotra i Pawła) (Okół), ul. Grodzka 52A, Mon–Sat 9am–5pm, Sun 1.30–5pm
Church of St. Adalbert (Kościół św. Wojciecha) (Old Town), Rynek Główny, Mon–Sat 9am–3pm, 4–6pm, Sun 9am–6pm
Church of St. Andrew (Kościół św. Andrzeja) (Okół), ul. Grodzka 54, daily

9am – 6pm (5pm during Winter); no visits during Mass

Church of St. Anne (Kościół św. Anny) (Old Town), ul. św. Anny 11, Mon, Wed & Fri 1.30–7pm, Tue, Thu & Sat 9am–7pm, Sun 2–7pm

Church of St. Benedict (Kościół św. Benedykta) (Podgórze), Lasota Hill, St. Benedict's Day (March 31st), Rękawka (Tue after Easter), and limited hours during Summer

Church of St. Barbara (Kościół św. Barbary) (Old Town), Mały Rynek 8, Mon–Sat 9am–6pm, Sun 2–3.30pm

Church of St. Bartholomew (Kościół św. Bartłomieja) (Nowa Huta), ul. Klasztorna 11, Spring & Summer

Church of St. Bernard (Kościół św. Bernardyna) (Stradom), ul. Bernardyńska 2, Sun Mass 6.30, 8, 9, 10, 11am, noon, 4 & 6.30pm

Church of St. Casimir the Prince (Kościół św. Kazimierza Królewicza) and Monastery of Reformed Franciscans (Klasztor Franciszkanów Reformatorów) (Old Town), ul. Reformacka 4, daily 11am–6pm, no visits during Mass (crypt only open on All Souls Day (November 2nd) and by appointment by appointment)

Church of St. Catherine (Kościół św. Katarzyny) (Kazimierz), ul. Augustiańska 7, May–Oct

Church of St. Florian (Kościół św. Floriana) (Kleparz), ul. Warszawska 1B, Sun Mass 6.30am, 8am, 9.30am & 11am, 12.15pm, 3.15pm, 6.30pm and 8pm

Church of St. Giles (Kościół św. Idziego) (Okół), ul. Grodzka 67, Tue, Thu & Fri, Sun noon–4pm, English Mass Sun 10.30am

Church of St. John the Baptist (Kościół św. Jana Chrzciciela) (Nowa Huta), ul. Wańkowicza 35, Sun Mass only

Church of St. Joseph (Kościół św. Józefa) (Podgórze), ul. Zamojskiego 2, Mon–Sat 9am–5.30pm, Sun 1–5.30pm (no visits during Mass)

Church of St. Martin (Kościół św. Marcina) (Old Town), ul. Grodzka 58, Mon–Thu 10am–3.30pm, Sun 11am–noon

Church of St. Nicholas (Kościół św. Mikołaja) (Wesoła), ul. Mikołaja Kopernika 9, Sun Mass only

Church of the Annunciation (Kościół Zwiastowania Najświętszej Maryi Panny) (Piasek), ul. Loretańska 11, daily 6.30–11am, 4.30–8pm (no visits during Mass); Sklepik Klasztorny Mon–Fri 9am–6pm, Sat 9am–2pm

Church of the Holy Cross (Kościół św Krzyża) (Old Town), ul. św. Krzyża 23, Mon–Sat 10am–4pm, Sun 1–3pm, no visits during Mass

Church of the Holy Saviour (Kościół Najświętszego Salwatora) (Salwator), ul. św. Bronisławy 9, Sep–Jun Sun Mass only 11.15am, Jul & Aug 2nd, 4th & 5th Sun 11.15am

Church of the Immaculate Conception of the Blessed Virgin Mary (Kościół Matki Bożej Nieustającej Pomocy) (Warszawskie), ul. Rakowicka 18, Sun Mass 8.30, 10, 11.30am, 1 & 7pm

Church of the Lord's Ark (Kościół Arka Pana) (Nowa Huta), ul. Obrońców Krzyża 1, Mon–Sat 9am–6pm, Sun 3–4pm (no visits during Mass)

Church of the Transfiguration (Kościół Przemienienia Pańskiego) (Old Town), ul. Pijarska 2,

Church of the Visitation of the Blessed Virgin Mary (Kościół Na Piasku) (Piasek), ul. Karmelicka 19, daily 5.30am–8pm, no visits during mass

Cloth Hall (Sukiennice) (Old Town), Rynek Główny 3, Tue–Sun 10am–6pm; Gallery of 19th Century Polish Art, National Museum in Krakow (Muzeum Narodowe w Krakowie), Tue–Fri 9am–5pm, Sat 10am–6pm, Sun 10am–4pm

Contemporary Art Gallery Bunker (Galeria Sztuki Współczesnej Bunkier) (Old Town), plac Szczepański 3A, Tue–Sun 11am–7pm

Cracow Poster Gallery (Galeria Plakatu w Krakowie) (Old Town), ul. Stolarska 8–10, Mon–Fri noon–5pm, Sat 11am–2pm

Cricoteka (Podgórze), ul. Nadwiślańska 2–4, Tue–Sun 11am–7pm

Crown Treasury and Armoury (Skarbiec Koronny i Zbrojownia) (Wawel Hill), see Wawel Royal Castle (Zamek Królewski na Wawelu)

Cukiernia Jagiellońska (Old Town), ul. Jagiellońska 5, Mon–Thu 9am–7pm, Fri & Sat 9am–8pm, Sun 10am–7pm

Cukiernia Karmelowa (Piasek), ul. Karmelicka 23, Mon–Fri 8am–6pm, Sat 8am–2pm

Cybermachina (Old Town), ul. Stolarska 11, daily 2pm–2am (Fri, Sat & Sun 4am)

Czapski Museum (Muzeum Czapskich) and Czapski Pavilion (Pawilon Czapskiego) (Nowy Świat), National Museum in Krakow (Muzeum Narodowe w Krakowie), ul. Marszałka Józefa Piłsudskiego 12, Tue–Sat 10am–6pm, Sun 10am–4pm

Dawno Temu Na Kazimierzu (Kazimierz), ul. Szeroka 1, daily 9.30am–10.30pm

De Revolutionibus (Old Town), Bracka 14, Mon–Fri 8.30am–9pm, Sat & Sun 10am–7pm

Defence Walls (Mury Obronne) (Old Town), Museum of Krakow (Muzeum Krakowa), ul. Pijarska, Apr–Oct daily 10.30am–6pm (closed 2nd Mon each month)

Dragon's Den (Smocza Jama) (Wawel Hill), see Wawel Royal Castle (Zamek Królewski na Wawelu)

Drukarnia (Podgórze), ul. Nadwiślańska 1, Sun–Thu 9am–1am, Fri & Sat 9am–2am

Dydo Poster Gallery (Nowy Świat), Hotel Cracovia, al. Marsz. F. Focha 1, daily 2.30–6.30pm

Eagle Pharmacy (Apteka pod Orłem) (Podgórze), Museum of Krakow (Muzeum Krakowa), plac Bohaterów Getta 18, Mon 10am–2pm, Tue–Sun 9am–5pm (closed 2nd Tue each month)

Empik (Old Town), Rynek Główny 23, Mon–Fri 9am–8pm, Sat 10am–6pm, Sun 11am–6pm

Eszeweria (Kazimierz), ul. Józefa 9, Sun–Wed 10am–2am, Thu–Sat 10am–5am

Ethnographic Museum (Muzeum Etnograficzne) (Kazimierz), plac Wolnica 1, Tue–Sun 10am–7pm; Dom Esterki, ul. Krakowska 46, Tue–Sun 10am–7pm

Europeum Centre for European Culture (Ośrodek Kultury Europejskiej Europeum) (Old Town), National Museum in Krakow (Muzeum Narodowe w Krakowie), plac Sikorskiego 6, Tue–Fri 9am–6pm, Sat 10am–6pm, Sun 10am–4pm

Family Home of John Paul II (Dom Rodzinny Ojca Świętego Jana Pawła II) (Wadowice), plac Jana Pawła II 5, May–Sep daily 8.30am–5.30pm, Nov–Mar daily 8.30am–2.30pm, Apr & Oct daily 8.30am–4.30pm

Football Heaven Sports Bar (Kleparz), ul. św. Filipa 7, Mon–Fri 7–11pm, Sat & Sun 1–11pm

Forum Designu (Nowy Świat), Hotel Cracovia, al. Marsz. F. Focha 1, Mon–Sat 11am–7pm

Forum Mody (Nowy Świat), Hotel Cracovia, al. Marsz. F. Focha 1, Mon–Sat 11am–7pm

Forum Przestrzenie (Dębniki), ul. Marii Konopnickiej 28, daily 10am–2am

Frania Café (Kazimierz), ul. Stradomska 19, daily 7.30am–midnight

Galerie d'Art Naïf (Kazimierz), ul. Józefa 11, Mon–Fri 1–5pm, Sat 1–3pm

Galicia Jewish Museum (Żydowskie Muzeum Galicja) (Kazimierz), ul. Dajwór 18, daily 10am–6pm

Garrison Shooting Range (Strzelnica Garnizonowa) (Wola Justowska), ul. Królowej Jadwigi 220, Projekt Strzelnica Restaurant daily 11am–10pm; Museum of Photography (Muzeum Fotografii), Tue–Fri 11am–6pm, Sat & Sun 10am–3.30pm

Geology Museum (Muzeum Geologiczne) (Old Town), ul. Senacka 3, Thu & Fri 10am–3pm, Sat 10am–2pm

Grand Hotel Café (Old Town), ul. Sławkowska 5/7, daily 7am–11pm

Hawełka (Old Town), Rynek Główny 34, daily noon–10pm

Hevre (Kazimierz), ul. Beera Meiselsa 18, Sun–Thu 9am–2am, Fri & Sat 9am–4am

High Synagogue (Synagoga Wysoka) and Austeria Bookshop (Kazimierz), ul. Józefa 38, Mon–Thu 9.30am–7pm, Fri, Sat & Sun 9.30am–8pm

Hipolit House (Kamienica Hipolitów) (Old Town), Museum of Krakow (Muzeum Krakowa), plac Mariacki 3, Nov–Mar Wed, Fri–Sun 9am–4pm, Thu noon–7pm, Apr–Oct Wed–Sun 10am–5.30pm; Café Bar Magia, daily 9am–1am

Home Army Museum (Muzeum Armii Krajowej) (Warszawskie), ul. Wita Stwosza 12, Tue–Sun 11am–6pm (last entry one hour before closing)

International Cultural Centre (Międzynarodowe Centrum Kultury) (Old Town), Rynek Główny 25, Tue – Sun 10am–6pm

Izaac Synagogue (Synagoga Izaaka) (Kazimierz), ul. Kupa 18, Sun–Thu 8.30am–6pm, Fri 8.30am–2.30pm

Italicus (Piasek), ul. Kremerowska 11, daily 9am–7pm, Sat 10am–4pm
Jagiellonian Library (Biblioteka Jagiellońska) (Czarna Wieś), al. Adama Mickiewicza 22, Mon–Fri 8.15am–8.50pm, Sat 9am–4pm
Jagiellonian University Museum (Muzeum Uniwersytetu Jagiellońskiego) (Old Town), Collegium Maius, ul. Jagiellońska 15, standard guided tour every 20 minutes Nov–Mar Mon–Fri 10am–2.20pm, Sat 10am–1.30pm, Apr–Oct Mon, Wed & Fri 10am–2.20pm, Tue & Thu 10am–5.20pm, Sat 10am–1.30pm; full guided tour Mon–Fri 1pm
Jak Wam Się Podoba (Stradom), ul. Stradomska 10, daily 10am–7pm
Jama Michalika (Old Town), ul. Floriańska 45, Sun–Thu 9am–10pm, Fri & Sat 9am–11pm
Jan Matejko House (Dom Jana Matejki) (Old Town), National Museum in Krakow (Muzeum Narodowe w Krakowie), ul. Floriańska 41, Tue–Fri 9am–4pm, Sat 10am–6pm, Sun 10am–4pm
Jan Matejko Manor House (Dworek Jana Matejki) (Nowa Huta), ul. Wańkowicza 25, Tue–Sun
Jarema (Old Town), plac Matejki 5, daily noon–11pm
Jarden (Kazimierz), ul. Szeroka 2, Mon–Fri 9am–6pm, Sat & Sun 10am–6pm
Jewish Community Centre (Centrum Społeczności Żydowskiej w Krakowie) (Kazimierz), ul. Miodowa 24, Mon–Fri 10am–8.30pm, Sun 10am–6pm
John Paul II Centre (Centrum Jana Pawła II) (Łagiewniki), ul. Totus Tuus 34, Sanctuary of Blessed John Paul II (Sanktuarium św. Jana Pawła II) daily 8am–6pm, John Paul II Institute (Instytut Jana Pawła II) daily 9am–5pm, Archdiocesan Museum (Muzeum Jana Pawła II) Wed–Sat 10am–4pm, Sun 10am–3pm
Józef Mehoffer House (Dom Józefa Mehoffera) (Piasek), National Museum in Krakow (Muzeum Narodowe w Krakowie), ul. Krupnicza 26, Tue–Fri 9am–4pm, Sat 10am–6pm, Sun 10am–4pm; Meho Café daily 10am–10pm (garden Apr–Oct)
Jubilat Department Store (Handlowa Spółdzielnia Jubilat) (Nowy Świat), al. Zygmunta Krasińskiego 1, Mon–Fri 9am–8pm, Sat 9am–7pm; food and drink department all hours
Judaica Foundation (Fundacja Judaica) (Kazimierz), ul. Beera Meiselsa 17, Mon–Fri 10am–10pm, Sat & Sun 10am–6pm
Juliusz Słowacki Theatre (Teatr im Juliusza Słowackiego) (Old Town), plac Świętego. Duża 1, guided tours only Jul Thu–Sun 11am–2pm
Kawiarnia Literacka (Kazimierz), ul. Krakowska 41, daily 11am–11pm
Klezmer Hois (Kazimierz), ul. Szeroka 6, daily 7am–9.30pm (concerts at 8pm)
Klub Kulturalny (Old Town), ul. Szewska 25, daily 3pm–3am
Klub Re (Old Town), ul. św. Krzyża 4, noon–2am

Kobalt Pottery (Okól), ul. Grodzka 62, daily 10am–8pm
Kopernik (Old Town), ul. Grodzka 14, Mon–Thu 10am–7pm, Fri & Sat 9am–8pm
Kościuszko Mound (Kopiec Kościuszki) (Zwierzyniec), al. Jerzego Waszyngtona 1, summer daily 9am–dusk (exhibitions 9.30am–7pm), winter 9.30am–6pm (last entry 30 minutes before closing)
Krakow Arcade Museum (Interaktywne Muzeum Gier Wideo) (Czyzyny), Centralna 41a, Wed–Fri 4–9pm, Sat & Sun 10am–10pm
Krakow Pinball Museum (Interaktywne Muzeum Flipperów) (Stradom), ul. Stradomska 15, daily noon–10pm (Fri & Sat 11pm)
Krakow Zoo (Ogród Zoologiczny w Krakowie) (Zwierzyniec) at ul. Kasy Oszczędności Miasta Krakowa 14, daily 9am–7pm (last entry 6pm)
Krakowski Antykwariat Naukowy (Old Town), ul. Sławkowska 19, Mon–Fri 10am–6pm, Sat 10am–2pm
Krakowski Kredens (Wesoła), Galeria Krakowska, ul. Pawia, Mon–Fri 10am–9pm, Sat & Sun 10am–8pm
Krzysztofory Palace (Pałac Krzysztofory) (Old Town), Museum of Krakow (Muzeum Krakowa), Rynek Główny 35, Tue–Sun 10am–5.30pm
Kuchnia u Doroty (Kazimierz), ul. Augustiańska 4, daily 10am–9pm
Kupa Synagogue (Synagoga Kupa) (Kazimierz), ul. Warszauera 8 (entrance from ul. Miodowa 27), Sun–Thu 9.30am–4pm, Fri 9.30am–2pm
Kurant (Old Town), Rynek Główny 36, Mon–Fri 9am–7pm, Sat & Sun 10am–4pm
Lipowa 3 Glass & Ceramics Centre (Centrum Szkła i Ceramiki Lipowa 3) (Zabłocie), ul. Lipowa 3, Mon–Fri 10am–6pm, Sat 10am–4pm
Lokator (Kazimierz), Mostowa 1, daily 10am–8pm
Lost Wawel (Wawel Zaginiony) exhibition (Wawel Hill), see Wawel Royal Castle (Zamek Królewski na Wawelu)
Małopolska Garden of the Arts (Małopolski Ogród Sztuki) (Piasek), ul. Rajska 12, daily 10am–7pm; Pauza In Garden café Mon–Fri 9am–11pm, Sat 10am–10pm, Sun 11am–9pm
Manggha Museum of Japanese Art and Technology (Muzeum Sztuki i Techniki Japońskiej Manggha) (Dębniki), ul. Konopnickiej 26, Tue–Sun 10am–6pm
Massolit Books & Café (Nowy Świat), ul. Felicjanek 4, Mon–Thu 9am–9pm, Fri & Sat 9am–10pm, Sun 10am–8pm; Massolit Bakery & Café, ul. Smoleńsk 17, Mon–Fri 7am–7pm, Sat 10am–7pm
Mauretania (Kazimierz), Bulwar Kurlandzki, daily 11am–10pm
McDonalds (Old Town), ul. Szewska 2, Mon–Wed 7am–4am, Thu 7am–5am, Fri & Sat 8am–5am, Sun 8am–4am
Metaforma Design Café (Nowy Świat), ul. Powiśle 11, daily 9.30am–10pm

Metrum Restobistro (Old Town), Academy of Music (Akademia Muzyczna w Krakowie), ul. św. Tomasza 43, Mon–Fri 8am–4pm
Milkbar Tomasza (Old Town), ul. św. Tomasza 24, Tue Sat 8am–8pm, Sun 9am–8pm
Mleczarnia (Kazimierz), ul. Beera Meiselsa 20, Sun–Thu 10am–1am, Fri & Sat 10am–2am
Monastery of the Camaldolese Fathers in Bielany (Klasztor Ojców Kamedułów na Bielanach) (Zwierzyniec), al. Konarowa 1, men permitted daily 10–11am, 3.30–4.30pm; women only Feb 7th, the Annunciation, Easter Sunday, Pentecost Sunday, Pentecost Monday, May 31st, first Sun following Jun 19th, Jun 24th, Aug 15th (Assumption of Mary), Sep 8th (Nativity of Mary), Dec 8th & 25th
Monastery of the Norbertine Sisters of Krakow (Klasztor Sióstr Norbertanek w Krakowie) (Salwator), ul. Kościuszki 88, Church of SS. Augustine and John the Baptist (Kościół św. Augustyna i św. Jana Chrzciciela), Sun Mass only 6.30am, 7.30am, 9am, 10.30am, noon, 1.15pm, 7pm
Mostowa Artcafe (Kazimierz), ul. Mostowa 8, Sun–Thu noon–10pm, Fri & Sat noon–midnight
Museum of Anatomopathology (Muzeum Anatomopatologiczne) (Wesoła), ul. Grzegórzecka 16, visits by appointment www.en.uj.edu.pl
Museum of Anatomy of the Jagiellonian University (Muzeum Anatomii Uniwersytetu Jagiellońskiego) (Wesoła), ul. Mikołaja Kopernika 12, visits by appointment only www.www.en.uj.edu.pl
Museum of Contemporary Art (Muzeum Sztuki Współczesnej) (MOCAK) (Zabłocie), ul. Lipowa 4, Tue–Sun 11am–7pm (last entrance 30 minutes before closing)
Museum of Municipal Engineering (Muzeum Inżynierii Miejskiej) (Kazimierz), ul. św. Wawrzyńca 15, Tue 9am–5pm, Wed–Fri 9am–8pm, Sat & Sun 10am–8pm
Museum of Pharmacy (Muzeum Farmacji) (Old Town), ul. Floriańska 25, Tue noon–6pm, Wed–Sat 9.30am–3pm (last entry 45 minutes before closing)
Museum of Photography (Muzeum Fotografii), see Garrison Shooting Range (Strzelnica Garnizonowa)
Museum of the Armed Act (Muzeum Czynu Zbrojnego) (Nowa Huta), os. Górali 23, Mon–Fri 10am–3pm
Museum of the Faculty of Medicine of the Jagiellonian University (Muzeum Wydziału Lekarskiego Uniwersytetu Jagiellońskiego) (Wesoła), ul. Radziwiłłowska 4, visits by appointment only www.www.en.uj.edu.pl
National Museum in Krakow (Muzeum Narodowe w Krakowie) (Czarna Wieś), Main Building (Gmach Główny), al. 3 Maja 1, Tue–Fri 9am–5pm, Sat 10am–6pm, Sun 10am 1pm
Natural History Museum of the Institute of Systematics and Evolution of Animals (Muzeum Przyrodnicze Instytutu Systematyki i Ewolucji

Zwierząt) (Stradom), ul. św. Sebastiana 9, Tue–Fri 9am–3pm, Sat & Sun 10am–6pm

New Jewish Cemetery (Nowy cmentarz żydowski) (Kazimierz), ul. Miodowa 55, Sun–Fri 9am–4pm

New Podgórze Cemetery (Nowy Cmentarz Podgórski) (Podgórze), ul. Wapienna 13, daily 7am–8pm

Nowa Huta Cultural Centre (Nowohuckie Centrum Kultury) (Nowa Huta), al. Jana Pawła II 232, daily 8am–10pm; Zdzisław Beksiński Gallery Tue–Sat 11am–7pm, Sun noon–7pm

Nowa Huta Museum (Dzieje Nowej Huty) (Nowa Huta), Museum of Krakow (Muzeum Krakowa), os. Centrum E 1, Tue–Sun 10am–5.30pm; Nowa Huta Underground, group guided tours only, Tue–Sun 10am–5pm

Nowa Prowincja (Old Town), ul. Bracka 3–5, Mon–Thu 8am–midnight, Fri & Sat 8am–1am, Sun 9am–midnight

Nowy Kleparz Market (Kleparz), corner of ul. Długa & al. Słowackiego, daily 7am–8pm

Obwarzanek Museum (Żywe Muzeum Obwarzanka) (Kleparz), ul. Paderewskiego 4, Mon–Thu 10am–4pm, Fri, Sat & Sun 9.30am–5.30pm; English-language sessions available Wed at 2pm and Sat at midday

Old Podgórze Cemetery (Stary Cmentarz Podgórski) (Podgórze), corner of ul. Bolesława Limanowskiego and al. Powstańców Śląskich, daily 7am–8pm

Old Synagogue (Synagoga Stara) (Kazimierz), Museum of Krakow (Muzeum Krakowa), ul. Szeroka 24, Apr–Oct Mon 10am–2pm, Tue–Sun 9am–5pm, Nov–Mar Mon 10am–2pm, Tue–Thu 9am–4pm, Fri 10am–5pm, Sat & Sun 9am–4pm

Oriental Art (Sztuka Wschodu) exhibition (Wawel Hill), see Wawel Royal Castle (Zamek Królewski na Wawelu)

Orthodox Church of the Assumption of the Blessed Virgin (Cerkiew Zaśnięcia Najświętszej Maryi Panny) (Old Town), ul. Szpitalna 24, Mon–Fri 1–6pm, Sat & Sun noon–3pm

Oskar Schindler's Enamel Factory (Fabryka Emalia Oskara Schindlera) (Zabłocie), Museum of Krakow (Muzeum Krakowa), ul. Lipowa 4, Mon 10am–2pm, Tue–Sun 10am–6pm (timed tickets in advance only www.bilety.mhk.pl; last entrance 90 minutes before closing)

Pauza Bar and Gallery (Old Town), ul. Stolarska 5/3, Mon–Thu 10am–3am, Fri & Sat 10am–4am, Sun noon–2am

Palace of Art (Pałac Sztuki) (Old Town), plac Szczepański 4, Mon–Fri 8.15am–6pm, Sat & Sun 10am–6pm (last entrance 30 minutes before closing)

Palace of Bishop Erazma Ciołek (Pałac Biskupa Erazma Ciołka) (Okół), National Museum in Krakow (Muzeum Narodowe w Krakowie), ul. Kanonicza 17, Tue–Sat 10am–6pm, Sun 10am–4pm

Palarnia Kawy (Piasek), Karmelicka 17, Mon–Fri 9am–9pm, Sat 9am–2pm

Pasaż 13 (Old Town), Rynek Główny 13, Mon–Sat 11am–9pm, Sun 10am–7pm

Piec'Art (Old Town), ul. Szewska 12, daily from noon

Piekarnia Mojego Taty (Kazimierz), ul. Beera Meiselsa 6, Mon–Sat 6am–2am, Sun 7pm–2am

Piekarnia Pochopień (Piasek), ul. Krupnicza 12, Mon–Fri 6am–8pm, Sat 7am–4pm

Piwnica Pod Baranami (Old Town), Rynek Główny 27, daily 11am–2am; literary cabaret Sat 9pm

Plac na Stawach Market (Salwator), plac na Stawach 7, Mon–Fri 6am–8pm, Sat 6am–6pm

Plac Nowy 1 (Kazimierz), plac Nowy 1, Mon–Wed noon–midnight, Thu & Fri noon–2am, Sat 9am–2am, Sun 9am–midnight

Plac Targowy Unitarg (Grzegórzki), ul. Grzegórzecka 3, daily 6am–6pm; flea market Sun only; Kiełbaski z Niebieskiej Nyski, Mon–Sat 8pm–3am

Pod Aniołami (Okół), ul. Grodzka 35, daily 1pm–midnight

Pod Baranem (Stradom), ul. św. Gertrudy 21, daily noon–10pm

Pod Filarkami (Kazimierz), ul. Starowiślna 29, daily 7am–7pm

Pod Papugami (Old Town), ul. św. Jana 18, noon to 2am

Pod Temidą (Okół), ul. Grodzka 43, daily 9am–8pm

Podgórze Museum (Muzeum Podgórza) (Podgórze), Museum of Krakow (Muzeum Krakowa), al. Powstańców Wielkopolskich 1, Tue–Sun 9.30am–5pm

Pojnarówka Art & Coffee Bar (Piasek), al. Adama Mickiewicza 21b, Mon–Fri 7.30am–8pm, Sat 9am–7pm, Sun 10am–7pm

Polish Aviation Museum (Muzeum Lotnictwa Polskiego) (Rakowice), al. Jana Pawła II 39, Tue–Sun 9am–7pm

Polski Pub (Old Town), Rynek Główny 44, daily 9am–1am

Popper Synagogue (Synagoga Popper) and Austeria Bookshop (Kazimierz), ul. Szeroka 16, Mon–Thu 10am–7pm, Fri–Sun 10am–8pm

Princes Czartoryski Library (Biblioteka Książąt Czartoryskich) (Old Town), National Museum in Krakow (Muzeum Narodowe w Krakowie), ul. św. Marka 17, Mon–Fri 9am–3.45pm, Sat 9am–1.45pm

Princes Czartoryski Museum (Muzeum Książąt Czartoryskich) (Old Town), ul. Pijarska 6, reopening December 2019

Projekt Strzelnica Restaurant (Wola Justowska), see Garrison Shooting Range (Strzelnica Garnizonowa)

Propaganda (Kazimierz), ul. Miodowa 20, Sun–Thu noon–2am, Fri & Sat noon–5am

Rakowicki Cemetery (Cmentarz Rakowicki) (Warszawskie), ul. Rakowicka 26, daily 7am–6pm

Regionalne Alkohole (Kazimierz), ul. Miodowa 28A, Mon–Wed 10am–10pm, Thu–Sat 10am–midnight, Sun 10am–9pm

Remuh Synagogue (Synagoga Remuh) (Kazimierz), ul. Szeroka 40, Sun–Thu 9am–4pm, Fri 9am–2pm; Shabbat services on Fri for local community members and others by appointment only

Restauracja Starka (Kazimierz), ul. Józefa 14, Sun–Thu noon–11pm, Fri & Sat noon–midnight

Rydlówka (Bronowice Małe), Museum of Krakow (Muzeum Krakowa), ul. Tetmajera 28. Tue–Sat 9.30am–5pm

Rynek Underground (Podziemia Rynku) (Old Town), Museum of Krakow (Muzeum Krakowa), Rynek Główny 1, Nov–Mar Mon, Wed–Sun 10am–8pm, Tue 10am–4pm, Apr–Oct Mon 10am–8pm, Wed–Sun 10am–10pm, Tue 10am–4pm; closed every second Mon of each month

Salwator Cemetery (Cmentarz na Salwatorze) (Salwator), al. Jerzego Waszyngtona 1, daily 7am–6pm; Chapel of All Saints (Kaplica Wszystkich Świętych), Mass May & Jun, Sep & Oct 10am

Sanctuary of Divine Mercy (Sanktuarium Bożego Miłosierdzia) (Łagiewniki), ul. św. Siostry Faustyny 3, Basilica daily 7.30am–7.30pm; viewing tower daily 8.30am–8pm (from Sep 7pm); Eternal Adoration Chapel all hours except St. Faustyna's tomb Mon noon–9pm, Tue–Sun 6.30am–9pm

Sąsiedzi (Kazimierz), ul. Miodowa 25, daily noon–11pm

Schubert's World of Amber (Okól), ul. Grodzka 38, daily 9am–8pm

Singer (Kazimierz), ul. Estery 20, daily 9am–3am (Sat 6am)

Skałka Sanctuary (Sanktuarium Skałka) (Kazimierz), ul. Skałeczna 15, Basilica of SS. Michael the Archangel and Bishop Stanislaus the Martyr (Bazylika św. Michała Archanioła i św. Stanisława Biskupa i Męczennika), Mon–Sat 7am–7pm, Sun 7am–8pm, no visits during Mass; crypt as Basilica but closed Dec–Feb

Skansen Smaków (Kryspinów), ul. Cholerzyn 424, daily 11am–9pm

Sklep Podróżnika (Old Town), ul. Jagiellońska 6, Mon–Fri 11am–7pm, Sat 10am–2pm

Społem (Old Town), ul. św. Tomasza 4, Mon–Thu 5pm–4am, Fri 5pm–5am, 6pm–5am, Sun 6pm–4am

Stained Glass Museum (Muzeum Witrażu) (Nowy Świat), al. Krasińskiego 23, Tue–Sat 11.30am–6pm; guided tours in English on the hour

Stanisław Lem Science Garden (Ogród Doświadczeń im. Stanisława Lema) (Czyżyny), al. Pokoju 68, Apr–Jul Mon–Fri 9am–8pm, Sat & Sun 10am–8pm, Aug Mon–Fri 9am–8pm, Sat & Sun 9am–8pm, Sep Mon–Fri 9am–6pm, Sat & Sun 10am–7pm, Oct Mon–Fri 9am–4pm, Sat & Sun 10am–7pm

Stara Zajezdnia (The Old Depot) (Kazimierz), ul. św. Wawrzyńca 12, Mon–Thu noon–11pm, Fri & Sat noon–midnight, Sun noon–10pm

Starka (Kazimierz), ul. Józefa 14, daily noon–11pm

Starmach Gallery (Galeria Starmach) (Podgórze), ul. Węgierska 5, Mon–Fri 11am–5pm and during exhibitions www.starmach.eu

Stary Kleparz Market (Kleparz), Rynek Kleparski 20, Mon–Fri 7am–6pm, Sat 7am–3pm, Sun 8am–3pm

Stary Port (Old Town), ul. Straszewskiego 27, Mon–Wed 10am–1am, Thu & Fri 10am–3am, Sat noon–3am, Sun noon–1am

Studio Qulinarne (Kazimierz), ul. Gazowa 4, Mon–Sat 6–9.30pm

Szambelan (Old Town), ul. Bracka 9, Mon–Thu 11am–10pm, Fri & Sat 11am–9pm, Sun noon–6pm

Szara Gęś (Old Town), Rynek Główny 17, daily noon–11pm

Szołayski House (Kamienica Szołayskich) (Old Town), National Museum in Krakow (Muzeum Narodowe w Krakowie), plac Szczepański 9, Tue–Fri 9am–5pm, Sat 10am–6pm, Sun 10am–4pm

Szpeje (Kazimierz), ul. Józefa 9, daily noon–7pm

Tadeusz Kantor Gallery – Studio (Old Town), ul. Sienna 7/5, Fri–Mon noon–6pm

TAURON Arena Krakow (Czyżyny), ul. Stanisława Lema 7, guided tours by appointment only Mon & Tue 11am & 3pm, Sat 11am & 1pm, www.tauronarenakrakow.pl

Temple Synagogue (Synagoga Tempel) (Kazimierz), ul. Miodowa 24, Sun–Thu 10am–4pm, Fri 10am–2pm

Termy Krakowskie Forum (Dębniki), ul. Marii Konopnickiej 28, Mon–Fri 3–11pm, Sat & Sun noon–11pm

The Stage (Piasek), ul. Łobzowska 3, daily noon–1am

Thesaurus Cracoviensis – Artefacts Interpretation Centre (Thesaurus Cracoviensis – Centrum Interpretacji Artefaktów) (Bielany), Museum of Krakow (Muzeum Krakowa), ul. Księcia Józefa 337, visits by reservation only Sat

10am, 11am, noon, 1.15pm & 2.30pm, www.muzeumkrakowa.pl

Town Hall Tower (Wieża Ratuszowa) (Old Town), Museum of Krakow (Muzeum Krakowa), Rynek Główny 1, Nov & Dec, Mar–Oct daily 11am–5pm (closed every first Tue of the month)

U Babci Maliny (Old Town), ul. Szpitalna 38, daily noon–11pm

U Muniaka (Old Town), ul. Floriańska 3, daily 7pm–2am

U Stasi (Old Town), ul. Mikołajska 16, Mon–Fri noon–5pm

U Ziyada (Zwierzyniec), Przegorzały Castle (Pałac w Przegorzałach), ul Jodłowa 13, café daily 10am–11pm, restaurant daily noon–10pm

Ulica Pomorska Museum (Nowa Wieś), Museum of Krakow (Muzeum Krakowa), ul. Pomorska 2, Apr–Oct Tue–Sun 10am–5.30pm, Nov–Mar Tue, Wed & Fri 9am–4pm, Thu noon–7pm, Sat & Sun 10am–5pm (last entry 30 minutes before closing)

Willa Decjusza (Zwierzyniec), Villa Decius (Willa Decjusza), ul. 28 Lipca 1943 17a, daily 1–9pm

Waste Thermal Treatment Plant (Zakład Termicznego Przekształcania Odpadów) (Nowa Huta), ul. Jerzego Giedroycia 23, guided tours only on the first Tue of each month at 2pm

Wawel (Old Town), Rynek Główny 33, daily 10am–7pm

Wawel Cathedral (Katedra Wawelska) inc. Sigismund Bell and Royal Tombs (Wawel Hill), Wawel Hill (Wawelskie Wzgórze), Apr–Oct Mon–Sat 9am–5pm, Sun 12.30pm–5pm, Nov–Mar Mon–Sat 9am–4pm, Sun 12.30pm–4pm; Museum Apr–Oct Mon–Sat , Nov–Mar 9am–4pm

Wawel Royal Castle (Zamek Królewski na Wawelu) (Wawel Hill), Wawel Hill

(Wawelskie Wzgórze), State Rooms (Reprezentacyjne Komnaty Królewskie) Apr–Oct Tue–Fri 9.30am–5pm, Sat & Sun 10am–5pm, Nov–Mar Tue–Sat 9.30am–4pm, Sun 10am–4pm; Royal Private Apartments (Prywatne Apartamenty Królewskie) same as State Rooms but guided tours only and closed Sun; Crown Treasury and Armoury (Skarbiec Koronny i Zbrojownia) Apr–Oct Mon 9.30am–1pm, Tue–Fri 9.30am–5pm, Sat & Sun 10am–5pm; Oriental Art (Sztuka Wschodu) exhibition Apr–Oct Tue–Fri 9.30am–5pm, Sat & Sun 10am–5pm, Nov–Mar Tue–Sat 11am–2pm; Lost Wawel (Wawel Zaginiony) exhibition Apr–Oct Mon 9.30am–1pm, Tue–Fri 9.30am–5pm, Sat & Sun 10am–5pm; Dragon's Den (Smocza Jama) Apr, Sep & Oct 10am–5pm, May & Jun 10am–6pm, Jul & Aug 10am–7pm; Sandomierska Tower (Baszta Sandomierska), as Dragon's Den; Wawel Architecture and Gardens Tour (Budowle i ogrody Wawelu) Apr–Sep 11am–4.30pm

Wieliczka Salt Mine (Kopalnia soli Wieliczka) (Wieliczka), Daniłowicza 10, daily 7.30am–7.30pm

Wierzynek (Old Town), Rynek Główny 16, daily 1–11pm

Wojtyła Apartment (Mieszkanie Wojtyłów) (Dębniki), ul. Tyniecka 10, Tue–Fri 10am–2pm

Wyspiański Pavilion (Pawilon Wyspiański) (Old Town), plac Wszystkich Świętych 2, daily 9am–5pm

Zdzisław Beksiński Gallery (Nowa Huta), Nowa Huta Cultural Centre (Nowohuckie Centrum Kultury), al. Jana Pawła II 232, Tue–Sat 11am–7pm, Sun noon–7pm

Zwierzyniecki House (Dom Zwierzyniecki) (Zwierzyniecki), Museum of Krakow (Muzeum Krakowa), ul. Królowej Jadwigi 41, Tue–Sun 9.30am–5pm

Bibliography

GUIDEBOOKS

Lonely Planet Pocket Kraków (Mark Baker), Lonely Planet, 2020

Tadeusz Pankiewicz's Pharmacy in the Kraków Ghetto (Monika Bednarek), Muzeum Historyczne Miasta Krakowa, 2013

Wokół Rynku Kleparskiego (Walery Bubień), Muzeum Historyczne Miasta Krakowa, 2017

The Routes of John Paul II (Krzysztof Bzowski & Jacek Tokarski), Bosz, 2008

A Visitor's Guide to Krakow: Old Krakow, Kazimierz and Krakow During the Holocaust (Alex Dancyg), Moreshet – The Mordechai Anielevich Memorial Holocaust Studies and Research Center, 2014

Żydowski Kraków (Jewish Krakow) (Eugeniusz Duda), Vis-a-vis/Etiuda, 2010

Kraków (Karol Estreicher), Nakładem Towarzystwa Miłośników Historii i Zabytków Krakowa, 1931

The Krzysztofory Palace (Piotr Hapanowicz), Muzeum Historyczne Miasta Krakowa, 2015

Kraków's Kazimierz: Town of Partings and Returns (Agnieszka Legutko-Ołownia), Wydawnictwo Bezdroża, 2004

Cracow: An Illustrated Guidebook (Bogusław Michalec), Pascal, 2007

Sakralny Kraków: Kompletny przewodnik od A do Z (*Sacred Krakow: A Complete Guide from A to Z*) (Małgorzata Pabis & Henryk Bejda), Rafael, 2016

The Kraków Ghetto 1941–1943: A Guide to the area of the former Ghetto (Anna Pióro), Muzeum Historyczne Miasta Krakowa, 2015

A Pilgrim's Guidebook to the Sanctuaries and Churches of Krakow, Wieliczka and the Surrounding Areas (Michael Rozek), Petrus, 2016

Przewodnik po zabytkach i kulturze Krakowa (A Guide to the Heritage and Culture of Krakow) (Michał Rożek), Wydawnictwo Naukowe PWN, 1997

Basilica and Convent of St. Francis of Assisi in Krakow (Franciszek Solarz), Wydawnictwo Franciszkanów Bratni Zew, 2018

Blue Guide Kraków (Jasper Tilbury), Blue Guides, 2000

Eyewitness Travel Guide Krakow (Various), Dorling Kindersley, 2018

Insight Guide Explore Krakow: The Best Routes Around the City (Various), Insight Guides, 2019

Marco Polo Perfect Days in Krakow (Various), MairDumont, 2017

Podgórze: A Guide to Krakow's Right Bank (Various), Vis-a-vis/Etiuda, 2008

Rynek Underground (Łukasz Walas),Muzeum Historyczne Miasta Krakowa, 2013

Visible Cities Krakow (Dorota Wąsik & Emma Roper-Evans), Somerset Ltd., 2003

SECRETS AND LEGENDS

Osobliwości Krakowa (The Peculiarities of Krakow) (Jan Adamczewski), Artystyczne i Filmowe, 1986

Legends and Stories about Krakow (Bronisław Heyduk), Wydawnictwo Literackie, 1972

Legends of Krakow (Anna Majorczyk), Bona, 2015

The Lajkonik: Legend and Tradition (Łukasz Olszewski), Muzeum Historyczne Miasta Krakowa, 2009

The Krakow Legends (Jaroslaw Skora), independently published, 2017

CULTURE

Culture Smart Poland: The Essential Guide to Customs and Culture (Greg Allen), Kuperard, 2015

Unfinished Utopia: Nowa Huta, Stalinism, and Polish Society, 1949–56 (Katherine Lebow), Cornell University Press, 2016

Polska Dotty: Carp in the Bathtub, Throttled Buglers, and other Tales of an Englishman in Poland (Jonathan Lipman), Jonathan Lipman, 2011

Klezmer's Afterlife: An Ethnography Of The Jewish Music Revival In Poland And Germany (Magdalena Waligorska), Oxford University Press, 2013

City of Saints: A Pilgrimage to John Paul II's Krakow (George Weigel), Image, 2015

ART AND ARCHITECTURE

Teodor Talowski (Tadeusza Bystrzaka), Attyka, 2018

Krakow – Rediscovering the Young Poland Movement (Genevieve Blondiau, Krysia Sobieski & Therese Sobieski), Civa Publishing, 2003

MOCAK Museum of Contemporary Art in Krakow (Maria Anna Potocka), Scala Arts & Heritage Publishers Ltd., 2018

Kraków: History & Art (Various), International Cultural Centre (Międzynarodowe Centrum Kultury), 2019

HISTORY

God's Playground: A History of Poland (2 vols.) (Norman Davies), Clarendon Press, 1981

The Krakow Diary of Julius Feldman (Julius Feldman), Quill Press, 2002

An Outline of Polish Culture (Jagiellonian University), Interpress, 1983

Searching for Schindler (Thomas Keneally),Sceptre, 2009

A History of Kraków for Everyone (Jan M. Małecki), Wydawnictwo Literackie, 2008

Here All Is Poland: A Pantheonic History of Wawel, 1787–2010 (Petro Andreas Nungovitch), Lexington Books, 2018

My Hometown Concentration Camp: A Survivor's Account of Life in the Krakow Ghetto and Plaszow Concentration Camp (Bernard Offen), Vallentine Mitchell & Co Ltd., 2008

The Krakow Ghetto Pharmacy (Tadeusz Pankiewicz), Literackie, 2017

Schindler's Krakow: The City Under the Nazis (Andrew Rawson), Pen & Sword Military, 2015

Poland: A History (Adam Zamoyski), William Collins, 2015

Cracow: An Illustrated History (Zdzislaw Zygulski), Hippocrene Books Inc., 2001

ILLUSTRATED BOOKS

Made in Krakow (Przemek Czaja), Copernicus Center Press, 2018

Cracow (Tomasz Fiałkowski & Elżbieta Jogażałła), Austeria Publishing House, 2018

FICTION

Schindler's Ark (Thomas Keneally), Sceptre, 2006

The Girl from Krakow (Alex Rosenberg), Lake Union Publishing, 2015

TOUR COMPANIES

City tours to a variety of destinations (www.cracowcitytours.com)

Cultural and historical tours (www.cracowtours.pl)

Small group walking tours (www.krakowwalkingtour.com)

WEBSITES

www.krakow.pl (Official Tourist Board)

www.inyourpocket.com/krakow (Indispensable online resource to all Krakow has to offer)

www.krakowpost.com (News, transport and weather service)

www.mpk.krakow.pl (Transport listings)

www.krakow4u.pl (Exhaustive treatment of Krakow's many churches)

Acknowledgements

For kind permission to take photographs, as well as for arranging access and the provision of information, the following people are most gratefully acknowledged:

Fred Baker, Bar Targowy, Katarzyna Ból (Thesaurus Cracoviensis/Muzeum Krakowa), Igor Brejc (Scalable Maps), Jonathan Carroll, Jacek Gancarczyk, Patrycja Gołdyn (Krakow School of Jazz and Contemporary Music), Adrian Grycuk, Brother Jakub (OFMConv), Robert Jagoda, Daniel Kennedy, Aneta Kopczacka and Natalia Fyderek (Muzeum Historii Fotografii w Krakowie), Michał Kopka (Projekt Strzelnica Restaurant), Jakub Kucharski (Browar Lubicz Restauracya), Massolit Bakery & Café, National Museum in Krakow (Muzeum Narodowe w Krakowie), Wojtek Ornat (Austeria Publishing House/Klezmer Hois), Urszula Ostrowska, Prof. Dr. Jan Ostrowski and Marta Golik-Gryglas (Zamek Królewski na Wawelu), Joasia Pietrzak (Restauracja Starka), Dr. Magdalena H. Rusek-Karska, Marcin Baran and Michał Niezabitowski (Muzeum Krakowa), Dr. Agnieska Rzepiela (Muzeum Farmacji), Olga Sabała, Ola Starmach, Jacek and Maria (Kino Pod Baranami), Jakub Steczko and Maciek Olesiak (Interaktywne Muzeum Flipperów), Yves Vieruzore, Gabriela Wierzbicka and Julianna Karp (Muzeum Witrażu), Maria Zimny (Opera Krakówska), and Agnieszka Ziolkowska (Teatr im J. Słowackiego w Krakowie).

Special thanks go to my old friend Marek Pryjomko for his invaluable assistance with translation and fact-finding. This book would not be what it is without his sterling support throughout the long period of research. Also Marek Zgórniak for the kind loan of useful reading materials and some stimulating conversation. Additionally Andreas Eberhart, Zoltán Farkas, Fiona Richards, James Linkogle, and Kristin Teuchtmann for their help with picture selection.

Also to Ekke Wolf (www.typic.at) for creating the layout, Simon Laffoley for his expert editing of several troublesome photos, and Jan Zgórniak for the comfortable accommodation.

Thanks also to my mother Mary and great cousin James Dickinson for bringing interesting news items to my attention, and to Digital Bits for managing my websites.

Finally, special thanks to Roswitha Reisinger for her tireless support of my work, and to my late father Trevor for inspiring me to track down things unique, hidden and unusual in the first place.

A rusting locomotive at the abandoned Płaszów Roundhouse (Lokomotywownia Płaszów) (see no. 65)

1st Edition published by The Urban Explorer, 2019
A division of Duncan J. D. Smith
contact@duncanjdsmith.com
www.onlyinguides.com
www.duncanjdsmith.com

Graphic design: Stefan Fuhrer
Typesetting, picture editing and cover design: Ekke Wolf, typic.at
Maps: www.scalablemaps.com
Printed and bound by GraphyCems, Spain